STRUCTURES OF
American Social History

STRUCTURES OF
American Social History

———————————

Walter Nugent

Indiana University Press

BLOOMINGTON

The Samuel Paley Lectures in American Civilization, delivered at the Hebrew University of Jerusalem, February 1979 (revised and expanded).

Distributed in Israel by the Magnes Press of the Hebrew University

Manufactured in the United States of America

Library of Congress Cataloging in Publication Data

Nugent, Walter T
    Structures of American social history.

    Bibliography: p.
    Includes index.
    1. United States—Social conditions. 2. Social history. 3. United States—Population. I. Title.
HN57.N83   973   80-8634
ISBN 0-253-10356-8   2 3 4 5 85 84

To our Baby-Boomers
Kath, Rachel, Dave,
Doug, Terry, and Sou
Imagines caveant.

CONTENTS

Illustrations

PREFACE

It seems appropriate to say where this extended essay on population growth and American history came from and what it is about. As a historian of the United States, I have been fascinated for a long time with population changes, the westward movement, urbanization, immigration, transformations in agriculture, and other mass movements which make up a large part of demographic history. The history of population has always seemed to me to be basic to the history of society in all but the most elitist respects. The chance to think through the subject and make a coherent statement about it arose when, in 1977, I was honored with an invitation to deliver the Samuel Paley Lectures in American Civilization at the Hebrew University of Jerusalem.

This book is a revised and expanded version of those lectures, delivered to a general audience in the Senate Room of the Hebrew University on Giv'at Ram in February 1979 under the title "The Graying of America: Population Change and American History." It is written in the hope of making the findings of demographers and demographic historians more accessible to others. The central observation of the book may be thought-provoking for anyone: that the rate of population growth, although nearly always declining since the seventeenth century, did not drop steadily or constantly. The decline instead forms a pattern of several sudden drops from higher to lower plateaus. That pattern allows us to divide American history into periods in a new way and on a solid factual base. This book is not a full-scale demographic history, but a framework for a social history based on a demographic observation. I hope to make explicit most of the long-term trends in the history of the American population, to suggest an empirically based framework for the periodization of that history, to show how population history intertwines with social and economic history and the history of values at a number of points, and to project historical patterns into the early twenty-first century more optimistically than is usually done.

In the study of the history of population, the assumption is implicit that the mass of people are worth studying. Population history is not the history of vocal elites whose publications or letters were kept, but rather of the ill-recorded, usually voiceless majority and minorities, which, until fairly recently, were mostly rural folk. About half of them were women. Demographic history does not feature great political leaders, or industrialists, or labor leaders, or composers and writers, who in most political, economic, or cultural histories appear to have been men. Demographic history does not feature individual names at all, but deals with millions of individuals, women and men, whose interaction, measured by vital rates, forms a principal determinant of population change and hence of all other historical change.

As the book proceeds, I draw on ideas of T. R. Malthus, Frederick Jackson Turner, Fernand Braudel, and others. I take note of natural resources and their plentifulness and scarcity, and of how the rate of population growth related to decreasing availability of land over the long term. I develop the idea that most Americans over the past three centuries have lived their lives within either a frontier-rural mode or a metropolitan mode, and that American history was particularly rich, confusing, and conflict-ridden during the roughly fifty years, from about 1870 to 1920, when these two modes existed simultaneously. I conclude, extrapolating from several centuries of history, with an optimistic prognosis.

I have incurred many debts along the way, not least to the people responsible over the years for taking and compiling the United States Census, and to the demographers and historians whose works I will cite. I am greatly in the debt of Yehoshua Arieli, Shlomo Slonim, and others in the Department of American Studies of the Hebrew University of Jerusalem for inviting me to deliver the Paley Lectures for 1979. For critical readings and comments on one or another version of the entire manuscript, I am deeply grateful to Charlotte Erickson, James J. Farrell, Martin Ridge, James C. Riley, and Selwyn Troen. I also benefited from the frank comments of an anonymous reader for the Indiana University Press in 1979. Annette Atkins helped in researching various references. Several people put me on to very useful references, and they include Robert G. Barrows, Wilbur Jacobs, Sholom Kahn, John Mayer, George Stolnitz, and Paul Zall. I benefited from questions and discussions at several places where I presented aspects of the work at various stages: the audiences at the Paley Lectures themselves, in Jerusalem; the seminar on North American history of the Polish Academy of Sciences in Warsaw; lecture audiences at Hamburg University, the University of Oregon, and the Huntington Library Seminar; and members of the National Endowment for the Humanities Summer Seminar for College Teachers which I directed at Indiana in 1979. I am fully responsible, of course, for the use, misuse, or nonuse I have made of all that input.

A Fulbright-Hays senior lectureship allowed me to stay at the Hebrew University for several delightful months in 1978–79, and I thank everyone connected with that award, including Daniel M. Krauskopf, executive director of the United States–Israel Educational Foundation. I also benefited greatly from an N.E.H.–Huntington Library fellowship in 1979–80, giving me several months at the Huntington, where scholars behave as intelligent and humane conversants. Of the Huntington staff, I thank them all, but especially Ray Allen Billington, Noëlle Jackson, Virginia Renner, and Martin Ridge. I have drawn on the resources of the Huntington, the Indiana University and Hebrew University libraries, and the U.S. Cultural Center in Jerusalem. The trustees and administrators of Indiana University graciously allowed me a leave of absence and a sabbatical leave, during which I was able to visit first the easternmost frontier and then nearly the westernmost frontier of Western Civilization, in the contemplation of the history of the American population over nearly five hundred years.

Hebrew University
Jerusalem, Israel
February 1979

Huntington Library
San Marino, California
May 1980

STRUCTURES OF
American Social History

"Others appeal to history; an American appeals to prophecy; and with Malthus in one hand and a map of the back country in the other, he boldly defies us to a comparison with America as she is to be."

—Note by Frederick Jackson Turner, Turner mss., Huntington Library. Thought to be copied from *Blackwood's Magazine*, 1821.

I

America, the "New Habitat"

Short-run Observations and the Long View

After the demise of the Kennedys' Camelot and Johnson's Great Society in the early and mid-1960s, Americans became glum about their culture, its internal weaknesses, its external vulnerability, and its future. The mood at the end of the 1970s and beginning of the 1980s was querulous. National self-confidence became unfashionable. Americans expressed nostalgia for the 1950s, the days of Eisenhower and of John Foster Dulles. The uncertainty rested on well-known events which need little rehearsing. It began with the urban and campus riots of 1964 and the assassinations of the Kennedys and Martin Luther King. The Tet offensive of January 1968 seemed to brand failure on the intervention in Vietnam. Lyndon Johnson removed himself from possible reelection, for which he was eligible but which he might not have achieved. The Democratic party tore itself apart over the war issue at its nominating convention in Chicago, opening the way for Richard Nixon's ascent to the presidency. Recessions and two devaluations of the dollar reinforced uncertainty in 1970–71.

Then came Watergate, the disgrace and resignation of the Vice President in 1973 and then the President in 1974. At the same time, the Arab oil embargo quadrupled the price of a vital commodity, and the unfamiliar, half-forgotten specter of scarcity began to materialize. Between the late 1960s and 1980 the purchasing power of the dollar shrank by more than half, and inflation worsened from another doubling of world oil prices in 1979. Inflation approached 20 percent in early 1980, a level without precedent (except for a few fairly brief wartime and postwar episodes) in American history and in the history of the North Atlantic economy since the seventeenth century.[1] American self-confidence was not bolstered when Iranian revolutionaries hijacked the United States embassy in Teheran and took as hostages many of its staff. Gas lines lengthened, interest rates pushed homes beyond the reach of young adults, and a 1979 accident at a nuclear power plant in Pennsylvania threw doubts over future development of a very important and promising energy source. In the short run—if 1963 to 1980 can be called a short run—Americans had real reasons to be unhappy, for during no comparably long period, except possibly from 1800 to 1817, had they been so variously buffeted.

Uncertainty, a grasping for "relevance," hand-wringing over weaknesses perceived to exist in domestic and foreign affairs: these were marks of the public mood through much of the 1970s and into the 1980s. A noted historian of nineteenth-century America, David Herbert Donald, lamented in a *New York Times* Op-Ed essay that America had changed so drastically by the late 1970s that "If I teach what I believe to be the truth, I can only share with [undergraduates] my sense of the irrelevance of history, and of the bleakness of the new era we are now entering." Donald based his attitude on the end of America's traditional abundance. "From that abundance," he wrote, "we have derived our most amiable American traits— our individualism, our generosity, our incurable optimism; to it we owe our wastefulness, our extravagance, and our careless self-confidence." The past, he declared, is "today not merely irrelevant but dangerous."[2]

The *Times* printed only two rejoinders to Donald's heresy. One, from a professor of literature, affirmed that ". . . the most noble commitment is the struggle of a man to comprehend what *has* happened, to know that [as Faulkner wrote] 'the past is not dead. It is not even past.' "[3] Donald's statement was a strange one for a historian to make. But the fact that it could be uttered at all by a scholar who has thought deeply and written well of the abolitionist movement, the Civil War, and Reconstruction—hardly minor crises—underscores the seriously pessimistic mood among some of the best minds in the country, and demonstrates how thin they found the soup of the past when they strained it for sustenance to meet the future.

I take a very different position from Donald's. Despite the evidence of the events listed in the opening pages, events which gave the recent past its confining, frustrating quality and the near future its gloominess, I maintain that, when set in the proper historical context, the present situation is much less dire and collapse or even severe scarcity is much less threatening than at certain times past. Historically uninformed views of the present almost always make it appear better or worse than it really is. The historical context, the place of the recent past and the near future in time, provides stability and balance, an anchored view rather than a storm-tossed one. With Faulkner, I believe that the past remains relevant for understanding the present and for thinking intelligently about the future. Profound changes have certainly taken place in the United States, some fairly recently. But more perplexing and dangerous ones were undergone long ago. This will become clearer as we look beyond the level of events to broader patterns of historical structures and conjunctures.[4]

To see the patterns I have in mind requires looking back

over three hundred years of history. It involves a perspective unfamiliar to many people, including many historians: the development of the population of America since about 1700. I call attention to this perspective, and the patterns it reveals, not as a demographer but as a social historian making use of demographic research. These patterns speak to the broad question of where American society has been, and where it may go. The answers suggest grounds for optimism.

The rest of this chapter will be a description of three models of large-scale social change somehow relevant to America, and an observation of a demographic pattern. Did America "modernize?"[5] Was it the "first new nation?"[6] Is Turner's frontier thesis of help any more? What did Malthus conclude from American experience?[7] Consideration of these questions leads to the observation about growth rates: that Malthus was at first ignored and then, in the marketplace and without central planning, was gradually discovered and obeyed. The first chapter represents—to borrow some words of Beethoven's—the "awakening of cheerful feelings upon going out into the countryside."[8]

The second chapter introduces the main story. It sketches the demography of early modern Europe, out of which the colonial empires in the New World were founded, it focuses on the sparsely populated English colonies in the seventeenth century, and then it describes the emergence of the frontier-rural mode of life, which became standard for the majority of Americans for the next two hundred years. The third chapter describes the period from the late eighteenth century to the late nineteenth, when the frontier-rural mode dominated. These chapters are the "scene at a brook" and the "merry goings-on of the peasants."

In chapter four an alternative mode of life is seen to emerge in the early and mid-nineteenth century. When fully developed later, it deserves to be called the metropolitan mode. We also look at three "misfits"—life patterns which stand apart from the frontier-rural or metropolitan modes—which affected the lives of many people, but which did not have the pervasiveness of the two main modes. These were frontier-urban, settled-rural, and slave societies. The fourth chapter then sketches the Great Conjuncture, the time from about 1870 to about 1920 when the frontier-rural and metropolitan modes both flourished. The two modes, revealed by two patterns of population change, overlapped tumultuously for several decades, like a bad thunderstorm.

The final chapter concerns the period since 1920, when the metropolitan mode became dominant, and it concludes with a demographic observation about changing age structures, and some extrapolation of population history into the early twenty-first century. That is the finale, "joyful and thankful feelings after the storm."

Has America Been Unique?—
Modernization, Turner, Malthus

Many theoretical models exist to help us understand American development and place it in the broader context of world history, either as a humanistic exercise or in a social-scientific pursuit of predictability. These models include, among other possible approaches, Marxian analysis based on class struggle, Gramsci's softening of Marxism to allow bourgeois control by ideological hegemony rather than by force or revolution, or classic non-Marxian social theories such as Ferdinand Tönnies's *Gemeinschaft-to-Gesellschaft* shift.[9] The list could go on. I single out modernization theory because of its apparently growing popularity among American historians, after its two decades of near seclusion among social scientists. Although some historians are familiar with it to the point of boredom or worse, evidence abounds that others are finding modernization theory seductively attractive, some as a catch-all term, others as something more.[10] Its most extensive application to American history up to 1980 was Richard D. Brown's *Modernization: The Transformation of American Life, 1800–1865*, which appeared in 1976.

The term began to appear in the books and journals of sociology, political science, development economics, and social psychology in the 1950s as a crudely dichotomous and ahistorical notion that nation-states that were economically developed and politically centralized—that is, "modern"— somehow changed into modernity from a "traditional" condition. The same process was supposed to change presently underdeveloped or less-developed societies. Modernization theory has been applied at the macrolevel to whole societies or nations, mostly by political scientists and economists, and also at the microlevel of individual adjustment to social change, mostly by social psychologists.

Despite its collective authorship, spread over two decades, modernization theory has certain consistent features and meaning. Several social scientists have defined it (indeed proclaimed it) vigorously, among them Calvin Goldscheider, the team of Peter Berger and his co-authors, the micro-level analysts Alex Inkeles and David H. Smith, and a number of others.[11] Let a definition by S. N. Eisenstadt serve for all, because it is more subtle than some of the others and because Eisenstadt has been an articulate theorist of modernization since the 1950s. Eisenstadt[12] stressed the centrality of the shift from traditional to modern in societies, politics, and cultures. He recognized general agreement about the meaning of "traditional" and "modern" in classic social theory, whether in the form of Tönnies's *Gemeinschaft-Gesellschaft*, Henry Maine's status-to-contract, Durkheim's mechanical solidarity to organic solidarity, or Max Weber's traditional-charismatic to legal-rational. All involve a shift from one type of society to another. Modernization theorists have usually assumed that the shift was progressive and irreversible. In all of these theories, traditional societies were "static, with little differentiation or specialization, a predominance of mechanical division of labor, a low level of urbanization and literacy, and a strong agrarian basis as [their] main focus of population." Modern societies, on the other hand, exhibit a "very high level of differentiation, a high degree of organic division of labor specialization, urbanization, literacy and exposure to mass media, and [are] imbued with a continuous drive toward progress." In politics, modernization means a move from rule by traditionally authoritative elites to mass participation. In culture it means a shift from tradition-boundness to dynamism "oriented to change and innovation."[13] Other writers, stressing the impact of modernization on personality, and trying to identify "modernizing" traits of personality, point to a "heightened sense of personal efficacy," the urge to set the terms of one's own life, to be "relatively open-minded and cognitively flexible," as key elements.[14]

Some recent applications of modernization theory have been more subtle than earlier ones. When applied to historical events by a master of archival detail and literary grace, it seems to work convincingly, bringing a vast mass of historical data into a structured, coherent whole, yet doing no apparent violence to past social complexities. Exhibit A, in this regard, is Eugen Weber's *Peasants into Frenchmen: The Modernization of Rural France 1870–1914*.[15] In it we see, throughout the west and south of France, across most of the nineteenth century (not just after 1870), time take on new meaning, national authority spread, dialects disappear, farming commercialize, people migrate. We see the patterns of life formed by accretion over hundreds of years change from "traditional" to "modern" in only half or three-quarters of a century, and in one of the world's most developed countries. For Britain in the late eighteenth and early nineteenth centuries, the idea of modernization may also work, though its elements were captured well enough by Phyllis Deane under the more traditional rubric of "industrial revolution."[16] It may work also for other parts of Europe or for Japan. But does it work for the United States? Certain writers have been warning that it may not, at least not in its stark, crude, early formulations. Eisenstadt himself admonished scholars to pay proper attention to "specific historical experiences" not taken into account by the modernization paradigms of the 1960s.[17] For the United States, two central problems preventing any easy application of modernization theory to its history are the lack of a traditional peasant society anything like those of preindustrial Europe or the present Middle East or Africa, and the difficulty in pointing out when, if ever, the shift from traditional to modern really happened.[18] If traditional society, and the departure from it, cannot be identified, then the usefulness of modernization theory for understanding the American experience—indeed the very validity of the theory itself as a universal construct, since the United States is a preeminently modern society whose case the theory should cover—is severely limited.

Furthermore, the classic "demographic transition" does not seem to have happened in the United States, the demographic corollary of modernization which asserts that countries go through four stages of changing birth and death rates as they proceed from traditional to industrialized: death rates fall, while birth rates remain high, resulting in unprecedented population growth, and only after a time do birth rates drop to restore traditionally slow net growth and more stable population size. Transition theory may describe what happened in England in the eighteenth and nineteenth centuries, or (with revisions) in France, but it does not reflect the demographic history of North America.[19]

Many critiques of modernization are now in print and it is pointless to mention more than a few. Raymond Grew, in an essay entitled "Modernization and its Discontents,"[20] reminded his readers that the term "is vague as well as unattractive, even offensive," has "serious built-in biases," is unclear about its units of analysis, and has been seen, not surprisingly, as "the political ideology of Western self-interest." Nowadays it "evokes the distrust of a crew-cut; both are seen as symbols of the fifties and sixties and of an optimistic American imperialism." In fact, Grew maintained, there has never been a single theory of modernization but only a lot of individual theories on often separate problems such as families, workers, and cities. But despite its faults, he concluded, "a kind of common sense makes one hesitate to throw the concept out. [It] can . . . help identify vital questions [although] it provides no methods of its own . . . [and] its most important findings in the future are likely to be about differences" among societies rather than similarities.[21]

Two other historians have recently pointed out, in different ways, that traditional and modern ways of life may coexist in the same society or person, that they are not necessarily sequential, that subcultural traditions may survive, adapted to some extent, in a modernized society.[22] One, Thomas Bender, urged a reemployment of Tönnies's *Gemeinschaft-Gesellschaft* idea, but in its pristine form, which allowed the two to coexist. Bender criticized Louis Wirth's well-known article on "Urbanism as a Way of Life" (1937) as ahistorical, as positing characteristics of urban society without allowing for how they might change over time. According to Bender, Wirth succumbed to "a vision of unilinear and inevitable progress." Modernization is simply "the foreign policy version of Wirth's theory," formulated in the 1950s "to facilitate the 'development' of Third-World nations in ways that would avoid the sort of political instability that might strengthen the Communist World at the expense of the Free World." Bender proceeded to examine the historical nature of "community" in America since the seventeenth century and built a "tentative and speculative" time framework for understanding it. He correctly pointed out that over a dozen recent books have discussed the "logic of decay" of community in America, and hence obliquely modernization, but have confusingly dated it in the 1650s, 1690s, 1740s, 1780s, 1820s, 1850s, 1880s, and 1920s. He himself saw the years 1870 to 1920 as the central time when "social experience became bifurcated into what Tönnies called Gemeinschaft and Gesellschaft."[23]

This discussion of modernization theory suggests a frame for seeing how the United States does, and does not, fit into a transnational pattern. Modernization theory contains over-simplifications from a historical standpoint, especially in its unidirectional, progressive, dichotomous projections. A second problem, in the American case, is to what if any extent Americans have been "traditional." This must be solved by those who would apply modernization to American experience. Yet the historical record does not provide much evidence for traditional patterns in the sense used by Tönnies or Max Weber or the modernizers. America was never a "less-developed country." Nondeveloped surely, but not less- or under-developed. Although the seventeenth century (especially in New England) may have been a special case,[24] Americans were usually expansive, planners-ahead, money-makers, restless, "efficacious"[25] about their environment and its future. New England merchants and Chesapeake planters were deeply involved in the emerging transatlantic economy, and, in less dramatic ways, farmers and villagers were also involved in the marketplace and in small-scale agricultural entrepreneurship. American colonists in the eighteenth century had, as James Henretta wrote, an "aggressive psychological outlook which most clearly differentiated the inhabitants of eighteenth century America from a traditional peasantry."[26]

Not every American, all the time and everywhere, shared these modern traits, but then, not all do today. The point is that modern traits were present early and often. In 1836 a report to the New York State Medical Society fretted that "The population of the United States is beyond that of other countries an anxious one . . . we are an anxious, care-worn people."[27] Michel Chevalier, that great French liberal of the nineteenth century, visited the United States in the early 1830s and noticed how businesslike everybody was. In Cincinnati, "Public opinion is on the lookout to banish any habits of dissipation, however innocent, that might get a footing in society, and make a life of leisure tolerable." In New York City, "Nothing . . . is more melancholy than the seventh day . . . after such a Sunday, the labour of Monday is a delightful pastime."[28] Chevalier's more famous touring compatriot, Alexis de Tocqueville, found much the same thing:

> An American, instead of going in a leisure hour to dance merrily at some place of public resort, as the fellows of his calling continue to do throughout the greater part of Europe, shuts himself up at home to drink. He thus enjoys two pleasures: he can go on thinking of his business, and he can get drunk decently by his own fireside.

And, unlike European peasants,

> Almost all the farmers of the United States combine some trade with agriculture; most of them make agriculture itself a trade. It seldom happens that an American farmer settles for good upon the land which he occupies . . . [but] brings land into tillage in order to sell it again.[29]

Tocqueville exaggerated somewhat; some farmers, especially older ones, did put down roots. American workers resisted the work ethic from Franklin's time to the present, to various degrees,[30] and farmers only gradually shifted from semisubsistence production to production largely for markets.[31]

The traditional-modern patterns were (and are) seldom exclusive of each other. But compared to European peasantries[32] Americans were modern at least as early as the first half of the eighteenth century. We could write this off to Anglo-Saxon moneygrubbing or to the Protestant work ethic or to some other myth, but the traits of modernity also characterized

Germans, Swedes, Irish, and later immigrants. As Marcus
Hansen, the pioneering historian of immigration, put it,
"They were Americans before they landed." The same was definitely true of Poles and southern Italians who began arriving
in the United States in some numbers in the 1880s: they were
truly migrant workers, responding to marginal differences in a
transatlantic labor market in order to improve their situations
as entrepreneurs or landowners at home.[33]

Classic social theory, and specific theories of modernization derived from it, will not apply strictly to the American
historical experience. This is not to say that Americans failed
to "modernize" in some sense. Agriculture changed in the
nineteenth and twentieth centuries, traditional and modern
traits intermingled in subcultures and in the general culture,
and of course beyond those facts is the more general truth that
social structures like those suggested by "traditional" or
"modern" do not hold still over long time periods. Sociological
terms may be argued as if they were static, but the realities
they represent are not. All social realities change over time,
though some change very slowly.[34] So it was in America. But
from early times, America evidenced modernity, sharing in
England's already-begun modernization of the eighteenth century,[35] being not so much the "first new nation" as the
first nation that was never old. The concept of modernization
thus has some suggestive or heuristic value for students of
American social history. But it is certainly not faultless or
exhaustive.

A very different explanation of social change is the frontier
thesis of Frederick Jackson Turner. Rather than revolving about
transnational and universal processes like modernization, it
stresses the uniqueness of American development. The frontier thesis fits the pre-1890 American experience rather well,
and though it stops at that point, it has with some justice been
called the only comprehensive explanation of American history
that anyone has yet devised. Historians are familiar with it,

but it will do no harm to quote a few passages from Turner's paper of 1893, "The Significance of the Frontier in American History," his fullest enunciation of his frontier thesis.

"The existence of an area of free land," he declared, "its continuous recession, and the advance of American settlement westward, explain American development." A sweeping statement. Furthermore, the frontier, that area of free land, was pushed westward and was transformed into a civilized region by a continuing, repeating social process:

> The United States lies like a huge page in the history of society. Line by line as we read this continental page from West to East we find the record of social evolution. It begins with the Indian and the hunter; it goes on to tell of the disintegration of savagery by the entrance of the trader, the pathfinder of civilization; we read the annals of the pastoral stage in ranch life; the exploitation of the soil by the raising of unrotated crops of corn and wheat in sparsely settled farming communities; the intensive culture of the denser farm settlement; and finally the manufacturing organization with city and factory system. This page is familiar to the student of census statistics, but how little of it has been used by our historians. Particularly in eastern states this page is a palimpsest.

Further, "The growth of nationalism and the evolution of American political institutions were dependent on the advance of the frontier." And it was

> to the frontier [that] the American intellect owes its striking characteristics. That coarseness and strength combined with acuteness and acquisitiveness; that practical, inventive turn of mind, quick to find expedients; that masterful grasp of material things, lacking in the artistic but powerful to effect great ends; that restless, nervous energy; that dominant individualism, working for good and for evil, and withal that buoyancy and exuberance which comes with freedom—these are traits of the frontier, or traits called out elsewhere because of the existence of the frontier.

Turner was struck by the statement in the report prefacing the

federal census of 1890 that a continuous frontier line had
ceased to exist during the 1880s. Pockets of land remained
empty, but for the first time, a line from Canada to Mexico,
west of which was virtually unsettled land, there for the taking, could no longer be drawn on the map. Since Columbus
first sailed, Turner reminded his listerners, "America has been
another name for opportunity . . . [and] movement has been
its dominant fact." But in 1893, "four centuries from the discovery of America, at the end of a hundred years of life under
the Constitution, the frontier has gone, and with its going has
closed the first period of American history."[36]

That is the nub of the Turner thesis. It has had many crit-
ics, not least because Turner seemed to overargue the role of
the frontier in shaping American personality, to underargue
urban and industrial history and class conflict, and to attribute
to the influence of the frontier too many social and personal
qualities (though these were by no means all flattering or
romanticized). But these and other criticisms aside, does
Turner still have anything to tell us? I think he does, and I
think he might have told us more had he lived into our own
time and been able to see more clearly how the frontier became significant in an even longer time span and larger context
than he realized, either in 1893 or by the time he died in 1932.
In any case, it is obviously true, *grosso modo*, that the existence
of a very large virgin wilderness, accessible (the more so after
the building of the railroads), inexpensive, and easily
exploited, was a uniquely important difference between American development and that of other First World countries in the
eighteenth and nineteenth centuries, and of "less-developed"
countries in the twentieth, possibly excepting Brazil. Though
the role of the frontier in American history has been exten-
sively evaluated, more can be said, and the point about available land reapplied. Also, the frontier idea reflects on modernization theory: although it is a kind of modernization scheme
of its own, the frontier idea is particular to America while

modernization theory, in its classic formulations, is transnational and transtemporal. Yet if we understand both ideas broadly, they may complement each other.

Modernization theorists have stressed increased control over the environment, the "efficacy factor," as a mark of modernization. They associate efficacy with the break from traditional peasant or rural ways and the entry into urban life, mass politics, and other modern behavior. But if the essence of this process is the presence of efficacy rather than the place where it was exercised, then we can find it not only in the rural-to-urban movement on which modernizationists focus so often, but also in the rural-to-rural movement, the rapid expansion, the aggressive exploitation of land and resources typical of the United States in the eighteenth and nineteenth centuries. Another point: education is a key to modernization, according to its theorists. If we concede that education can take place outside of classrooms, laboratories, or libraries, all of which were strikingly absent from American frontier regions, then possibly the United States might yet squeeze under the modernization umbrella. As William Appleman Williams once wrote, the frontier as an exploitable area was an educator, not the least of whose lessons was expansionism. In America it did not teach peasant ways, but entrepreneurial ones. "The frontier in some ways took the place of formal education," according to Williams; "a kind of non-intellectual learning by surviving and succeeding became part of the American attitude at an early date."[37]

The frontier also had much to do with the early establishment and continued predominance of property owning or property seeking among Americans. Marx and Engels thought that class struggle could not break out in the United States until "undeveloped social conditions" and easy ownership of land had ceased. Engels wrote in 1886 that in America, "every one could become, if not a capitalist, at all events an independent man, producing or trading, with his own means, for his own account. And because there were not, *as yet*, classes with opposing interests, our [English] . . . bourgeois thought that America stood *above* class antagonisms and struggles." He took the Haymarket riot and the strikes of that turbulent year to mean that the class struggle had finally begun in America—"I only wish Marx could have lived to see it"—but events did not bear this out, as he later realized. Available land acted as a social safety valve, as part of the answer that Werner Sombart found to his famous question, "Why is there no socialism in the United States?"[38]

Turner's point of departure, as already noted, was what he took to be the closing of the frontier by 1890, when the Census Bureau reported the nonexistence of a frontier line. He later admitted that that was overstatement, and that frontier conditions did survive in limited areas for a time. Nonetheless, "the period around 1890 . . . was a real turning point."[39] The first great period of American history, beginning with Columbus, was over. A second period, fraught with unknowns, was beginning. Turner thus presented a two-stage scheme of American history. The first was known or knowable, because it was already accomplished. Its essential element was the frontier. The second period was a book not only yet to be opened but yet to be written. Who would write it, and what would they say? Many of Turner's listeners, and others like himself who reflected after World War I on diminishing world resources and rising population, found the question frightening. A comfortable past, irrecoverable because the frontier was used up, was about to be overtaken by an unknown, resource-scarce future.[40]

But then, as Yehoshua Arieli once remarked, "Up to the twentieth century, the American experience was predominantly future-directed," always anxious to experience change, to greet the new, to achieve rather than to contemplate. In some ways that would continue.[41] Turner assured his listeners in 1893 that despite the sharp separation he was making between the (past) stage one and the (future) stage two, the future was "not *tabula rasa*"; certain American attitudes and ways of meeting reality would surely persist.[42] Turner might have been more reassured and reassuring if he had lived farther in time from the end of the frontier line, that simple geographic and demographic fact from which he succeeded in drawing such enormous historical significance. Now, on the edge of the 1980s, we may revise Turner by placing the frontier, significant as it was, in a larger context, simply because we know much more of the story than Turner did almost ninety years ago. We can now see that in the long view, American history can be understood, on the basis of evidence as concrete as Turner's, as a three-stage rather than a two-stage scheme. American history looked at as three stages (described later in this chapter) may afford comparisons to other societies: Instead of applying modernization theory to the American experience, which it fits at best awkwardly, the American experience may suggest something useful for understanding other national histories.

Consider one more approach to social change, that offered by Robert Malthus. His is a classic discussion, first published anonymously in 1798, when he was a young fellow of Jesus College, Cambridge, from which he had graduated in mathematics a few years before. Malthus was not the first to ponder the relation of population to social change, and some of his most famous ideas were "in the air" in Europe when he wrote at the close of the eighteenth century.[43] But he formulated his ideas with force and clarity. Appearing when American national life under the Constitution was less than ten years old, his theory owed much to demographic events in the former English colonies in North America.

Malthus is probably better known than any other classic social theorist except Marx, in part because few problems are as persistent and threatening as population and food, and in part because few theories are as simple as his. The basic points should be familiar. "I think I may fairly make two postulata," Malthus began.

> First, that food is necessary to the existence of man.
> Secondly, that the passion between the sexes is necessary, and will remain nearly in its present state.
> These two laws ever since we have had any knowledge of mankind, appear to have been fixed laws of our nature, [and we can expect no change] . . . without an immediate act of power in that Being who first arranged the system of the universe; and for the advantage of his creatures, still executes, according to fixed laws, all its various operations.

On these two observations Malthus rested his grim and famous conclusion:

> Assuming, then, my postulata as granted, I say, that the power of population is indefinitely greater than the power in the earth to produce subsistence for man. Population, when unchecked, increases in a geometrical ratio. Subsistence increases only in an arithmetical ratio. A slight acquaintance with numbers will shew the immensity of the first power in comparison of the second.[44]

Malthus's entry in the *Dictionary of National Biography* was written by no less eminent a Victorian than Leslie Stephen, who assured us that Malthus was "a singularly amiable man."[45] But Malthus, the graduate of the mathematics tripos, could not shrink from a Q.E.D.: the great disparity between geometrical population growth and arithmetical subsistence growth argued conclusively

> against the perfectibility of the mass of mankind. . . . And, that the superior power of population cannot be checked without producing misery or vice, the ample portion of these two bitter ingredients in the cup of human life, and the continuance of the physical causes that seem to have produced them, bear too convincing a testimony.[46]

In the second and expanded edition of the *Essay*, which Malthus brought out in 1803, he urged another alternative besides vice and misery, the voluntary one of "moral restraint," by which he meant delaying marriage (and staying celibate before marriage), thereby reducing the number of births. This offered some hope for progress and human improvement, though that was by no means certain.[47]

Malthus at one point considered whether emigration might be an "adequate remedy" to overpopulation, but he did not think much of it. "When we revert to experience, and to the actual state of the uncivilized parts of the globe . . . it will appear but a very weak palliative." To support this view he recited several disastrous attempts to colonize in the New World, efforts that led to famine and death, as in early Virginia, New England, and "the Barbadoes."[48] Nassau Senior, an English economist of the next generation, criticized Malthus in the 1840s for disregarding emigration as a check on population. Senior, like many English thinkers and doers (though not enough of them), was concerned about Ireland and its overpopulation, and declared emigration to be the only remedy. He made the interesting observation that while populations for whom property holding is easy—the Americans of the eighteenth or nineteenth century, for whom land was abundant—have high birth rates, it is paradoxically true that poverty, verging on destitution, leads also to high birth rates, as in Ireland: ". . . when men are so indigent that they cannot become poorer, and so abject that they cannot be more degraded, they naturally seize whatever pleasures are within their reach without caring for the consequences."[49]

Malthus did, however, allow for certain prosperous colonies to provide a solution to threats of overpopulation. Ever since the time of the classical Greeks, colonies occasionally provided an escape from the vice and misery that inevitably overtook populations that outdistanced their food supplies. Malthus called such places "a plenty of rich land to be had for little or nothing," and in another place, "a great plenty of fertile uncultivated land."[50] Such words described the former

English colonies in North America, as they had developed in the eighteenth century, and Malthus was very much aware of that. Citing Ezra Stiles of Connecticut and other eighteenth-century American observers, Malthus graciously concluded,

> In the United States of America, where the means of subsistence have been more ample, the manners of the people more pure, and consequently the checks to early marriage fewer, than in any of the modern states of Europe, the population has been found to double itself in twenty-five years. This ratio of increase, though short of the utmost power of population, yet as the result of actual experience, we will take as our rule; and say,
> That population, when unchecked, goes on doubling itself every twenty-five years, or increases in a geometrical ratio.[51]

In fact, he pointed out, back-country areas doubled in only fifteen years in America.[52] But he took a conservative twenty-five as his average, and it became the famous "Malthusian ratio," the natural, unchecked rate of increase of human populations when the means of subsistence are plentiful.

Presently available data for the eighteenth century are much the same as Malthus's and have not improved enough to upset his figures. If a population grows at a rate of 3 percent per year, it will double in just under twenty-five years. American population in the eighteenth century increased in some areas at 4 percent, doubling in nineteen years, or even 5 percent, doubling in fifteen years. Rates above 3 percent were true in the nineteenth century of Americans, of both English and French Canadians in the St. Lawrence Valley,[53] and even of Sioux Indians on the northern Great Plains.[54] When would this staggering growth stop? Malthus knew:

> Even civil liberty, all powerful as it is, will not create fresh land. The Americans may be said, perhaps, to enjoy a greater degree of civil liberty, now they are an independent people, than while they were in subjection to England; but we may be perfectly sure, that population will not long continue to increase with the same rapidity as it did then.[55]

Yet an English traveler who published his impressions in 1821 wrote, "Mr Malthus would not be understood here."[56] In fact, Americans were able to ignore Malthus, to continue to increase almost as rapidly, for several more decades. More precisely, they were able to multiply in their "new habitat," which Malthus clearly understood was very different from Europe in a demographic sense.

Malthus made a great contribution. As Australian political economist Ian Bowen put it, Malthus "once and for all [drew] mankind's attention to the fact that there were limits to expansion. Once the postulate is granted that food . . . cannot be indefinitely expanded, then it follows that population cannot be indefinitely increased."[57] In the process of stating his population theory, Malthus became the chief founder of modern demographic theory and historical demography. Not that no one before him had remarked on population. Many had.[58] But no one clarified for English readers, as Malthus did, questions about fertility, mortality, migration, income, resources, and class—the stuff of sociology, economics, and much of history. After the population essay and other works, it was possible for Malthus's friend and critic, David Ricardo, to marry population and economics,[59] for Nassau Senior to revise the theory to apply to Ireland and to account for population growth among the destitute, and for later scholars to continue working on the research agenda that Malthus had explored. Malthus himself wrote that we know too little about the oscillations between times of plenty and times of misery, because "the histories of mankind that we possess are histories only of the higher classes."[60] As for whether America was unique, Malthus as a student of population knew that it was a "new habitat," but he expected that it would become more and more like Europe as land became less available, the means of subsistence less abundant, and population growth less rapid. The story became more complicated than that, but, like modernization theory and Turner's frontier, Malthus (and Ricardo and Senior) ad-

vanced the understanding of America in both its uniqueness
and its transnational context.

Structures and Conjunctures: The French Connection

Malthus's call for histories of all classes, not just the elites,
was not really heeded by any large group of professional historians until Marc Bloch and Lucien Febvre founded the journal *Annales d'histoire sociale et économique* in Strasbourg in
1929, and when they and others coalesced into the "*Annales*
school," centered in Paris after World War II.[61] *Annales* history
encompasses more than demographic history, but has helped
it flourish in France and Britain. Demographic history, hardly
thought of in the United States before 1965, since developed
after that into a substantial body of scholarly literature.[62] To a
few historians before then, the importance of a history of
population, in itself and for other histories, was not in doubt.
Turner, in notes for a lecture delivered in 1923, refers to census data and to prominent demographers, and to Malthus.
Population was a concern of Turner's, as were the "Nordic
alarmists" of that time, neo-Malthusians who feared that
population in the United States and the world would outrun
food supplies, minerals, petroleum, and other necessities
within a generation or two. Turner's frontier observation of
1893 was itself demographic and geographic.[63] Nearly ninety
years later, an American demographic historian pleaded for
more studies meeting "the historical demographer's ideal . . .
informed speculation and models for explanation, a knowledge
of demographic methods and comparative findings, and hard
work in the sources."[64] At about the same time, Robert Parke,
of the Social Science Research Council, cited areas where policy makers should take better account of demographic studies;
very regrettably he omitted historical work.[65]

European authorities on the importance of population in
history include England's H. J. Habakkuk, who said in 1958
that

for those who care for the overmastering pattern, the elements are evidently there for a heroically simplified version of English history before the nineteenth century, in which the long-term movements in prices, in income distribution, in investment, in real wages and in migration are dominated by changes in the growth of population.[66]

Similarly, Fernand Braudel of the *Annalistes,* in his masterpiece *The Mediterranean and the Mediterranean World in the Age of Philip II,* reflecting on the doubling of population around the Mediterranean between 1500 and 1600, wrote,

> . . . this biological revolution was the major factor in all the other revolutions with which we are concerned, more important than the Turkish conquest, the discovery and colonization of America, or the imperial vocation of Spain. Had it not been for the increase in the numbers of men, would any of these glorious chapters ever have been written?[67]

Other prominent witnesses abound who will testify that population is important in history, that it should be "the starting point for constructing an *histoire totale,*"[68] and that Americans have not absorbed it well enough into their thinking about the past.

Embedded in Braudel's book is an ingenious scheme for looking at history and relating passing events and longer-run patterns. His terms should clarify what I want to say about the periodization of American history based on population changes. In *The Mediterranean* and other of his writings, Braudel seeks to isolate immediate, concrete events, the *événementielle,* as surface happenings on more lasting units of time, periods of twelve to fifty years, which he calls *conjonctures.* These in turn rest on much longer-lasting *structures.* Events are short-run (*courte durée*), *conjonctures* are middle-run (*moyenne durée*), and *structures* are long-run (*longue durée*). Everything changes. Nothing in human society is absolutely static over time. But *longue durée* patterns may change very slowly, lasting with little measurable change for centuries.[69]

The challenge which Braudel throws at historians is to identify the *moyenne* and *longue durées* out of the chaos of passing events. In what follows, the entities I call the frontier-rural mode and the metropolitan mode are akin to Braudel's *structures*. I use the word "mode" because it is less ambiguous than the cognate English word "structure" for *structure*, but I still mean a set of long-lasting social (and therefore economic and cultural) patterns, changing slowly over ten or twenty decades, shaping the lives and behavior of the great majority of people who lived in that place in that period. "Mode" means *structure*, and period, as when I say "frontier-rural period," means the span of time when that mode was prevalent. "Conjuncture," as I will use it, refers to the briefer time when two modes coexisted and interacted.[70]

A Demographic Observation: Growth Rate Plateaus

At one point in his book, Braudel was writing about violence, poverty, brigandage, and piracy in Italy and Germany in the sixteenth century. This provoked the thought that the terrorism of the 1970s in those countries—the work of the Baader-Meinhof gang, the P.L.O. at the Munich Olympics in 1972, the Red Brigades who killed Aldo Moro, the kneecappers, and others—may be explainable in part by long-term historical structures of those areas. Braudel's point was more philosophical, however; out of a series of instances of violence he reflects on the task of historians. "Are these incidents," he asks,

> trivial happenings in themselves, the surface signs of a valid social history? . . . . Is this evidence meaningful at some deeper level? That is the historian's problem. To answer yes, as I intend to do, means being willing to see correlations, regular patterns and general trends where at first sight there appear only incoherence, anarchy, a series of unrelated happenings.[71]

With this mandate (and keeping in mind the useful ideas on

social change provided by the modernization theorists, Turner, and Malthus) we now seek "regular patterns and general trends" in the history of the American population. I offer an observation which is simple and concrete, but which has not been remarked upon as far as I know. It divides American history into periods on the basis of mass population data and may therefore help solve such questions as when Americans modernized, if ever; where the frontier ended and what it meant; even where the balance of population and resources may go in the near and middle future.

Total figures of the United States population exist for ten-year intervals back to 1790, thanks to the Census, and well back into the colonial seventeenth century, thanks to historians. These figures are reliable within the reasonable limits demanded for comparing the speed of population growth. When the increases in each decade are translated into percents, and are graphed, three distinct plateaus appear (see table 1 and figure 1).[72] Wild fluctuations occur before 1670, when the colonial population was less than 100,000, or before 1700, when it reached 250,000. Before those dates the sparseness of people made the seventeenth century into a sort of statistical *Vorzeit*, or prehistory.[73] From (very roughly) 1720 until just after 1860, population in America increased at exceedingly rapid rates. This period, from the early eighteenth century until the early 1860s, may be considered, from a demographic standpoint, to be the first phase of American history.

From the 1670s through the 1850s, a period during which the total population rose from 112,000 to 31,443,000, the average rate of growth per decade was 34.6 percent. The rate fluctuated within a wide range in the early decades when population was small, between a low 19.5 percent in the 1690s to a high 41.3 percent in the 1780s. But after 1790, with the population at about 4 million and rising, the fluctuations fell within the high but narrow range of 33 to 36 percent, averag-

TABLE I

Population of the United States, 1630–1980

Year	A: total population (in thousands)[1]	B: percent increase in preceding decade[2]	C: percent rural[3]
1630	4.6	—	
1640	27	487.0	
1650	50	85.2	
1660	75	50.0	
1670	112	49.3	
1680	152	35.7	
1690	210	38.2	
1700	251	19.5	
1710	332	32.3	
1720	466	40.4	
1730	629	35.0	
1740	906	44.0	
1750	1,171	29.2	
1760	1,594	36.1	
1770	2,148	34.8	
1780	2,780	29.4	
1790	3,929	41.3	95
1800	5,308	35.1	94
1810	7,240	36.4	93
1820	9,638	33.1	93
1830	12,866	33.5	91
1840	17,069	32.7	89
1850	23,192	35.9	85
1860	31,443	35.6	80
1870	39,818	26.6	75
1880	50,156	26.0	72
1890	62,948	25.5	65
1900	75,995	20.7	60
1910	91,972	21.0	54
1920	105,771	14.9	49
1930	122,775	16.1	44
1940	131,669	7.2	43

1950	150,697	14.5	36
1960	179,323	19.0	30
1970	203,235	13.3	26
1980	221,500	9.0	

[1]Source: *Historical Statistics* 1975, series Z1-Z19, A2. 1980 approximate, from Census report P-25, no. 881.
[2]Source: Computed from column A.
[3]Source: *Historical Statistics* 1975, series A203. "Rural" means the proportion living on farms or in villages smaller than 2,500 (after 1940, not including suburban fringes, which have been counted as "urban").

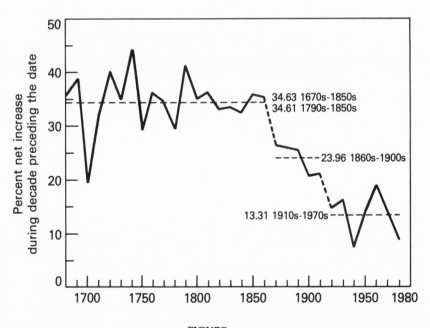

FIGURE I

The three plateaus: Rates of
population growth, by decade

ing 34.6 percent from the 1790s through the 1850s. That rate
of growth was slightly higher than the Malthusian ratio. The
American population doubled about every twenty-two years.
But no Malthusian disaster happened. Famine and pestilence
did not sweep the land. Epidemics of yellow fever, cholera,
and smallpox hardly made a dent except among Indians. Wars
were few and relatively local.[74] Sufficient food and land were
available to satisfy physical and economic cravings, and to
encourage rapid expansion of territory and population.

As the land area of the United States was extended to include the trans-Appalachian West by the Treaty of Paris of
1783, ending the Revolutionary War, and then into the immense regions of Louisiana in 1803, the Floridas by 1819,
Texas in 1845, Oregon in 1846, and the Southwest in 1848,
the density of the population barely doubled while the numbers of population doubled and redoubled and re-redoubled in
an exuberant drive to fill these regions productively with
Anglo-Americans. The extremely rapid growth, although it involved tens of millions of individual people, had certain features that were practically constant. Although we are employ-
ing aggregate data from censuses, aggregates which flatten out
a wide range of individual behavior by the averaging and col-
lecting process, nonetheless we can make some valid general
statements. The expanding population was rural, (see table 2)
and its expansion rarely involved town-building except as
supply centers and jumping-off points into exploitable rural
areas were demanded.[75] Expansion sprang from high birth
rates rather than dropping death rates, or from heavy net migration, at least until the late 1840s. The areas growing most
rapidly in population were those just behind the frontier,
areas of six to forty-five people per square mile:[76] not the
rawest frontier, or the more settled areas, but areas with
enough cultivation and available land to permit new families
to form and to build farms. The long period from the early
eighteenth century to about 1860, with its very rapid (and,

after 1790, very steady) growth, deserves to be called the frontier-rural period in American history.

In the 1860s, the rate of population growth suddenly dropped. From the customary increase of over 35 percent in the 1850s, the increase in the 1860s fell to just over 26 percent. It remained at about that level through the 1870s and 1880s. It fell again in the 1890s and from 1900 to 1910, but not as steeply, to about 21 percent. During the half century from the early 1860s to about 1915, growth per decade averaged 24 percent, or about a third slower than the growth rate prevailing for more than a century and a half before then. A distinct and sudden change had taken place around 1860, signaling a new period in demographic and social history. It was a bi-level period, lasting about fifty years, and, for reasons to be seen, it can be called the Great Conjuncture.

After 1915, population never again grew as much as 20 percent in a decade.[77] The census of 1920 placed the total population at 15 percent higher than 1910. From 1920 until the beginning of the 1980s, increases have averaged 13 percent, ranging from a high of 18 during the baby-boom years of the 1950s to lows of 7 or 8 percent during the depression-ridden 1930s and the 1970s. Thus the years from just before 1920 to the early 1980s—and perhaps well beyond—form a third phase in American history. The first period consisted of growth in the frontier-rural mode almost exclusively. The third has seen virtually no frontier-rural growth, but almost purely a metropolitan mode, involving industry, interregional trade and business organization, urbanization, and suburbanization. Agricultural population has stabilized in absolute numbers, or fallen, while urban population has continued to eat into the total at a rate of about 5 percent per decade (as has happened since the 1840s). Almost four out of five Americans lived in urban areas by 1980—and practically all the rest were touched by metropolitan life via the media and the market-place, even though some were moving away from the physical,

TABLE 2

Rural and urban population growth, and rural
as a proportion of total U.S. growth,
by decade, 1790s–1960s

Decade ending	A. Rural % increase	B. Urban % increase	C. % of total growth acc'ted for by rural
1800	33.7	59.4	96.0
1810	34.7	63.0	95.3
1820	33.2	32.0	100.3
1830	31.2	62.6	93.1
1840	29.7	63.7	90.8
1850	29.1	92.1	81.1
1860	28.4	75.4	78.1
avg. 1790s–1850s	31.4	64.0	90.7
1870	13.6	59.3	51.1
1880	25.7	42.7	98.8
1890	13.4	56.4	52.5
1900	12.2	36.4	58.9
1910	9.0	39.3	42.9
avg. 1860s–1900s	14.8	46.8	60.8
1920	3.2	29.0	21.5
1930	4.4	27.3	27.3
1940	6.4	7.9	88.9
1950*	7.9/−5.2	19.5/29.6	54.5/−35.9
1960	−0.9	29.9	−4.7
1970	+0.2	19.2	−0.2
avg. 1910s–1960s	2.7	22.7	27.2

Column C is arrived at by dividing percent rural
increase (column A above) by percent total increase
(column B of table 1—not by column B above).

Rate of rural increase declines. So does rate of urban
increase. But rural increase accounts for more than
half of the total U.S. increase until almost 1920.

Sources: *Historical Statistics* 1975. Column A, series A69;

geographic metropolises. But few could escape the mode. Urban growth has always been slower than rural growth in the United States, and the decline in the rate of growth through most of American history forms two parallel lines, the urban below the rural.[78]

As the metropolitan mode became established in the middle and late nineteenth century and then became predominant after 1915 or so, population growth was typically much slower than during the frontier-rural and Conjuncture periods, in spite of boom towns of the recent past like Los Angeles and Houston, in spite of the exodus of blacks from the South to northern and midwestern cities between 1915 and 1970, and in spite of the emergence of a suburban-dwelling majority. Metropolitan growth differs from frontier-rural not only in its slowness but also in its causes, outcomes, and economic and demographic character.

From 35 percent per decade in the first period, to 24 percent in the second, to below 14 in the third: that is the regular pattern for nearly three hundred years. The regularity is admittedly less stark if we leave aside net migration from Europe, Africa, and Asia, as Malthus did, and deal only with the natural increase from the surplus of births over deaths in the existing population. Without immigration the step-wise pattern of downward plateaus of growth rates is a little less clear. But it is only slightly blurred, not fully eroded by any means. And certainly immigration cannot be left out of any general treatment of the American experience without violating the story irreparably.[79]

A leading demographic historian reviewed the state of his field in 1979, noted as have others that much good work has been done since the mid-1960s, but lamented that "there is no

---

column B, series A57; column C, series A69 divided by series A2.
*Census definition of "urban" changes. This decade is omitted in calculating averages of 1910s–1960s.

consensus on periodization, and 'linear' notions of every sort are now questioned."[80] One can add that much of that work is specialized, and attempts at comprehensive histories are rumored but not published. The three-phase periodization, based on plateaus of growth, may be helpful in this regard. The question arises as to why the decline in growth was steplike rather than steady, and I will not answer that to a demographer's satisfaction. But it evidently happened, and in succeeding chapters I will describe the modes and conjuncture that the plateaus represent. Components of change, including decline in the rural growth rate, decline in the urban growth rate, the relation between the two, the baby-boom anomaly, changes in mortality rates and in migration patterns, and other aspects of demographic history, have been remarked upon and continue to be studied. Enough is now understood, I believe, to permit a comprehensive look, even if it is tentative. What is offered here, then, is a framework for social history based on a demographic observation involving the American population throughout its history. The framework might well accommodate many other elements—politics, economics, *mentalités*[81] —but on this occasion they appear, if at all, as suggested byroads.

Frederick Jackson Turner might have seen the three-stage pattern of growth rates had he lived into our own day, conscious as he was of demographic patterns and graphic techniques.[82] But he died in March 1932, before the pattern became clear. He might have seen that American history did not divide into two periods, frontier and postfrontier, but into three: frontier-rural, metropolitan, and the conjuncture of the two modes to form a period in between. He did see that the existence of a vast mass of readily available land was a fact of cardinal importance for a long time, as no one considering American history can seriously deny, though many have given it too little weight. Turner called attention to the frontier in 1893. In 1923 he warned of the "likelihood that we in New

England and the Midwest in general will not appreciate the importance of the rural factor in our history and in the problems of the future."[83] In the 1980s we may run that risk, immersed in the metropolitan *mentalité* as we are, and we should remind ourselves that the rural past is not dead, or, as Faulkner said, is not even past.

Turner was conscious that the frontier did not end "with a bang" in 1890, as he once put it, that 1880–1900 formed some kind of transition phase which had not fully ended until the early twentieth century, that homestead patents were still being issued in 1920. But the Census of 1920, with its evidence of rising farm tenancy, depressed him, and he worried that population pressure and rising costs of farmland would create an American peasantry for the first time. He was well aware of changes in agriculture during the eighteenth and nineteenth centuries, and at one point (in 1926) declared that "frontier advance . . . went on until not only the frontier *line,* as mapped by Henry Gannett [of the Census] could no longer be depicted, but until the frontier *phase* of our history drew to its close." And he dated that phase from Bacon's Rebellion (1676) to La Follette's presidential candidacy (1924)—dates based on nondemographic events but which mark the limits of the frontier-rural mode very closely to the rates-of-growth pattern.[84] In his final days, however, Turner did not clearly see that new forms of opportunity, especially white-collar jobs, had begun to replace the lost opportunities of frontiers, and that the metropolitan mode had arrived, bringing new ways of living which were not deserving of the pessimism with which he, and more alarmist observers of the 1920s, regarded it. The end of the frontier was not the end of America, and by the time Turner died, the transitional phase was already past.[85]

The most interesting part of our observation about growth rates is the emergence of a transition phase of about fifty years, with the end of the frontier line falling almost exactly at the midpoint of that phase. Instead of a simple, dichotomous shift from frontier to postfrontier, or from traditional to modern, or (most popularly and oversimply) from rural to urban, we find rapid frontier-rural growth continuing after 1890 and through much of the Conjuncture, and at the same time the spread of metropolitan growth, especially in the northeastern quarter of the country. In the final years of the Conjuncture, frontier-rural growth breathed its last, giving up the field before 1920 to exclusively metropolitan patterns of life. Because both modes operated between the 1860s and about 1915, those years deserve the name "Great Conjuncture." The crucial point is that the newer form of growth was not simply replacing the older. Both happened at once in those years.

Through much of their population history, Americans ignored Malthus. They exhibited hardly any sign until well into the twentieth century of the "moral restraint" he preached, but on the other hand they suffered little of the "vice and misery" of which he warned.

II

From Prehistory to the Frontier-Rural Mode,

1500 – 1720

This chapter treats of the European demographic matrix from which colonies sprang in the sixteenth and seventeenth centuries, and the impact of colonization on aboriginal Americans; of the social-demographic nature of English colonies in New England and astride the Chesapeake in the seventeenth century, a period I term *Vorzeit;* and of the emergence of the frontier-rural mode in the early eighteenth century. The dates 1500 and 1720 are approximate, and indicate general trends rather than precisely datable events.

Old World to New World in the Sixteenth Century

We begin in western Europe and surrounding waters in about 1500. A cycle of population expansion had begun in the late fifteenth century and was to continue through the sixteenth. The bubonic plague that had scourged Europe from the 1340s into the fifteenth century was mostly dormant and would not reappear widely until the seventeenth century. Harvests were generally good, markets reasonably efficient in bringing food to cities. For these and other reasons, not all of

35

them well understood as yet, the population of Europe rose from perhaps 70 million to over 100 million in the sixteenth century. In the Mediterranean countries it may have doubled between 1530 and 1590.[1] In many respects sixteenth-century Europe remained medieval. The Mediterranean was a world to itself, taking sixty days to cross just as it had in Roman times, and remained "the centre of the world, a strong and brilliant universe . . . for a hundred years after Christopher Columbus and Vasco da Gama."[2] Still, the brilliant universe was beginning to shed its light in new places. In the sixteenth century the Spanish and Portuguese established their vast empires in North and South America. The French began to create one only slightly smaller, an empire ultimately stretching from the Caribbean and the mouth of the Mississippi northeastward to the Great Lakes and the Gulf of St. Lawrence, almost the entire eastern two-thirds of North America.[3]

These empires, however, did not swarm with Europeans, because Europe could not yet provide them. The startling thing is not how many people left Europe, but how few. The early parties that went to Mexico and Peru numbered in the hundreds, and they confronted an indigenous population numbering in the millions. In all of the Americas in 1500 somewhere between 50 million and 100 million native people lived, the great majority of them in the coastal or Andean mountain regions from the Tropic of Cancer southward to below the Tropic of Capricorn.[4] With amazing speed and ease, the few hundred Spaniards conquered the Mexican and Peruvian Indians, who outnumbered them more than one hundred thousand to one. How was it possible? The Spanish did have horses and gunpowder, which were formidable advantages, but not enough to account for their victory after the initial shock was past. The Spanish, however, also had the silent and terrible weapon of European contagious diseases. As happened to the peoples of Europe when plague struck in the fourteenth century, the Indians of Mexico and Peru were devastated by exposure to diseases for which they had no internal immunity whatsoever, genetic or otherwise.

By 1500, western Europe "had much to give and little to receive in the way of new human infections."[5] It gave much to the native inhabitants of Central and South America. Smallpox ravaged central and coastal Mexico in 1522, killing millions. From then on, smallpox, together with diseases mild to a European (measles, chicken pox, whooping cough), or more serious (malaria and influenza), or carried by African slaves of Europeans (yellow fever, which appeared in the seventeenth century), wiped out most of the native peoples. The population of Mexico, probably over 25 million when Cortez arrived in 1519, plunged hideously. By 1568 it numbered no more than 3 million. Another epidemic in 1576–77 cut it in half, and by 1605 only about a million were alive. Moreover, European diseases more often struck down young adults than the aged or the children. The ancient gods were silent. Indian society fell apart, famine followed epidemic, and "a demographic disaster with no known parallel in human history" was complete.[6]

To the north, in what became the United States and Canada, no such destruction took place; tropical and Mediterranean diseases made less headway, and far fewer Indians lived there.[7] The "decimation factor"—the ratio of Indian population at its pre-Columbian height compared to its lowest point thereafter—may have been 25 to 1 in coastal-tropical Mexico, but 10 to 1 in most of the future United States and 5 to 1 in future Canada.[8] Colder climate and, more importantly, a more primitive and nomadic culture scattered over large areas allowed Indians farther north to avoid epidemics with a little more success than did the Inca, the Aztecs, and other densely populated cultures. A recent and cautious estimate put the Indian population of the future United States and Canada at about 2.2 million in 1500.[9] In 1600 the density of native population never exceeded ten persons per square mile and was much less in most areas.[10] The Iroquois Confederacy, which caused so much difficulty in fact (and provided so much material for fiction) in the French and Indian War of 1754–63, almost surely never exceeded 17,000 people spread over hundreds of square miles. The Powhatans, who except for Pocahontas gave the early settlers in Virginia much grief, numbered perhaps 9,000.[11] The removals in the 1830s of the "civilized tribes" from Georgia, Florida, and adjacent states to present-day Arkansas and Oklahoma affected about a hundred thousand Indians, a very large group of people but few compared to the 3.5 million whites in the South Atlantic states at that time.[12] Everywhere, the Indians' contact with European-Americans, and with Africans, brought demographic disaster, from smallpox and other contagious diseases, from wars with the colonists, and from wars among themselves.

Warring among tribes had gone on long before Europeans arrived, although wars with the Europeans and their descendants have received greater attention, at the time and since. But the worst killer of Indians was the series of epidemics that struck them down from the seventeenth through the nineteenth centuries, across time and across the continent.[13] Peter Kalm, sent by the Swedish Academy of Science in 1748 to observe and report on American conditions, wrote that the Indian population had been thinning out since the late seventeenth century. Some supposedly sold their lands and went west,

> But in reality . . . most of them ended their days before, either by wars among themselves, or by the small-pox, a disease which the Indians were unacquainted with before their commerce with the Europeans, and which since that time has killed incredible numbers of them. For . . . they do not understand fever or other internal diseases.[14]

Ezra Stiles of Connecticut, writing in 1783, believed that there were no more than 40,000 Indians east of the Mississippi and north of the Ohio by that time, and Thomas Jefferson, in his *Notes on Virginia* of 1782, attributed the decline in Indian population to "spirituous liquors, the small-pox, war, and an abridgement of territory."[15] While the colonists of European stock were ravaged by smallpox, yellow fever, malaria, cholera, and other diseases (though never the plague) in the eighteenth and much of the nineteenth centuries, the native population suffered far worse. The curious thing, in the long run of American history, is not that the English and later the Americans consistently defeated the Indians, but that they had so much trouble doing it, considering the incidence of debility, demoralization, and death resulting from European and African diseases, which reduced the Indians' already small numbers and drained them of resilience and spirit even when they lived.

Vorzeit *in English America: The Seventeenth Century*

Europe's tentative entry into the modern pattern of population growth in the sixteenth century stalled in the seventeenth. England and Holland grew but slowly, France hardly at all. The great age of the Baroque, of Louis XIV, and the Glorious Revolution it may have been, but in demographic terms it was gloomy, stagnant, and long. Death visited more frequently than in the centuries before and after, bringing a virtual halt to population growth. This stability lasted from about 1590 to 1720 and beyond.[16] The Thirty Years' War (1618–48) emptied parts of the Germanies by either death or emigration. Spain and Italy suffered at least ten epidemics of plague and other diseases, and their populations fell. France was battered by periodic epidemics and famines. Plague swept London in 1665, killing perhaps a hundred thousand, according to Daniel Defoe's *Journal of the Plague Year*, which he wrote in 1721 when another epidemic crossed Europe (but spared England). Bad harvests deprived the poor and weakened their resistance to disease. Braudel called the period a "biological *ancien ré-gime*," whose marks were "balance between births and deaths, very high infant mortality, famine, chronic undernourishment and virulent epidemics. These oppressions hardly relaxed with the advances of the eighteenth century. . . ."[17]

England did not suffer all of the hardships that afflicted Europe, but the century still compared unfavorably to the eighteenth. Yet during the seventeenth century, Englishmen founded the colonies that in 1776 became the United States: the first in Virginia in 1607 and the last in Georgia in 1732, all in 125 years, the precise period when much of Europe and England were at their demographic worst since the disastrous, plague- and war-ridden fourteenth century. Population pressure by itself did not provoke colonization. The numbers of poor, and the expenditure needed to care for them, did rise in England in the late sixteenth and early seventeenth centuries, and in certain areas population was perceived by some to be overabundant.[18] But religion in New England and commerce in the Chesapeake were much more important motives for colonization. France, with 18 million people in 1600 to England's 4.5 million, sent her first colonists up the St. Lawrence about then, just a few years before Englishmen went to Virginia, Plymouth, and Boston. But the French colonists were even fewer than the English.

In the first years of most colonies, deaths outran births, and migration to them was a last resort of the destitute or spirit-struck. Population increased slowly if at all, especially in the southern colonies, for many reasons: Indian warfare, epidemics, malnutrition, a shortage of women, the cost of passage, rules against acquiring land and thus against forming a family, and a very sane fear of the howling wilderness.[19] The puzzling fecklessness of the first settlers at Jamestown, who according to reports preferred a short workday and playing games to raising the wheat essential for their survival, may have resulted from sheer malnutrition. In the first three years, according to the newly-arrived Sir Thomas Gates, only sixty men survived out of six hundred, and the sixty were almost too weak to walk. The first years at Jamestown were truly "starving times."[20] That was the worst case, but experiences of other colonies in their earliest years suggest that desperation had to be a motive for facing the ocean and the wilderness. In the seventeenth century, England's North American colonies were for the most part rude and fragile places, intrusions on the edge of a vast empty land mass, put and kept there for marginal economic advantage to their stockholders or proprietors or, in the case of the New England Puritans, because the settlers were too quarrelsome to get along with the Crown, the Church of England, or even with each other.[21] By 1700 the total colonial population, from Maine to Georgia, was only 250,000.

Students of seventeenth-century America will doubtless be outraged to be told that the century of Jamestown, Plymouth, the Puritans, and so forth, is prehistory. But in a demographic sense, it is. As Richard Hofstadter wrote, "So many volumes have been written on the very earliest settlements that their bulk tends to conceal the important fact that the population in these settlements was negligible in number."[22] There were too few people, even at the close of the seventeenth century, to interact in patterned ways, at least in the frontier-rural pattern they would shortly exhibit and continue to exhibit for nearly two more centuries. New England's early practice of settlement by town-congregation was weakening by the early eighteenth century, and did not survive long beyond the Great Awakening and other events around 1740. The plantations of the Chesapeake continued to exist, but smallholdings far outnumbered them once native-born population began to increase by the end of the seventeenth century. Demographically, the European-derived population of the entire future United States was smaller than present-day Winnipeg, Wyoming, or Wichita.[23] Granted, early New England had much more institutional impact than those places; demographic patterns are not the whole of history. But the evident facts that the early settlements grew very slowly, remained tiny, hugged the coastline, and depended for their social shape about as much on European ideas as on American realities and the possibilities which these settlements had yet to exploit,[24] separates them from the pervasive frontier-rural mode that was about to take shape, just as a prehistory is separate from a history.

Nevertheless it is worth a glance at New England and the Chesapeake in their seventeenth-century *Vorzeit* in order to see the differences they had with each other and with the frontier-rural mode to come, and in what ways they bore the seeds of that mode. From a demographic standpoint, early New England and the Chesapeake were very unlike eighteenth-century and later America. The first years at Jamestown were murderous: four out of five settlers in the first fifteen years died, and by 1624 the mortality rate was 252 per thousand (in the 1970s it was just under 9 per thousand in the United States). The crude death rate dropped to perhaps 35 to 55 per thousand in Maryland and Virginia in 1650–1700, and was somewhat lower (15 to 25) in Massachusetts by 1700. Life was short, especially in the Chesapeake.[25]

Vorzeit in the Chesapeake exhibited a very odd demographic regime by American standards. Such population increase as there was resulted from continued immigration, not from natural growth. It could hardly have been otherwise since the sex ratio was six males per female around 1650 and still about five to two in 1700. Indentured servitude, the condition of the majority of immigrants, delayed the age of marriage well into the twenties and thus reduced the number of children a couple would have, which was just as well since the average marriage lasted only seven years before one partner died. Infant and child mortality was high; almost half of those born would never see adulthood.[26] For the growing slave population the sex ratio was about 1.5 males per female, marriages were uncommon, and disease lowered the birth rate.[27]

The condition of women was unlike that in England or New England, or in the southern colonies later. If a woman survived her period of indenture, which was probably the condition under which she came to Maryland, she would almost certainly become the wife of a "planter," a male ex-indentured servant with a certain amount of land. The sex ratio almost guaranteed marriage for women. Premarital pregnancy was common (about one case in three, twice the incidence in England or New England), but the stigma was slight or absent if the couple married before the child was born. Women "were less protected but also more powerful than those who remained at home." On the other hand the death rate among women in the child-bearing years was higher than among men. High mortality afflicted slave women as well.[28]

For both men and women, life was shorter in the Chesapeake than in England at the same time, and if the localities so far researched represent the general pattern, "Most men who lived in Maryland in the early colonial period died well before they reached age fifty."[29] Only when a native-born generation came into being, which happened quite slowly, and when the native-born began to outnumber the English-born or African-born, which happened only after 1680 or 1700, did natural increase become rapid. Then the age of marriage fell, the sex ratio became less skewed, fertility rose, families formed, and the raising of children to adulthood became more normal. Native-born women did not arrive in Maryland under indenture and therefore could marry younger than their immigrant mothers. That brought more children, distributed normally as to sex. Marriage became more possible for the next generation of males. "By the mid-1680s, in all probability, the population thus began to grow through natural increase . . ." The same sort of thing happened to slaves, allowing for some degree of "stable family life" not present in the "isolating and dehumanizing experience" of slavery in the earliest decades.[30] In the Chesapeake, the turn of the seventeenth century into the eighteenth signaled the end of the *Vorzeit* as measured by demographic events.

New England also had its *Vorzeit* in the seventeenth century, but a different one. In fact, the outstanding differences between New England in the *Vorzeit* and the frontier-rural mode that became prevalent in the eighteenth and nineteenth century were less demographic, except for mobility, than social, specifically in social organization and settlement patterns. New England in the seventeenth century was a region of small, tightly knit communities, their civic form the town meeting and their religious form the congregation. The birth rate in Dedham, Massachusetts, for example, was about 40 per thousand, a little higher than in seventeenth-century French or English villages, and a little lower than in the United States at the end of the eighteenth century. The death rate, however, was considerably lower than in Europe: 27 per thousand compared to 30 or 40. People lived longer in New England than in the Chesapeake, often past fifty or even seventy. This, together with an average age of marriage of around twenty-two to twenty-four for women and twenty-five to twenty-seven for men, perhaps two years earlier than in Europe or the Chesapeake, and the high frequency of marriage, led to larger families, more rapid natural increase, and almost certainly more two-parent families during the childhood and adolescence of the offspring. In the early generations, when available property was still well beyond subsistence requirements, longer parental lives meant more parental control over children's marriages and inheritances.[31]

Mobility was very low in every sense except the method of establishing new towns, which was by clusters of families authorized to take up new land as a congregation. Immigration into New England in the seventeenth century (and much of the eighteenth) was meager after the first years. Emigration was also rare. In the case of Dedham, eight of ten people born there would live and die there, "still oblivious to the continent that waited to the westward."[32] Three features separating seventeenth- and early eighteenth-century New England from the Chesapeake and from the later frontier-rural mode appeared throughout Puritan New England from Maine to extreme southwestern Connecticut, where twenty-nine people founded Stamford in 1641:

> All were veterans of previous New England plantings, and all shared a commitment to the assumptions of non-separating Congregationalism, to the open field pattern of landholding, and to the system of autonomous community government that constituted the Puritan way of life in early Connecticut.[33]

The open-field economic system, with settlers living in a village community, encouraged them "to turn their backs on the wilderness," to stay put. Why not, as long as land was abundant? For most of the seventeenth century and beyond, towns usually had not fully cultivated their holdings.[34] The usual inheritance practice was to leave property equally to all children, with perhaps a double share to the oldest son.[35] This could not continue indefinitely, and in fact partible inheritance became rarer as land became scarcer and farms smaller by the third and fourth generations, that is, by the early eighteenth century. In eastern Massachusetts a man could acquire one or two hundred acres around 1650, but by the time of the American Revolution, the average farms in four towns near Boston were 56, 44, 38, and 17 acres. In Andover, the first generation bequeathed its property to all male heirs in 95 percent of the cases, but this was so of only 75 percent from second to third generation, 58 percent from third to fourth, and "less than half of the male members of the fourth Andover generation [maturing in the mid-eighteenth century] remained in the town for the rest of their lives." Some went into trades, some moved to other towns, some took up land elsewhere.[36]

Mobility out of the early towns thus increased in the eighteenth century as land became scarcer. The breakdown of the congregational communities had already begun, as farmers moved from the village to their increasingly distant farmlands. The original open-field, common land system was already breaking up by 1700 in some places.[37] Population rose rapidly in many towns. Women married later by a couple of years, a practice resulting in lower birth rates and declining family size (from 7.6 births per marriage in Andover in the 1690s to 5.7 in 1710–19 to 3.0 in 1785–94).[38] Mortality also rose and life expectancy decreased. The natural growth of New England's seventeenth-century population undermined its cherished congregational mode of settlement. Values, and the control of society by elites, were severely strained.[39] The Great Awakening, around 1740, further loosed the bonds of the congregation, as the population-conscious Ezra Stiles lamented:

> One source of different [anti-congregational] sentiment, were the unhappy excesses into which our churches have been transported in the late enthusiasm that prevailed since the year 1740. In the public mistaken zeal, religion was made to consist in extravigancies [sic] and indecencies, which were not according to the faith once delivered. Multitudes were seriously, soberly, and solemnly out of their wits.

That led to the forming of unauthorized assemblies, although a hundred and fifty authorized ones were also built, "not on the separations but natural increase."[40] Still, the *Vorzeit* was over in New England by the middle of the eighteenth century, often decades earlier. Massachusetts grew from 56,000 in 1700 to 91,000 in 1720, Connecticut from 26,000 in 1700 to 59,000 in 1720, straining the old ways past the breaking point. New Englanders either stayed in their sheltered towns, "old, stable, concentrated," and "clannish," or they looked at long last to frontier-rural opportunities.[41]

The Emergence of the Frontier-Rural Mode

Between the 1720s and 1740s, the eighteenth century—in demographic terms—started in Europe, and with it Europe's great population explosion that was to last into the twentieth century. Unlike the expansion of the sixteenth century, the takeoff of the eighteenth century was not stopped by epidemic or famine.[42] The reasons for the increase are not fully understood, but falling death rates were a key element, because of the absence after 1720 of famines, epidemics, or wars like those of the seventeenth century that ravaged civilian populations.[43] Smallpox inoculation was widely practiced. Agriculture became more productive, at least in England, and the first signs of industrialism appeared. With the development of markets, towns and villages became more certain of sufficient food and shelter to ensure survival and subsistence, which raised the limits on reproduction. It was safer than before to have children. Birth rates rose while death rates kept dropping. England's population grew by about 300,000 in the first half of the eighteenth century, by 3 million (from 6 to 9 million) in the second. Much of this increase the industrializing English economy could absorb, but some of it went to the colonies. Their populations rose abruptly. The 250,000 of 1700 became 1,250,000 by 1750, or one colonist for every five people in England. After 1750 the rate accelerated.

Who were these people, the American colonists? Immigration accounted for many, though it is impossible to say how many. Benjamin Franklin, writing in 1751, estimated "upwards of One million *English* souls in *North America* (tho' 'tis thought scarce 80,000 have been brought over Sea)."[44] This estimate of immigrants seems low. A more likely figure is 200,000 English, and to that should be added an almost equal number of Scotch-Irish, 100,000 Rhineland Germans, small groups of French Huguenots, Swedes, Finns, and Sephardic

Jews, and at least 250,000 black Africans. By 1770, 21 percent of the whole population of the future United States were Africans or their descendants, virtually all slaves in the southern colonies: the highest proportion ever of black people. The total of immigrants (including Africans) between 1700 and 1775 was probably between 700,000 and 900,000, though the figures are obviously indefinite.

The scale of immigration may conjure up a mind's-eye view of eighteenth-century American population growth, a picture of ships disgorging boatload after boatload of Europeans on the docks of Boston or New York or Philadelphia, and Africans in Charleston and along the tidal rivers of Maryland, Virginia, and the Carolinas. We might picture, leaving out the Africans, the eastern seaboard filling up with an Anglo-Saxon, Protestant, freedom-loving, idealistic people fleeing European poverty and despotism. A handsome picture, but aside from the Anglo-Saxon Protestant part, a romantic one. The realities were that New England neither wanted nor got many immigrants. The only large non-British group other than the Africans were the Germans who settled in Pennsylvania between 1720 and 1750. Indisputably Protestant (Moravian, Reformed, or Lutheran), they nevertheless did not assimilate into the English majority. Franklin gave one reason in a comment he made in 1753. Though he favored intermarriage between English and German, or so he claimed, it was unlikely to happen.

> The German women are generally so disagreeable to an English eye, that it wou'd require great portions to induce Englishmen to marry them. Nor would the German Ideas of Beauty generally agree with our Women: *dick und starcke* . . . always enters into their Description of a pretty Girl.

Franklin was reputed to be an experienced judge.[45]

Our mind's-eye view errs also by not recognizing that most of the population increase in eighteenth-century America was natural, the excess of births over deaths. Perhaps one-fourth resulted from immigration,[46] and Franklin thought it was less. For one thing, many who immigrated did not stay. More important, natural increase was very rapid and was well established by 1720. It was the most obvious demographic indicator of the frontier-rural mode of life. Life expectancy from age twenty in New England was about forty more years.[47] Smallpox inoculation among whites was widely accepted and practiced.[48] The death rate was much lower than in European cities such as Berlin, Paris, Breslau, and Vienna,[49] the birth rate was surely much higher, and both birth and death rates compared favorably to rural areas in Europe, where mortality was well below that of the cities. Potter's pioneering survey of American population history before 1860 set total per-decade increases at 35 percent, with natural increase accounting for 26 to 30 percent.[50] Mortality was high and life was short, but only by late twentieth-century standards, not by the standards of eighteenth-century Europe. Americans lived longer, married younger, had more children, saw more of them live to maturity, than Europeans did.

As a result of this natural increase, the number of colonists passed 1 million sometime in the 1740s, although that was a relatively slow decade. By the time they declared their independence from England in 1776, they numbered over 2.5 million, one for every three English men and women. The slow or negative growth of the *Vorzeit* had been replaced by a new demographic regime marked by very rapid natural increase. Once the American population approached significant size, say the 250,000 of 1700, it looked nothing like the traditional regime of Europe before the "demographic transition."[51] It already enjoyed lower mortality and higher fertility, a gap between rates of births and deaths which would have caused population to grow even without any immigration.[52] Recorded instances of premarital conception of the first child rose in the eighteenth century, perhaps because of crumbling social restraints among young New Englanders,[53] perhaps because resources permitted family formation more readily. For whatever set of reasons, the American demographic regime was already different from Europe's. In James Cassedy's words,

> Operating with little restraint in an exceedingly favorable natural environment, human reproduction ultimately was sufficient to ensure a steady rise in population. By mid-18th century, with assistance from immigration, this growth had achieved what seemed to be an astonishing rate.[54]

The eighteenth-century sources on American population are scattered but consistent. Franklin wrote his *Observations concerning the Increase of Mankind* in 1751 and published it in 1755, to prove that Britain should allow colonial manufacturing, since it was no threat to the mother country because colonial consumers were getting so numerous. The tract is therefore tendentious, but some of its points are probably correct:

> . . . Marriages in *America* are more general, and more generally early, than in *Europe*. And . . . we may here reckon 8 [births per marriage compared to 4 in Europe], of which if one half grow up, and our Marriages are made, reckoning one with another at 20 Years of Age, our People must at least be doubled every 20 Years.[55]

Ezra Stiles, writing in 1760, agreed. He estimated that New England's increase from a few thousand souls in 1643 to a half million in 1760 was totally the result of natural increase, because "since that time more have gone from us to Europe, than have arrived from thence hither." Stiles realized that net migration, not gross, was the important number. Stiles also noticed that the interior grew faster than the coast: "The increase of the maritime towns is not equal to that of the inland ones. . . . While on the sea-coast it [the rate of doubling] is above 25 years, yet within land it is 20 and 15."[56] Thus rural life and farming meant the fastest population growth. This perceptive observation was echoed in 1771 by Richard Price, a fellow of the Royal Society who published a book on life contingencies called "Observations on Reversionary Payments." Price noted that burials exceeded births in Boston between 1731 and 1762, and the city would have shrunk but for replenishment from farms.[57]

The English victory in the French and Indian War, largely a fact by 1760, opened the way for new farms in Maine and New Hampshire, in New York just west of Albany, and in central Pennsylvania. By then the movement of people into adjacent unsettled areas, their creation of farms, and very rapid population growth, constituted a general pattern. Benjamin Rush, the noted Philadelphia physician, presented a paper in 1774 to the American Philosophical Society on Indian medicine. Noting the very rapid population growth of white Americans, he argued that

> . . . the universal prevalence of the protestant religion, the checks lately given to negro slavery, the general unwillingness among us to acknowledge the usurpations of primogeniture, the universal practice of inoculation for the smallpox, and absence of the plague, render the imposition of government for that purpose [population growth] unnecessary. These advantages can only be secured to our country by AGRICULTURE. This is the true basis of national health, riches, and populousness.[58]

The Proclamation Line of 1763, west of which the Crown forbade settlement, had succeeded poorly in preventing trans-Appalachian growth, and the repeal of the line by independent Americans removed even that slight brake. Indeed, rapid growth existed already, and kept up. Even the dislocations of the Revolutionary War (1775 –81) did not stop the surge. The South, the Middle States, and New England were all combat theaters, on the coast and on the frontier. Thousands perished. Seventy to a hundred thousand left the rebellious colonies for Canada, Florida, or the Caribbean islands out of loyalty to the Crown, and in the last two cases often took slaves with them.[59] Immigration probably ceased, as it has during every other major American war. For these reasons, population grew between 1770 and 1780 "only" 29 percent, slow for the eighteenth or nineteenth centuries but faster than during the post-World War II baby boom, the fastest-growing period in living experience. In the 1780s, any lost ground was made up by growth of over 41 percent.

The rate continued to be remarkable. Jefferson calculated in 1782 that his Virginia had doubled in population every twenty-seven and a quarter years.[60] Jeremy Belknap, in his *History of New Hampshire* (1792), figured that despite seven years of war and 1,400 deaths because of it, his state had grown between 1767 and 1790 at a rate that would double its population every nineteen years.[61] By 1790, fewer than 10,000 Indians roamed east of the Alleghenies. In 1798, Malthus published his essay, drawing on Franklin, Stiles, and other Americans for data, and concluded that the natural rate of unchecked population increase doubled it every twenty-five years.

By Malthus's time, the pattern of rapid rural growth in America had long since been set. How did it work? Why did it happen? Two early descriptions, about forty years apart, suggest an answer like that proposed by Franklin and Rush. The Swedish observer Peter Kalm explained from his notes of 1748 why American population grew faster than European:

> December the 7th. In the morning I undertook a little journey again to Raccoon, New Jersey. It does not seem difficult to find out the reasons why the people multiply faster here than in Europe. As soon as a person is old enough he may marry in these provinces without any fear of poverty. There is such an amount of good land yet uncultivated that a newly married man can, without difficulty, get a spot of ground where he may comfortably subsist with his wife and children.[62]

Jeremy Belknap made a similar point in 1791:

> Where land is cheap, and the means of subsistence may be ac-

quired in such plenty, and in so short a time as is evidently the case in our new plantations, encouragement is given to early marriage. A young man who has cleared a piece of land, and built a hut for his present accommodation, soon begins to experience the truth of that old adage, "It is not good for man to be alone." Having a prospect of increasing his substance by labour, which he knows himself able to perform, he attaches himself to a female earlier than prudence would dictate if he had not such a prospect. Nor are the young females of the country averse to a settlement in the new plantation. . . . [63]

Available land, the prospect of owning their own farms, a young population, early marriage, a people spread thinly across a vast land area so that even contagious diseases could not easily erupt into general epidemics: these were the ingredients of exceptional growth. The frontier-rural mode became just that: the mode, the norm. It lasted for many decades, affecting tens of millions of people and setting the main terms of their lives. By the 1860s, the United States was in almost every respect different from what it had been in the 1760s, but change had taken place within a *structure* of the *longue durée:* most people still lived their lives according to the frontier-rural mode, and not yet according to the metropolitan mode.

III

The Frontier-Rural Period,
1720 – 1870

Demographic Features of the Period

By the late eighteenth century the frontier-rural mode was the established social and demographic norm in most of English-speaking North America. The frontier-rural period included an early phase, from around 1720 (very approximately) to 1780 or 1785, still a time of emergence out of the *Vorzeit*, a time of immigration and the slave trade and of the struggle for political recognition within the British Empire to 1775 and then outside of it. It was also a time of restricted settlement, as the frontier line moved to, but rarely beyond, the Appalachian chain of mountains.[1] The 1780s onward were the later phase, the eighty-year heyday, of the frontier-rural period. Total population rose from over 3 million in the 1780s to over 30 million in the 1860s, mostly from natural increase. Western settlements proliferated, and the formative years of the American republic unfolded, increasingly innocent of foreign involvements and disturbances.

As a demographic regime the frontier-rural period, in its later phase, displayed several characteristics. The most striking is the high birth rate. At the beginning of the nineteenth century it was almost certainly over 50 live births per thousand people per year.[2] It may have reached 65 in some areas of fresh settlement.[3] Fertility in Canada, both French- and English-speaking, was slightly higher.[4] The American birth rate in the early nineteenth century was higher than that of any country in the world in the 1970s. None except a few in Africa and the Middle East even approached it. From that peak in 1800, which is as far back as we can be reasonably certain of figures, the birth rate declined slowly, not dropping below 40 per thousand per year until the 1860s. The decrease was very slight before 1820, but was 9 or 10 percent in the 1840s and again in the 1850s, which were decades of unprecedented city growth. After the 1860s the national birth rate fell more quickly than before, but remained high in freshly settled areas.[5]

Death rates are less clearly known. For want of data, death rates, life expectancies, and infant mortality in many places, and how they changed over time, may never be determined.[6] Mortality research has many questions yet to answer, but at this point the following seem to be established facts. In the *Vorzeit*, about 1700, death rates in the Chesapeake were much higher, perhaps 50 per thousand per year, than in Massachusetts, at 15 to 25 per thousand. Malaria has been suggested as the cause of mortality and morbidity in the Chesapeake.[7] As in Europe, cities in the English colonies were much less healthy in the eighteenth century than were small villages or farms,[8] but the differences lessened in the first half of the nineteenth century. The evidence now available tells us that for the better part of the frontier-rural period the crude death rate of the white population stayed around 20 per thousand per year, and for the slave population it was about 30.[9] Life expectancy seems to have increased by a few years in the eighteenth century, but may not have changed much at all in the early nineteenth, up to 1860.[10] In truth, length of life probably did not increase or decrease very much through the entire frontier-rural period.[11] Infant mortality remained high, though we cannot be certain since deaths of infants and children, especially in rural areas, were poorly recorded. But the rate may not have been far from 200 per thousand live births, and for the slave population between 1810 and 1860 it appears to have averaged about 230 for girls and 272 for boys. For frontier-rural areas a reasonable guess would put infant mortality at a fourth of all live births, with perhaps another fifth dying before reaching adulthood. A person who reached age twenty was reasonably certain of another thirty to forty years, but the first few years of life were very hazardous.[12]

Lives began to last longer, on the average, and death rates dropped, in the 1880s but not before.[13] Stability is more impressive than change through the frontier-rural period, and that should not be surprising since no major advances in medicine occurred except smallpox inoculation. Peter Kalm identified several killers as of 1748: it "appears that the diseases which are most fatal are consumption, fevers, convulsions, pleurisy, hemorrhages and dropsy."[14] Cholera and scarlet fever caused 34 percent of the deaths in 1860. Respiratory diseases, and gastric troubles such as dysentery and diarrhea with their resulting dehydrations, caused much of the high mortality, especially among infants and young children. Poor sanitation and impure food were the root problems, and they would not be corrected widely until sewer systems, pure water, and refrigeration arrived in the late nineteenth and early twentieth centuries. In the meantime, airborne infections such as tuberculosis, diphtheria, smallpox, influenza, measles, and mumps, and waterborne infections such as cholera, typhoid fever, and dysentery, kept mortality high by twentieth-century metropolitan standards.[15]

Frontier-rural people were young. The median age in the 1790s was about sixteen years, and did not reach twenty until the 1860s. In 1800, a third of the entire population was under ten years old, and in 1870, still a fourth.[16] The obvious result

was early marriage, rapid family formation, high fertility, and
large families. The age of first marriage may have been about
twenty-five for men and twenty-four for women through the
early nineteenth century,[17] though it almost certainly varied
considerably between coastal and frontier areas, as practically
all demographic variables did. In *Vorzeit* Virginia, "a girl seldom had the opportunity to get beyond her teens before she
married," and the planter William Byrd wrote a friend that
"his daughter Evelyn, aged twenty, was 'one of the most
antick Virgins' he knew of."[18] Part of the reason was the
abundance of males compared to females. Later, in more settled areas, the sex ratio would approach one to one. Then the
age of first marriage rose, at least for women. But in newly
settled areas in the nineteenth century where men outnumbered women, the age of marriage was probably lower,
perhaps as low as twenty-one for males, less for females.[19]
Young couples migrated together to new lands, having married
recently and at tender ages.

> Frequently, couples came to the frontier directly after getting
> married or directly after the birth of their first child. . . . new-
> lyweds usually brought no offspring with them, and young
> couples who had been married a year or two probably brought
> no more than one or two.[20]

Fertility was enormously high as long as the young couple
could form their own household on their own land.[21] Females
reached menarche at about age fifteen in 1800 and perhaps a
few months earlier in 1850.[22] If a woman married soon after
that, as many did, the ultimate size of her family could be
prodigious. The American and Canadian census manuscripts
are crowded with cases of women marrying at sixteen or seventeen and producing a child every eighteen to twenty-four
months—about the biological maximum because of breast-
feeding and pregnancy intervals—until reaching menopause
in their mid-forties. The average number of children born per

average woman in her lifetime, as of 1790, was almost eight. That number sank to four by 1930, but through the frontier-rural period the figure remained high.[23] Newly married women could look forward to twenty or even thirty fertile years. Young men often left home between seventeen and twenty-one, and married then or soon after, having "acquired enough capital to launch themselves upon the world, and [having seen] that there was no future for them on the [family] farm."[24] Women of similar age and prospects very often went with them.

Huge families were uncommon, to be sure, but the mean size seems to have been about five people at any one time, even as late as 1880, which does not include children who had already left the hearth, who died shortly after birth, or who for whatever reason were not counted in censuses. The nuclear, two-parent family with several children over a lifetime (and one to three at any given time) was not only the norm but far and away the usual thing. Such families were the basic social unit, and also the basic economic unit, in newly settled areas as in older ones. Everyone did, or was supposed to do, such jobs as he or she could.[25] On the southern frontier, women performed "the multifarious duties of the household" and gained "the reputation of being more industrious than their husbands."[26] In the Midwest, wives and children did housework and lighter farmwork as they were able. Very rarely did they work in the fields. William Dean Howells, the eminent writer, recalled of his early years in rural Ohio that "The rule was, that whoever had the strength to work, took hold and helped. If the family was mostly girls, they regularly helped their father in all the lighter farm work."[27] On New England's frontier, and on the eighteenth and nineteenth century northern frontiers generally, the work of the women of the family was as important as, and complementary with, the men's— though one wonders if it was always so recognized. One historian recently thought so.[28] Others have argued that young women gained greater independence when they took up factory jobs, whose earnings gave them freedom to make more of their own decisions.

Another characteristic of the frontier-rural period was its ethnic sameness. Except for the Pennsylvania Germans who arrived in the early and mid-eighteenth century, the Africans, and the descendants of these groups, virtually all Americans were of English or Scotch-Irish stock until nearly the end of the frontier-rural period. In the years 1790 to 1810 and beyond, immigration was slight (the federal government did not even record arrivals until 1820), and English stock was "by far the most numerous and widely diffused" throughout the country.[29] Americans were also Protestant, and rarely Church of England but rather evangelicals of one kind or another: dissenters, Calvinists, or Arminians. A truly foreign element did not arrive until the late 1840s, when the great wave of Catholic southern Irish, and of Lutheran and Catholic Germans, began. The United States was not receiving many immigrants until the 1840s, and the donor countries of the first mass wave, Ireland and Germany, were not sending many. Despite terrible overpopulation in Ireland before the potato famine, few left; "Cobbett's comment on the English farmers in 1831 — 'they hang on, like sailors to the masts or hull of a wreck' — applied with much more force to the Irish peasants of 1815–45."[30] The proportion of foreign-born declined steadily after 1760, until it was less than one in twelve by 1845.

Migration of ethnic groups is a salient factor in American history. Much has been and more should be said about it, but I confine myself here to two points. The formative years of American nationhood, from the Revolution to the 1840s, the time when national ideals, self-images, rhetorics, and many social and political institutions took shape, happened to be the period of lowest immigration from foreign countries and smallest proportion of foreign-born in American history — except for the years following World War II, and by then immigrants may have been few but the country abounded with second-, third-, and fourth-generation ethnics of every description. Before 1845 the United States was ethnically one-dimensional. National ideals were formed during the several decades when ethnic and cultural homogeneity were most absolute. Secondly, when waves of immigrants did begin to arrive, in 1846 and after, waves which never stopped except for a few years of wars and depressions until 1924, the immigrants very often located in cities. Urban residence even claimed Germans and Scandinavians and others of the older immigration, who also contributed much to farm settlement from the 1850s to 1890. Yet cities were very rare when mass immigration began. By the late nineteenth century, one could safely guess that the larger a city, the higher its proportion of foreign stock. Many of the biggest, such as Chicago, New York, and Brooklyn, grew as fast as they did because of immigrants, not because of native-stock migrants from rural areas or because of natural increase. Cities were foreign in two senses to the Anglo-Protestant majority throughout the frontier-rural period and the Great Conjuncture: foreign in ethnicity and culture, and foreign to the normal rural experience.[31]

Besides the more strictly demographic characteristics of birth and death rates, age structure and fertility, and ethnicity, the frontier-rural mode displayed some other features related closely enough to its demography to warrant mention here. An obvious but important one is the expansion of the land area under United States sovereignty, the area effectively available for settlement. From a coastal strip about a hundred miles wide in the 1750s, that area spread to nearly all of the land east of the Mississippi by 1800. Louisiana, added in 1803, doubled the country's size.[32] Then came Florida, Texas, the Southwest, and Oregon. A land area without practical limits beckoned to a population increasing without practical parallel. Territorial expansion guaranteed that land would remain available, a crucial ingredient in the frontier-rural mode. From 1790 to 1860 the population doubled every twenty-one years, faster than Malthus's conservative ratio.

Indians were an annoyance to the whites, sometimes dangerous, sometimes fatal. But the aboriginal peoples never stopped the onrushing European-Americans for long, despite treaties guaranteeing exclusive rights of lands to the Indians, despite westward removal of tribes to the west, or despite any other policy. Treaties made by the federal government with Indian tribes were solemn undertakings, as with foreign nations, but neither state nor federal governments possessed the means of enforcing those treaties against the encroachments and over the political pressure of the sovereign squatters. Governments might propose, but the land-hungry settlers disposed. European and African diseases continued to ravage the Indians. Smallpox remained the worst killer, despite vaccination campaigns by the federal government. Intertribal warfare made the white Americans' conquests and settlements easier. These conflicts have been overlooked even more completely than epidemic diseases as a cause of Indian defeats, but they predated Columbus and lasted until after the Sioux receded from the northern Great Plains in the 1870s.[33] All things considered, white Americans met much less resistance from presettled peoples on their frontiers than other nations did on theirs.[34]

Good diet also supported the demographic regime. Food seems always to have been abundant in America, except in the early *Vorzeit*, and in this respect frontier-rural America contrasted sharply with preindustrial Europe. There, it appears, productivity was low and the work week short simply because nutritional deficiencies limited what peasants and laborers could do. The nutritional level of Europe, especially of England, rose in the late eighteenth century, and with it came a rise in energy levels and general health. In England this improvement underpinned the Industrial Revolution.[35] In

America, good diet underpinned frontier-rural expansion. Nineteenth-century descriptions of farm diets reveal consistently massive quantities of food if not of gourmet quality. A Norwegian woman in Wisconsin wrote home in 1847 that

> A breakfast here consists of chicken, mutton, beef, or pork, warm or cold wheat bread, butter, white cheese, eggs or small pancakes, the best coffee, tea, cream, and sugar . . . and my greatest regret here is to see the superabundance of food, much of which has to be thrown to the chickens and the swine.[36]

Michel Chevalier reported that Irish railroad workers, doing the roughest unskilled jobs of the 1830s, received three meals a day, with meat and wheat bread, coffee and sugar at two meals, butter once, and six to eight glasses of whiskey depending on the weather.[37] A Kansas teenager named Luna Warner, recently arrived in the Solomon Valley of Kansas from Massachusetts with her family in 1871, wrote in her diary that they regularly ate beef hearts, chicken, all kinds of vegetables, and fresh fruit.[38] Hamlin Garland's fictional but life-drawn farm workers in Wisconsin in the late 1880s consumed a midday meal during threshing season which included boiled chicken, potatoes, corn cakes, gravy, tea, doughnuts, milk, and more.[39] A daughter of Bohemian immigrants in Iowa recalled that as a child in 1910 or so,

> we always had plenty to eat even if the fare was not always fancy. Cornmeal was cheap; so we had cornmeal mush for breakfast, fried mush for lunch, and corn bread or "Johnny cake" (which to this day I have to force myself to eat) for dinner. The chickens provided the eggs as well as meat. . . . We had our own milk, all that we wanted to drink, butter, cream, cottage cheese, and plenty of pork, fish, and rabbit meat. . . . Roasted squab was a rare treat. In the fall when the weather was colder, Dad butchered a hog. . . . [40]

Good diet was as essential to American population growth as it was to European after 1750.[41]

A final characteristic of the frontier-rural mode was the overwhelmingly rural location of the people. In residence and occupation they were even more homogeneous than in ethnicity and religion. Cities certainly existed, and 20 percent of the people lived in cities of 2,500 or more by 1860. But before that, for the great mass, rural life was universal. In 1790, 95 percent lived on farms or in villages so tiny that the countryside was visible everywhere and never farther than a two-minute walk. In 1860, after the urban take-off of the preceding fifteen years, 80 percent of the people remained rural, and the great majority made their livings as farmers or in farm-related industries such as tanning, milling, ironmongering, distilling, or otherwise processing farm products.[42] The one effective exception to homogeneity was whether a person lived in a place where the enslavement of black people was prohibited, or where it was protected. That was indeed a big difference, and the argument over the extension of slavery to the territories of Kansas and Nebraska split the political parties in the 1850s and split the nation in 1860–61, plunging it into the Civil War of 1861–65. Even with this difference in view, however, the demographic experiences of northerners and southerners were more alike than not, during the frontier-rural period.

From the beginning of the period the great majority were not only rural but middle-class, property-owning rural. In New England, in the Middle colonies, and in most of the South, as early as 1750, America was "peopled mainly by farmers and small planters and by those who bought from them, supplied them, worked for or slaved for them."[43] Formal education, if only a modicum, distinguished the middle-class from lower-class children who were bound out or apprenticed.[44] Although wealth in America began to concentrate in fewer hands in the nineteenth century—one historian states that 10 percent of the people held half the wealth in 1780, but increased its share to 70 percent by 1850—it was distributed more broadly in frontier areas, where 10 percent of the people held around 35 percent of the property. People believed that they could go west and get a foot in the capitalist door, and they were right.[45]

The Process of Expansion and Settlement

With the principal characteristics of the frontier-rural mode in mind, we look now at the process of expansion. Since the mode existed in the *longue durée* from the early eighteenth century to the 1860s, we could choose from any number of times and places to demonstrate how the process worked. Vermont in 1785 will do. A small, landlocked region of harsh climate, Vermont was then beginning to collect enough people to be admitted to statehood six years later, the first state after the original rebellious thirteen. The Revolutionary War had just ended, and with it several years of economic and social dislocation. Few Indians remained even in that remote part of New England, and in neighboring New York they had been subdued; they were not a barrier to white settlement.[46]

Connecticut and western Massachusetts lay to the south. That region had been settled from one to several generations earlier, and in some places along the Connecticut River since the 1640s. As a farming area it was becoming crowded. The town-congregation method of settlement, typical of the New England *Vorzeit*, had been breaking down as farmers moved away from the central village to their outlying lands. Production was becoming more efficient, making young farmhands less needed, and the size of farms declined as family holdings were subdivided in the passage from one generation to the next.[47] When the state governments' close control of new settlements relaxed in the eighteenth century and tracts were sold to speculators, and when the speculators offered good terms to settlers, Vermont and western New Hampshire beckoned. Cold and rocky they may have been, but they were also fertile, timbered, well watered, and full of empty, available land. Into

Vermont poured boys and young men, mostly from Connecticut and western Massachusetts, males in their teens and twenties, some bringing brides the same age and others anxious to return and fetch brides as soon as they made clearings in the forest and raised their cabins. Some came as families or groups of families, some as individuals, but seldom did people come as authorized congregations as in the Massachusetts and Connecticut of the seventeenth and early eighteenth centuries.[48] Vermont and western New Hampshire "began about 1760 to take on brimming vigor and self-confidence," wrote Charles E. Clark:

> From the western parts of Connecticut and Massachusetts, rustic pioneers who had already tried one frontier and were ready now to tackle a new one, some of them religious dissidents whose side had come off badly in the local church fight occasioned by the Great Awakening, migrated into some of those townships in Wentworth's "New Hampshire grants" that lay west of the Green Mountains. . . . Rhode Island, eastern New Hampshire, and even Scotland contributed to the stream of settlers that swelled the population of Vermont from 120 families in 1763 to about 20,000 people in 1776.[49]

Some had the wherewithal to buy the cheap land right away, while others probably worked for other farmers until their cash and credit accumulated to a point at which they could get their own places. They moved for a simple reason: their parents' farms in Massachusetts offered them a dull future, one with little property even if the parental farm were divided among the heirs, or no property if it were not. Yet the middle-class, property-owning urge was powerful. In New England tradition, and in English tradition before that,[50] the yearning for land cried for satisfaction. Vermont would make independent landowners of these young men and women.[51]

Inheritance practices in late eighteenth-century New England were much more liberal than feudal primogeniture, in the sense that each son and daughter was usually recognized as entitled to some share in a parent's estate. That says nothing about whether there was to be an estate; or whether a share, equal or not, was large enough to be worth something; and if the share was in land, whether large enough to support the heir and his family. Nonetheless, as far as we know,[52] parents normally felt some responsibility for helping establish their children in life and in dealing with several children equitably if not equally. Daughters probably received half to a third as much as sons did, perhaps in cash or goods rather than land,[53] and the oldest son seems frequently to have received a double share, at least before the nineteenth century.[54] Or so it may have been in New England. In the South, primogeniture ended legally between 1776 and 1796, and in western North Carolina, if nowhere else, fathers left the family farm to the youngest son, not the oldest.[55] In the nineteenth century, farm parents probably wanted to help their children get started in life. They were probably willing to subdivide their property up to a point to do so, and if the farm was too small or unproductive to bear any more subdividing, they might help their children apprentice to an artisan. The limits on parental aid became quite narrow, obviously, in large families. Consciously or unconsciously, farm families with not much to give their children, or whose optimism about the future value of their property was slight, had fewer children than farm families in areas to the west where land was more abundant and its value likely to rise.[56]

As of the late 1970s we knew more about inheritance practices in Ontario than in the northern or southern United States in the nineteenth century, and about the relations between inheritance, land availability, migration, and fertility changes. The majority of Canadian farm families seem to have been very reluctant to divide their farms among the heirs, but rather than limiting the bequest to the oldest son and excluding the other children, they bequeathed the land to one or perhaps two heirs, who were then obliged by law to provide the others with a roughly equal amount of property or income other than the family land. If a father died, the farm went to the oldest son and not the widow, but the oldest son was required to provide for the widow and his brothers and sisters from the product of the farm. The system was fair in one sense, but in another it essentially mortgaged the future of the oldest son and the farm, led to the uncomfortable dependence of widows on their oldest sons, and often deprived siblings of their full share, sometimes any share, of their patrimony. By 1860 or 1870, demand for land pushed values up. Many younger siblings had long since left for western regions where land was more available. Fertility in eastern Ontario began dropping and the area resembled the settled-rural pattern of the eastern United States.[57]

To sum up: We do not yet know as much about inheritance practices as we would like to. What we do know suggests a variety of arrangements, including the Canadian pattern just described, the impartible (legally or effectively), and the partible (to all heirs, to just the males, or randomly to some). What eighteenth- and nineteenth-century farm parents felt they ought to do to start their children in life, on farms or with other kinds of property or apprenticeships, is virtually unknown. The commonsense guess is that inheritance patterns and feelings of parental responsibility both varied enormously. The overriding fact is that large landholdings were never common, nor were large holdings of other forms of property. Therefore it was simply not possible for parents to provide for all of their many offspring. The result is clear: in view of the decline of available land in settled areas, enough land for a "decent" living, the forces pushing young people away from home and toward areas where land was easier to get—in short, the frontier-rural migration pattern—were very strong, and waned only by 1910 or 1915 when new land was no longer there.

The shortage of available land in longer-settled areas, and

its availability farther west, had two demographic results: westward migration, and the ability to maintain very high fertility rates in newly settled areas while fertility dropped rapidly in the older areas. By the mid-eighteenth century, areas on or near the Atlantic coast, either in New England or in the Chesapeake, were crowded. Farms could be subdivided no further without reducing the heirs to or below the subsistence level. Landholding took on a "European" look.[58] By 1790 the sex ratio in Massachusetts, Rhode Island, and Connecticut was female-dominated, because of "the great emigrations of young men from these overcrowded areas to Vermont and western New York."[59] The frontier-rural pattern evident in so many places in the late eighteenth and much of the nineteenth centuries was that crowding in the east raised the age of marriage and lowered the birth rate there, while abundance farther west, among migrants and especially among the children of migrants—the second generation in a newly settled area—lowered the age of marriage, raised the birth rate, and increased the number of fertile years within marriage.[60] Other factors such as level of literacy or illiteracy, cultural heritage, sex ratio, and urban residence almost certainly had some effect on fertility, but land availability had more.[61]

The teenage or twentyish young man and woman moving to Vermont became adults quickly. They had little time for adolescence, for formal education even if it had been available, or for "finding themselves." Yet land-hungry young people streamed into Vermont in the 1780s, 1790s, and 1800s, making it the California of that age. Its population grew five times over between 1790 and 1810. In those days, as on later frontiers, success depended on cleverness. The couple had to be good judges of fertility of soil, water, accessibility, and other qualities of their new farm.[62] They had to be lucky and avoid crippling diseases and accidents. They had to put forth constantly the hard physical labor that only youth and good health would permit, because their kind of farming was almost completely unmechanized. It depended not on machines but on the brawn of people and animals. The settlers cleared the land, cut down trees, pulled stumps, built cabins and outbuildings by hand after hewing the boards from logs, planted and harvested, and subsisted very largely on the produce of their own land. Indians seldom bothered them. All the while they brought forth, besides crops and livestock, astonishing numbers of children, "about as fast as was naturally possible," according to Stilwell, and probably "the original 30,000 pioneers of 1781 were quite capable of filling Vermont with their own children and grandchildren without the aid of any further immigration whatever."[63]

In Vermont at the close of the eighteenth century, the connections between land availability, new settlements, and high fertility were clear. Scarcity of available land in settled areas south of Vermont in 1785 pushed the young into migrating. Abundant land in Vermont pulled them toward it. When population became dense, fertility dropped, and where it was sparse, as in the country just behind the edge of the frontier, the country filling up with farms, fertility was highest.[64] The same was true in nearby Canada, where the fertility of the English-speakers, contrary to legend, was even higher than that of the French, famed for their *vitalité*.[65] This pattern continued for decades after the settlement of Vermont and was central to the frontier-rural regime. Land availability, together with availability of jobs—farm-laborer jobs as well as jobs in towns—correlated closely with mobility and population growth in the nineteenth century.[66] The Vermont settlers of 1785 to 1810 may in their later years have grown spade beards and American Gothic faces, but the truth is that they were very young—two-thirds under twenty-six in 1800, probably more in 1785. They were not constrained by much in the way of good manners; often enthusiasts, religious or irreligious; somewhat given to new fads and possessing the room to embrace those fads; providing their own livelihoods and living only partly on a money economy; often ready, at least until they were over thirty-five, to move on and start over if they got a good price for their place. As one scholar of the frontier put it, "it was the more radical of the New England farmers who emigrated to the West." Emigrants fell into two classes:

> a. The poorer folk, those who have the small and infertile farms;
> b. The young men coming of age and wishing to start out for themselves. The first of these classes, having been troubled with debts and poverty, are very apt to be of the restless, nonconformist type. The second class have the characteristics of youth, one of which, of course, is radicalism.[67]

Before long Vermont became crowded. By 1810, thirty years after the first mass waves of settlers, their sons and daughters were in much the same position as the emigrants from Massachusetts were a generation before. The choices were to stay on the family farm, probably subdividing it, where resources would not easily extend at the same level to themselves and a third generation, or to find new land on a new frontier. But again, new land there was, 50 or 100 miles away in New York, easily reachable, timbered, well-watered, less remote, and usually more fertile than Vermont. As land prices rose in Vermont, out-migration began, and the birth rate started dropping even as in-migration was still going on.[68] The rush into northern, central, and western New York partly overlapped the rush into Vermont, and was partly fed by Vermont emigrants, bringing an avalanche of settlers into the St. Lawrence and Mohawk valleys from the 1790s to the 1830s. The Holland Land Company, to pick but one example, started selling farms around Batavia, in west-central New York, in 1802 at a dollar and a half and two dollars an acre, with no down payment and liberal credit terms, and the market responded vigorously.[69] Vermont, which had increased in population by 9 percent a year between 1771 and 1810, virtually stabilized at 0.9 percent per year between 1810 and

1840.[70] By 1810 to 1820 Vermont was donating people to northern New York,[71] and New York State's population soared by 73 percent in the 1790s, 63 percent from 1800 to 1810, and another 40 percent during the 1820s, when the Erie Canal opened fully. This rush may have been "reckless prodigality," but it gave New York an almost instant population. As Judge Cooper of Cooperstown stated, in May 1786, "I opened the sales of 40,000 acres which, in sixteen days, were all taken up by the poorest order of man." A comment of 1791 was more flattering: "Immigrants are sweeping into this fertile region in shoals like the ancient Israelites seeking the land of prom-ise."[72] The population rush to New York continued to be fed in later decades by immigration when the frontier-rural rush for land pushed farther westward.

The reasons for emigration were not obscure. In general, land scarcity was at the root of it. Three-fourths of emigration from Vermont from 1790 to 1810 came from the older counties in the south, and three-fourths of the emigrants were under thirty. High birth rates plus already occupied land meant emigration. After 1810 the same equation pushed the young of the middle and northern counties to New York and elsewhere. More specifically, Stilwell adduces President Jefferson's em-bargo of 1808, which stopped trade between northern Ver-mont and Canada; the collapse of the state bank in 1811–12; the War of 1812, the effect of which resembled that of the em-bargo, but lasted longer; and cold weather in 1816, when "the summer was so cold and dry that almost nothing matured." Stilwell did not know it, nor did the Vermonters of 1816, but volcanic eruptions in Indonesia so filled the air of the Northern Hemisphere with particulate matter that 1816 became "the year without a summer." In northern places where the grow-ing season was short in any year, the threat of famine spurred migration. So it was in Vermont, and so it was in southwest-ern Germany, where emigration fever swept the starving peasantry. The customary substantial diet returned after that

awful year, but by 1820 the prodigal exploitation of land,
game, and forests for more than thirty years reduced Vermont's natural resources to the point of exhaustion. "Agricultural methods were biblical in their crudeness," according to
Stilwell, and involved wooden plows and flails, but no fer-
tilizers or crop rotation. "Unconsciously and cheerfully the
pioneers ruined the soil—raising the same crops on the same
fields until the humus left from the forests was well-nigh
exhausted." Diminishing soil fertility compounded the decline
in land availability. Young men and women moved west,
young women (by the thousands) to the factories of Massachusetts in the 1840s.[73]

As New York's frontier-rural phase overlapped Vermont's,
it was in turn overlapped by immigration into Ohio, and in
the 1830s into Indiana and Michigan. Pushing the frontier line
westward with great speed, settlers breached the Mississippi
in the 1840s and the Missouri in the 1850s, and finally opened
up to cultivation the vast garden of Kansas, Nebraska, and the
Dakotas in the 1870s and 1880s. By 1860 Illinois, Indiana, and
Ohio had become net exporters of native-born people, and the
ratio of males to females in New York and New England
shifted in favor of females, reflecting out-migration from those
areas.[74] The migration was often in two steps, a young man
finding a place and then returning to bring back his wife and
their one or two children. That may account for the slightly
male-biased sex ratio in new areas and the slightly female-
biased ratio in more settled areas. Once founded, however, the
farm was a family operation. "Nuclear families with both
spouses present, and their minor children," a social and economic unit usually of five to seven people, were the norm.[75]

Everywhere during the frontier-rural period the pattern
was one of available land attracting settlement, then slow con-
striction of available land and rising prices for land, high fertility, then land hunger and population pressure from a large
and unpropertied second (then third) generation, and finally

migration of the young to a new area full of cheap and empty land. Few could hope to inherit their fathers' farms or large enough parcels of land to afford the expected standard of living. Many others would work as farm laborers to accumulate enough capital and command enough credit to buy their own places.[76] It cost somewhere between five hundred and one thousand dollars to establish a forty-acre farm in Illinois or Iowa in the 1850s, a considerable sum, but within reach of a young man "if he could borrow money or if he were willing to develop the farm over a number of years, perhaps while he was hiring himself out."[77] The young settlers "were self-reliant and impatient of control to the point of lawlessness," exploited the abundant soil without much regard to the future, and regarded each other suspiciously if they came from different regions, New York or New England versus the upland South.[78] But they did the work, and by 1860 the geographical center of the American population had crossed the Ohio River into southern Ohio. By 1890 it was in Indiana, which a half-century earlier was largely wilderness.[79]

The United States in the nineteenth century was built largely from the enormous, uncounted numbers of man-hours and woman-hours of hand labor expended in creating frontier farms. The settlement phase lasted thirty or thirty-five years, whether in Vermont at the turn of the eighteenth century or across the continent until Oklahoma experienced typically rapid frontier growth from 1890 to about 1920, and then actually lost people in the 1930s. The frontier phase also lasted about three or four decades in Alabama and Mississippi, from 1810 to the 1840s, and again in Kansas from the 1850s to about 1890.[80] Outside of the South, regional metropolises of 50,000 to 100,000 usually appeared by the fourth decade after initial settlement.

With the coming of family farms, the sex ratio gradually came into balance.[81] The frontier-rural woman spent her time with her husband and children. Upper-middle-class notions of domesticity, the genteel "cult of true womanhood," were developing at that time in settled eastern towns and cities, but they did not shape the lives of women living in the frontier-rural mode.[82]

Literary testimony to the frontier-rural process dates back at least as far as James Fenimore Cooper's *The Pioneers*, first published in 1823 but set in 1793 in Cooper's home country between the Mohawk River and the Catskills in central New York. Cooper opened his novel with a word-picture of the region and how greatly it had changed between the Revolution and 1793:

> The expedients of the pioneers who first broke ground in the settlement of this country, are succeeded by the permanent improvements of the yeoman, who intends to leave his remains to moulder under the sod which he tills, or, perhaps, of the son, who, born in the land, piously wishes to linger around the grave of his father.—Only forty years have passed since this whole territory was a wilderness.
>
> Very soon after the establishment of the independence of the United States by the peace of 1783, the enterprise of their citizens was directed to a development of the natural advantages of their widely extended dominions. . . . Within the short period we have mentioned, [New York's] population has spread itself over five degrees of latitude and seven of longitude, and has swelled to the powerful number of nearly a million and a half, who are maintained in abundance, and can look forward to ages before the evil day must arrive, when their possessions will become unequal to their wants.[83]

Ninety years later, Hamlin Garland described the frontier-rural process in the Wisconsin and Dakotas of the 1880s. Younger sons were leaving Wisconsin for the Dakotas because land in Wisconsin was then fetching ten dollars to fifteen dollars an acre, a sum beyond their means. The result, says one of his characters: "Gone West. Most all the boys have gone West. That's the reason there's so many old maids." Again, "Girls are thicker'n huckleberries" back east in Wisconsin, according to some of those boys who emigrated to the lonely Dakotas.[84] A demographer could have told them to expect the sex ratio to be unbalanced in both places. In another story, Garland wrote of a Wisconsin lad who went to Dakota Territory, started a farm, found (as Jeremy Belknap said of New Hampshiremen almost a century before) that it was not good for man to be alone, and as soon as he could returned to Wisconsin to seek a bride. He found a Norwegian girl, plowing the cornfields for her father. Liberating her, he carried her off to the new promised land of Dakota—a place so inhospitable, cold, flat, and remote that it peaked in population in 1930 and has been stable ever since.[85] It was also incredibly boring, as most frontiers were, and could drive people mad, as happened to the heroine of Ole Rølvaag's *Giants in the Earth*, the great novel of immigrant farm life on the Plains. "Loneliness was, by all accounts, the most oppressive of hardships" for women, and the endless physical work at least occupied the mind.[86]

But even the Dakotas were beyond the reach of most of Garland's poor Wisconsin farmers before long. Another character talked about farm conditions in Wisconsin.

> "I s'pose it pays reasonably?" he was asked by a visitor. "Not enough to kill," said one of the younger men. "You c'n see that by the houses we live in—that is, most of us. A few that came in early an' got land cheap, like McIlvaine, here—he got a lift that the rest of us can't get. . . . Ten years ago Wess, here, could have got land in Dakota pretty easy, but now it's about all a feller's life's worth to try it. I tell you things seem shuttin' down on us fellers."
>
> "Plenty of land to rent," suggested someone.
>
> "Yes, in terms that skin a man alive. More than that, farmin' ain't so free a life as it used to be. This cattle-raisin' and butter-makin' makes a nigger out of a man. Binds him right down to the grindstone and he gets nothin' out of it—that's what rubs it in. He simply wallers around in the manure for somebody else. I'd like to know what a man's life is worth who lives as we do. How much higher is it than the lives the niggers used to live?[87]

The man was talking about the intrusion of marketplace considerations into the lives of small farmers, the necessity of concentrating more and more on the product with the best cash return, even though dairy farming tied a farmer to a daily schedule far more than corn or other grains did. By the time such sentiments were being expressed—the setting was the late 1880s—the end of the frontier-rural mode was in sight.[88]

All of the foregoing has described the frontier-rural process in the Northeast and the Midwest, from Massachusetts and Vermont westward across New York and Pennsylvania through the Old Northwest to the Great Plains. It also went on in the South, sometimes differently but more often similarly. Beginning in western Virginia and the Carolinas in the 1760s, people reproduced abundantly, pressed their children and each other for increasingly valuable (or crop-exhausted) land, and recognized the attractions of raw but cheap land beyond the mountains, in Kentucky, Tennessee, and Georgia. Many thousands chose to grasp the frontier opportunity and open up those places just after the American Revolution. Georgia was one of the original thirteen states but was almost empty in 1780. For the next thirty years its population was almost the same as Vermont's, but for some time beyond that, Georgia kept growing while Vermont stabilized for lack of space. The 1820s and 1830s saw "the flush times of Alabama and Mississippi,"[89] when the black belt came under the plow, and cotton became king.

Virginia was the largest state at the time of the Revolution, with about a fifth of the whole American colonial population. In the 1830s it became the first large state to decrease in population as it exported whites, and black slaves in even larger numbers, to the new cotton lands to the southwest.[90] After 1830 the South Atlantic coastal states grew very slowly, but the Gulf states to the west of them exhibited all the classic signs of frontier-rural boom. The East South Central states (Alabama, Mississippi, Tennessee, Kentucky) rose 53 percent in overall population and 98 percent in black population during the 1820s, and in the 1830s 42 percent overall and 50 percent in blacks. In Mississippi alone the black population jumped 198 percent in the 1830s. The Indians of the Southwest, most of them members of the "Civilized Tribes"—called that because they were farmers and many had intermarried with whites—were uprooted from Georgia and adjacent areas and removed, with the army escorting them, to the Indian Territory far to the west on the edge of the Great Plains. Some resisted, a few with success (the Florida Seminoles), but for the most part Indians were once more only a mild hindrance to white frontier-rural growth, and they were not even present after the removals in the 1830s. In the 1840s and 1850s Arkansas and Missouri and the interior of Louisiana, all already states, began to be heavily settled, as did east Texas just before the Civil War. After the war the central Texas prairies opened to cotton farming.[91] The Oklahoma Territory first yielded to homesteading in the land rush of 1889, and with the adjoining Indian Territory it became the final frontier after the 1890s.

The frontier-rural process in the South was much like that of the North except that a minority of southern landholdings were larger than northern ones. Also, southern migration included the involuntary resettlement of slaves. Towns and villages were rarer than in the Midwest, but some did exist.[92] Birth and fertility rates were a little higher among southern whites than among northern, as far as we know, but average household and family size was only slightly larger if at all than in the North.[93] Property in land and slaves was concentrated; a small minority of slave- and land-holders lived in both the settled and the frontier regions of the South, a minority missing in the frontier North. This "gave the planter a social and economic significance far beyond his relative numerical standing."[94] One-ninth of white families by the 1850s held 80 percent of the slaves; two-thirds had none. The mass of families were small planters, with a few slaves, or small farmers, with one or none. In the South as in the North, frontier-rural people were a rural lower middle class.[95] The large plantations were commercial operations, but the average farmer is better described as semisubsistence, producing a bale or two of cotton each year, which he might take to a nearby large plantation for ginning and then sell to the factor at the country store. He was not a commercial farmer in the modern sense, although part of his diversified output might ultimately reach the international cotton market.[96]

Blacks did not play a large role in the frontier-rural process except as they were shipped involuntarily to the black-belt cotton region. Less than 10 percent of the southern frontier population in 1800, blacks made up about a third of it in 1840. These proportions were always lower than the black proportion in the settled South. In the North, despite the presence of a few hundred slaves in Indiana and Illinois before the 1820s, black settlers were mostly freemen. But there were hardly any of them, about 0.5 percent at any time between 1810 and 1840.[97] American black people were overwhelmingly southern in residence and slave in condition during the frontier-rural period, and consequently did not live within the frontier-rural mode except, for some, in a strictly locational sense, not as true participants. Their birth rates may have been higher than those of whites in the South, though this is not certain. It does seem probable that their mortality was higher because of prevalent tuberculosis brought on by poorer diet and housing.[98] Thomas Jefferson noted in 1782 that slaves increased "as fast or faster than the whites," but that a new Virginia law against importing slaves "will in some measure stop the increase of this great political and moral evil, while the minds of our citizens may be ripening for a complete emancipation of human nature."[99] Slavery did not stop, of course, and the natural increase of the slave population nearly matched that of the whites. Yet blacks never realized another Jeffersonian dream, that of smallholder independence. With that great exception, the frontier-rural mode shaped the lives of Americans in the late eighteenth and much of the nineteenth centuries. A growing scarcity of reasonably priced land, the inability of parents to provide farms for all of their many children, and the pull of newly settled areas were the common facts of life in the United States and also in Canada.[100]

Change in Agriculture, Change in Life

Abundant land, good diet, weak resistance from Indians, the means of transportation to new areas: these factors led to a margin above subsistence, and to the raising of large families. Gradually, during the course of the nineteenth century, agriculture changed. The frontier-rural mode, a structure of the *longue durée,* developed internally, especially as the possibilities emerged of a family producing and selling more than it needed for its own survival. Farmers became increasingly sensitive to the marketplace and able to reach it as transportation improved. They increasingly oriented their efforts toward it. By 1840 in the Ohio Valley, and from then to 1860 in the Mississippi Valley and the Great Lakes regions, farms became partly commercial as a rule. Farmers settling behind the frontier line looked more quickly and steadily toward markets, and improved their methods; "pioneering took on a more capitalistic form" in both North and South.[101] Family size and composition on the northern frontier began to resemble that in more settled areas.[102] Tocqueville had already noticed how farmers combined "some trade with agriculture" in the 1830s.[103] He was not seeing true commercial farming, which was little more than embryonic then, but a combination of artisanship and farming.

The change toward commercial agriculture was very gradual. In northern frontier areas, 90 percent of the work force were farmers in 1820, and 84 percent still were in 1840. The southern frontier was even more agrarian, at 96 and 95 percent in 1820 and 1840.[104] For some families the change probably involved a shift in attention from social concerns to economic ones, or at least an increasing share of attention to the marketplace rather than to family ties as such. But there are recorded exceptions to even that cautious statement. The whole family of Luna Warner, the teenage diarist from Kansas, migrated in 1871 and took up adjoining farms. Brothers, sisters, uncles, and sons did so in Oklahoma after 1900. The family became more, not less, important in at least one part of northwestern Michigan as the nineteenth century wore on, past the time of first settlement and into the land-scarce 1870s and 1880s.[105] At this time we lack enough evidence to say confidently or simply that the market replaced the family at the center of life, or that commercial farms drove out semisubsistence farms in the nineteenth century.[106] In some sense, however, within the peculiar American context, some kind of modernizing may have been happening.

More likely the shift toward commerce was more subtle and complicated. For a few it had happened long since. In the *Vorzeit* and the eighteenth century, growing crops and stock for distant markets was no novelty. Witness the indigo and tobacco trade of the Chesapeake, exports of naval stores and other goods from the North, and the southern cotton economy before 1860. Wheat and cotton exports multiplied in the first half of the nineteenth century, and were being marketed through the Ohio-Mississippi and other waterways. All of these instances, however, involved elites and not the mass of farmers who, if they sold on markets, sold in small lots, perhaps without using money, and as a minor part of their farming effort. The existence of a commercial system for a few does not mean a modern economy for the many. Farmers gradually awoke to market possibilities, many in the North by the 1840s. The timing depended on increasing closeness of railroads, development of commodity markets and storage depots, and the invention of farming machines, better breeds, and better seeds, to increase productivity.[107] Output per man-hour multiplied. The gap widened between American and European staple-crop production, a reality that spurred migration to America. A recent book on Swedish emigration juxtaposes two photographs from the late nineteenth century. One shows a sugar plantation in southern Sweden. Nineteen women are hoeing a field, one to a row, as a male foreman directs the operation. The other shows a reaping-binding machine harvesting wheat in Minnesota. It was pulled by twenty-seven horses and was operated by three men.[108] The difference in productivity is obvious.

To repeat, however, it is easy to overstress the shift from semisubsistence to market agriculture. One can easily mistake the cutting-edge of technological innovation for the norm that continued long after a new invention became available. Not for a long time after McCormick started selling reapers did every farmer buy one. The same was true seventy years later of Henry Ford's gasoline tractors. Horses and mules remained in common use even in the 1940s.[109] It is easy to note the construction of a river and canal network throughout the Ohio Valley and the Great Lakes states by 1850 and assume that all farmers immediately began using it, gearing their output to it, and changing overnight from yeomen to businessmen. Similarly, the creation of a railroad network, including the first transcontinental route, by about 1870 did not mean that all farmers suddenly sold on interregional and international markets. The shift was not sudden and never complete. Some subsistence farmers still exist today.

Although the trend toward commerce was a major theme in nineteenth-century agricultural history, the proportion of farm products sold on nonfarm markets rose from 20 percent in 1820, when farmers made up more of the work force than ever before or since, to only 40 percent in 1870.[110] In most places farming went on in the 1860s as it had for a century or more: young people cleared land, scrimped, bought livestock, subsisted mostly on their own labor and produce, sold a little on the market, shared household and farm tasks, raised families. The ideal way of doing things—it may have been common but surely was not universal—was described in a U.S. Patent Office report of 1852. The specific setting referred to, the wooded part of northern Pennsylvania, was more than a generation beyond first settlement, but the frontier-rural process was still going on, and similar scenes happened at other times and places:

> A healthy man, with or without family, and no other property than an axe and hoe, might thus get possession of one hundred acres [by purchase for one dollar to six dollars an acre]; the first year he might erect a cabin, and clear and sow with wheat ten acres, besides earning sufficient in the vicinity for his subsistence;
>
> the second year he would have a crop to dispose of that would be sufficient to enable him to buy a cow, a yoke of oxen, twenty sheep, some hogs, a plough, and a harrow, besides increasing his household furniture and supporting his family;
>
> the third year he could clear fifteen acres more, and every subsequent year continue to clear and cultivate and on third-rate land could keep the increase of his flock, until in ten years, his one hundred acres would be cleared and fenced, and he might have ten cows, two yoke of oxen, ten hogs, and two hundred sheep.
>
> After which, suppose the profit of each cow to be annually twenty dollars; that of each sheep, including the lambs, to be one dollar and fifty cents; there would be two hundred dollars for the cows and three hundred dollars for the sheep—making five hundred dollars; the other proceeds would doubtless, support his family.[111]

Such an admirable story may have happened. One historian found recently that older farmers in the Midwest had more property than younger ones, which is not startling. Accumulation did happen. But the story just given assumed no crippling accidents, no infections or epidemics to harm man or beast, and (hardest to believe) no spending of accumulating resources until ten years were up. The question lingers as to how this farmer, notwithstanding all his industry and thrift, would provide for children who would then be approaching working age. The answer had to be hard work with axe and hoe for them too. Frontier-rural growth required an incalculable amount of hand labor, with primitive tools, aided by horses and mules. That labor gradually transformed a wilderness into millions of semisubsistence farms, and a very few farms or plantations of great size.

The small farms slowly changed into economic units devoted and bound more and more to the marketplace. Change happened over several decades, relatively fast in the long history of human agriculture, as Danhof wrote regarding the plow:

> The generation that about 1860 was deeding its farms to its sons had witnessed during its lifetime the transformation of the plow from a most primitive wooden implement of limited effectiveness to a modern iron or steel device available in a wide variety of special-purpose forms, capable of far better work with half the effort. [112]

Lincoln's law partner, William H. Herndon, interviewed an old farmer in the 1860s, who reminisced on this subject as follows:

> I came to Ills. 1818. . . . broke prairie with a bar shear plow— Carry plow soon followed about 1827–28—Diamond plow after that about 1836—. . . Plowed corn with old fashioned bar shear plow and shovel plow—now riding plows, double &c.—with 2 yoke oxen and a span of horses—6 animals in all. . . . Fanning mills [for wheat] came in use about 1834 or 5—second plow was the carry plow—Break 2 acres a day—have seen hand mills of 2 kinds—one with stones with a pole there worked in a socket over head—the rock at the end going close to another rock— corn between. The other was like a coffee mill. Mills used about 1810–12–16–18 in Ills. Went to mill 20 miles, ground about 20 bushels per day—Blacksmith shop about 20 miles. . . . [113]

So it went with reapers, seed drills, and the rest of the new technology. The frontier-rural process, after 1860, turned ever more quickly toward the marketplace as the railroad network spread. Land-hungry young people continued to move from crowded rural areas to emptier ones. The process was repeated in the upper Mississippi Valley in midcentury, in the Grand Prairie of Arkansas (fine cotton country yet) then and later, in the cotton fields of east Texas and the wheat fields of Minnesota in the 1870s, and finally by the 1880s in the sea-like expanses of the Great Plains, from central Texas north through Kansas, Nebraska, and the Dakotas, to the prairie provinces of Canada, where wheat, corn, and beef cattle began emerging in prodigious quantities.

Changes in agriculture and the rise in productivity bore a close (if not yet fully explained) relation to the slowing growth of population in the 1860s and later. Lack of available land had always signaled the movement of an area from frontier-rural to settled-rural. In addition to this, by the late nineteenth century the rise in output per worker reduced the need for quite so many children who would for a time provide extra hands for the family farm. They could increasingly be seen instead as extra mouths to feed, as consumers rather than producers, using resources that might otherwise be sent to the marketplace. The idea needs further proof, but it seems likely that family size and birth rates declined even in frontier-rural areas for these reasons. Easy transportation accelerated the shift from semisubsistence to market orientation, and thus probably contributed to declining family size. This happened first in the North, then in the South, as the railroads came.[114] The old practice of a young person or couple working for someone else until they could accumulate enough resources to get a toehold on their own farm, a practice traceable back to indentured servitude in colonial times, took new forms: by the mid-to-late nineteenth century in Iowa, "more farmers found it necessary to begin their careers as renters, awaiting the accumulation of sufficient capital to move into the ownership ranks."[115]

As marginal farmers were shaken out in the late 1880s and the 1890s by competition, drought, freight rates, falling prices, and undercapitalization,[116] agriculture was no longer as capable as before of absorbing almost limitless numbers of young would-be farmers from farther east. It was becoming slowly less labor-intensive, revealing the first signs of the highly capital-intensive agriculture of the late twentieth century. The incursions of the railroad network and the entrapments of the marketplace were ruling out repetitions of the semisubsistence farm, and thus were ruling out the frontier-rural mode itself. Even if another frontier had existed beyond the Great Plains, suitable for small farming as frontiers always had been, the absorptive capacity, the ability to ignore Malthus, was no longer there. Hence the stabilizing of Great Plains population after the early 1890s (Texas' and Oklahoma's farming areas slightly later). The frontier-rural mode, like anything else, changed over time. After 1900 and especially after 1920, the demographic signals of rising age of marriage and declining numbers of children appeared among farm women, marking the definitive end of the frontier-rural mode.[117]

One final point about social order. Some writers have argued that a breakdown in social order took place during the nineteenth century, when a presumably stable eighteenth-century order was shattered by excessive mobility.[118] The idea has persuasive elements, but overlooks demography. "Stable" describes only some eighteenth-century communities, and even these were liable to disruption by the Great Awakening, the Revolution, and of course shrinking availability of land for the young. More striking by far is the continuing story of movement, the migration of millions of young men and women, since the early eighteenth century or before. Given the fact that the young were more mobile than children or the over-thirty-fives, migration contributed to stability rather than shattered it. These young migrants might otherwise have contributed to instability, in forms such as poverty or violence, had they stayed in their native places. If certain behavior patterns are specific to age groups, and if one of these is a concentration of crime, violence, and disorder among people in their teens and twenties, then the removal of masses of these cohorts from settled communities must have rendered those places more socially tranquil. Further, the occupation of these cohorts in frontier farming "kept them off the streets," so to speak.[119] The frontier was a safety valve after all, though not because it attracted urban workers to the West and thus reduced labor conflict; that did not happen. But it may well have released disruptive youthful energies to the West. The frontier attracted the young. Migrants were disproportionately in the 17-to-35 cohorts, often obstreperous people who instead of getting into trouble on city streetcorners, as they have in the twentieth century, broke their backs and wore out their arms pulling stumps, cutting logs, chopping cotton, reaping wheat with a cradle, and, for the young women, having the maximum number of babies. Removing idle hands from settled places, frontier-rural opportunity kept those hands busy in farm and family-making. In this light, the frontier-rural process was a source not of disorganization but of order.

IV

The Great Conjuncture,
1870–1920

The Emergence of the Metropolitan Mode

When did patterns of social and demographic behavior other than the frontier-rural begin to appear? When was that mode first challenged? In an absolute sense, some alternatives had always existed. There were cities in the wilderness, to borrow Bridenbaugh's phrase, from the earliest times: for example, Boston, Philadelphia, Charleston. Settlement by town and congregation was the norm in *Vorzeit* New England. The people of cities played an important role in bringing on the Revolution. Yet, for the great majority of Americans from the seventeenth century to the late nineteenth, frontier-rural life (or, by the latter date, settled-rural for many) was the start and end of life.[1]

Not until the early nineteenth century did a truly different set of demographic facts begin to intrude. Cities began regularly to enjoy population growth from natural increases.[2] The settled-rural Northeast, long a donor of young people to frontier-rural areas, and increasingly distant from them as the nineteenth century passed, then began donating people to cities. Intimately bound up with these demographic patterns

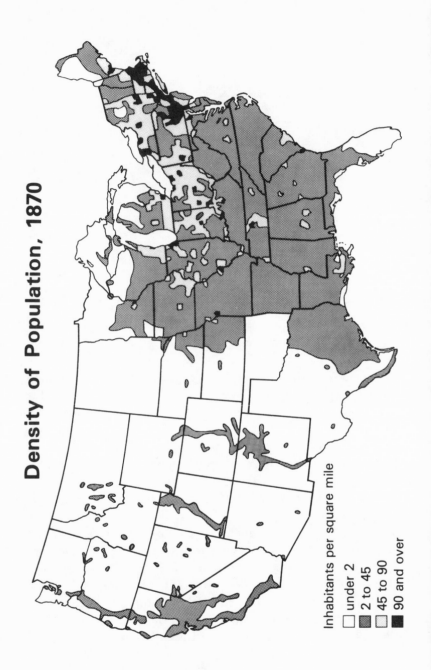

Density of Population, 1870

Inhabitants per square mile

- ☐ under 2
- ■ 2 to 45
- ▨ 45 to 90
- ■ 90 and over

Density of Population, 1920

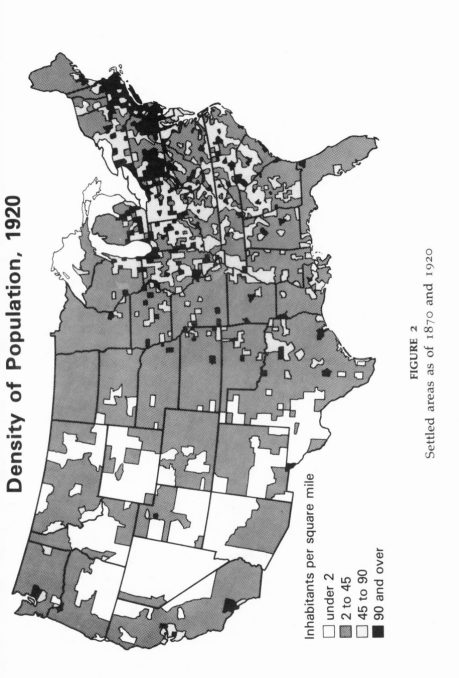

Inhabitants per square mile

☐ under 2
▨ 2 to 45
▧ 45 to 90
■ 90 and over

FIGURE 2

Settled areas as of 1870 and 1920

were changes in economic life. Minute but profound, they
were the harbingers of an entirely new mode of life in
America, a mode which would become firmly established in
the Northeast and parts of the Midwest by the late nineteenth
century, and which would become exclusively dominant after
1920: the metropolitan mode.

Before the War of 1812–15, textile mills had been established by Samuel Slater and others in Rhode Island and Massachusetts, but they employed few people, simple technology,
and a rural setting.[3] In 1813 the first seed of the metropolitan
mode, in its economic aspect, sprouted. Francis Cabot Lowell,
a Boston entrepreneur, and some associates, created the Boston Manufacturing Company and opened a cotton textile mill
at Waltham, Massachusetts. Lowell died young, four years
later, but the excellent profits of the Waltham mill encouraged
his associates to create other mills, notably in 1822 at the new
town of Lowell, on the Merrimack.[4]

These mills represented the beginning of the factory system and wage labor in the United States. They depended for
their labor force on young women from farm families and
small villages in Massachusetts and New Hampshire, people
who were literate, ambitious, interested in earning something
before they married, and willing to live in the supervised
dormitories that the factory owners were wise enough to provide so as to ensure a moral atmosphere satisfactory to the
young women and their parents. Of the thousands of women
who worked in the cotton mills in the early nineteenth century, the great majority were daughters of farmers, came from
farms or country villages, averaged eighteen or nineteen when
they started work and twenty-two or twenty-three when they
left, were not destitute but were seeking some independence,
and usually married soon after they quit the mills. But although two-thirds came from farms, less than one-third married farmers. Their rural-to-urban migration was ratified in

their marriages to artisans or factory workers. The demographic pattern was clear:

> Work in the mills functioned for women rather like migration did for young men who could see that their chances of setting up on a farm in an established rural community were rather slim. The mills offered individual self-support. . . . The steady movement of the family farm from a subsistence to a commercial basis made daughters relatively "expendable" and gave fathers who otherwise might have guarded the family labor supply reason to allow them a chance on their own.[5]

These women married later than did frontier-rural women, at over twenty-six in one set of cases,[6] and the number of children they bore in their lifetimes must have been fewer. Employment of women outside the home and farm contributed to a demographic regime of slower population growth, and it rested on the female-tilted sex ratio of settled-rural New England. Did they leave the parental farm because husbands were scarce by then in rural areas? The evidence is not yet clear. The more conscious reasons, at least, were the desire for independence and earnings for a time before they did marry. But when they married, it was usually to non-farmers, young men (native or immigrant) whom they met in the mill towns.[7]

Other signs of the incipient metropolitan mode emerged not long after the establishment of the factories of New England. The first steam railroad opened near Baltimore in 1830 with 13 miles of track. The building of factories and railroads spread quickly in the 1830s, until stopped by the depression of 1837–43. By that time (1840) New Orleans and Baltimore had just passed 100,000, Philadelphia 200,000, and New York 300,000. Urban residence was no longer nearly unknown. Yet only four other cities exceeded thirty thousand.[8] After the depression, the United States enjoyed one of the greatest economic growth phases in its history, from 1844 to 1860, accompanied by important demographic changes: an unprecedented spurt in urban population, based in small part on natural increases among those already in cities, in larger part on in-migration from settled-rural areas, and, for the first time in great numbers, on immigration from other countries. Between 1840 and 1860, U.S. urban population jumped from 1.8 to 6.2 million. New York State's urban population tripled in numbers, and rose from 19 percent to 39 percent of the state's total, even though New York's rural population also continued to rise. Massachusetts' urban population nearly tripled while its rural population held about stable, so that the urban percent rose from 38 to 60. Massachusetts and Rhode Island were the first states with urban majorities, both by 1850.[9] New York City rose in twenty years from 312,000 to 806,000, Brooklyn from 33,000 to 267,000, Buffalo from 18,000 to 81,000, and San Francisco and Chicago from virtual nonexistence to 57,000 and 109,000.[10] The conjuncture of simultaneous frontier-rural and metropolitan growth that was to spread across the country from 1870 to 1920 was hitting New York State and had already passed through eastern New England.

Birth rates dropped in each decade of the nineteenth century in the United States with increasing speed. The drop had been 6 or 7 percent nationally in the 1820s and 1830s, but became 9 or 10 percent in the 1840s and 1850s, a decline not matched again until the 1880s or surpassed until the 1920s, which were also exceptional decades of urbanization.[11] Economic changes accompanied demographic changes. Steam began to replace water as the power source for factories, freeing entrepreneurs from the need to locate them near waterfalls and permitting them to be placed in urban areas, closer to labor, materials, transportation, and markets. Factories could also be larger and could operate without reference to the seasons or changes in the water flow.[12] Between 1830 and 1860 the woolens industry of New England moved from home to factory, encouraging the wives and especially the daughters of farmers to leave for urban-located jobs. As Horace Bushnell told a group of farmers in Litchfield, Connecticut, in 1851,

> This transition from mother, and daughter, power to water, and
> steam-power is a great one, greater by far than many have as yet
> begun to conceive—one that is to carry with it a complete revo-
> lution in domestic life and social manners. [13]

The demographic and economic consequences were enormous
too. A true change in the mode of production, and the mode of
life, was taking place. Between the late 1840s and the Civil
War, manufacturing (value added) rose by hundreds of millions of dollars. By 1869, 2 million production workers toiled
in about 250,000 factories, an average of eight per unit: not
modern mass employment, yet the start of it. [14] Railroad tracks
expanded from 4,000 miles in 1844 to 53,000 in 1870, forming
a growing network throughout the Northeast and Midwest. [15]
    Immigration from Ireland and Germany ranged in most
years between 20,000 and 40,000 from each country between
1835 and 1845, but in 1846 each country sent more than
50,000 and the numbers rose thereafter to a peak of 221,000
Irish in 1851 and 215,000 Germans in 1854. From 1847
through 1858, 2.8 million immigrants came to the United
States, most of them to stay. Unlike many of the migrants of
the 1880s, or the great wave from 1905 to 1914, those of the
first wave were not interested in returning to an Ireland
scourged by the potato famine or a Germany whose farming
areas could not support them. They were the first large non-
British, mostly non-Protestant people to appear in the United
States except for blacks and Indians. In each year from 1849
through 1854 the number of arriving immigrants was greater
than 1 percent of the resident population, a proportion higher
even than in 1905–14, and in those years far more were transients. [16]
    Before the potato blight struck in late 1845, Ireland was a
country of upwards of 8 million people, 80 percent rural, half
of whose farms were ten acres or smaller, too small for any-

thing but the barest survival. Exorbitant rents kept the peasantry poor; ownership was illegal. The considerable agricultural product of the country was shipped to England, leaving the Irish increasingly dependent on potatoes for their diet. Without capital and without skills, though usually literate in English, intensely Catholic, family-oriented, and suspicious of political and economic authorities whom experience proved hostile, the Irish peasant could not protect himself when the potato blight struck. The choice was to starve or to emigrate. A million starved or died of epidemics between 1845 and 1852, and about 1.75 million emigrated in the ten years after 1845.[17] Nothing in the early nineteenth century American experience compared to the desperate condition of the Irish rural people before the famine, except perhaps the condition of the slaves. And famine even the slaves never had to undergo. Of those Irish who sailed, 10 to 20 percent died at sea or in the first year after leaving. The great majority of the survivors found themselves in cities large and small in New England, New York, Pennsylvania, and Maryland, "accustomed to a meager diet, mean raiment, gross domestic overcrowding, cold, and household squalor," and thus were "by no means unprepared for city slums."[18]

The emigrants from southwestern German states were not wealthy, but some of them brought a little capital and some true farming skills, with the result that perhaps half were able to proceed westward, either to cities or frontier-rural farms. They became a less urban, less northeastern, less poverty-stricken group than the Irish, though almost as numerous.[19] For both groups, the nuclear family was important, and families rather than individuals migrated more often than in later waves. Even so, the sex ratio was skewed somewhat toward males, and birth rates among immigrant women were perhaps only 30 to 40 percent of those for the native-born.[20]

Little wonder that for the first and only time a major political party arose on the basis of nativism, the antiforeign, anti-Catholic American or "Know-Nothing" party. It did not last long, but it was symptomatic of widespread hostility toward the newcomers. Worse than symptomatic were anti-foreign riots, as in Louisville when Know-Nothings attacked the Irish and Germans in 1855, burned down the Irish neighborhood, vandalized churches, prevented immigrants from voting, and killed over twenty people, most of them Irish.[21] Yet immigrants kept coming. Sustained by the influx, population growth remained above 3 percent per year until 1857, when it fell below that level, never to reach it again.

The most telling statistic about what was happening to the population in the middle of the nineteenth century is the change in the proportion living in cities. The curve of urban dwellers as a percent of all Americans swept upward. In 1840, about 10 percent of the whole lived in cities of any consequence (2,500 or more). These were almost never cities whose economic base was industrial, except for the new mill towns of New England. Instead they were commercial entrepôts which depended on the continuing output of farm products from the hinterlands around them and the sale of finished goods to the people in that hinterland.[22] Improved transportation linked city and hinterland. In a wholly unprecedent jump, the urban proportion rose to 15 percent in 1850, to 20 percent in 1860, to 25 percent in 1870. City population almost doubled in the 1840s alone, fed by Irish immigration. From that point on, until mass immigration ceased in the 1920s, the foreign-born and their descendants made up a disproportionate part of the population of large cities.[23] In the middle and late nineteenth century, the United States underwent the most spectacular urbanization in the world (see table 3). An urban middle class, nuclear families with few children, was already evident in Chicago in the 1870s.[24] The two-parent family was the norm for all groups.[25] Death rates declined somewhat, as did birth rates.[26]

By the end of the Civil War, the entire Northeast was approaching 50 percent urban in place of residence. The factory system was firmly entrenched in an industrial-urban band stretching from above Boston south to Baltimore along the east coast, jumping westward from new city to new city along the Great Lakes, through Rochester, Buffalo, Cleveland, Detroit, to Chicago and Milwaukee, and along the Ohio River from Pittsburgh to Cincinnati to Louisville to St. Louis. Within that parallelogram a process of population growth and economic development very different from the frontier-rural kind was operating. At the same time, frontier-rural life continued, as swarms of settlers pushed west of the Mississippi and Missouri rivers.

For eight years between the end of the Civil War and the Panic of 1873, railroad building went on at a frantic rate, and resumed when the ensuing depression ended in 1879. The railroads reduced travel time radically. Michel Chevalier marvelled in 1834 that it took him only seven hours by railroad and two more by steamboat to go from New York to Philadelphia, and only another eight hours to go to Baltimore by another railroad-steamboat combination. In 1840, before the railroads entered the Midwest, a traveler spent a week getting from New York to Cleveland, two weeks to New Orleans, three weeks to Chicago. By 1860 railroads were bringing passengers from New York to Cleveland in less than 24 hours and to Chicago in 48. By the 1880s even these times were cut in half.[27]

Further statistics would show changes in labor-force distribution, in output, in the number and sizes of cities, and in other demographic and economic areas, but they would only add detail to the general point: the metropolitan mode existed by 1870, and had become pervasive in the Northeast and in parts of the Midwest, after the dynamic years of 1844 to 1860. Yet the frontier-rural mode also persisted vigorously for several more decades.

TABLE 3

Cities of 100,000 or more, by census division, and when they reached that size

	1820	1830	1840	1850	1860	1870	1880	1890	1900	1910
New England				Boston			Providence		Worcester Fall River New Haven	Bridgeport Cambridge Lowell
Mid-Atlantic	New York Philadelphia				Brooklyn	Buffalo Newark	Jersey City Pittsburgh	Rochester	Paterson Scranton Syracuse	Albany
East North Central				Cincinnati	Chicago		Cleveland Detroit Milwaukee	Indianapolis		Dayton Grand Rapids
West North Central					St. Louis			Minneapolis St. Paul Kansas City Omaha	St. Joseph	
South Atlantic			Baltimore			Washington				Atlanta Richmond
East South Central						Louisville			Memphis	Birmingham Nashville
West South Central			New Orleans							
Mountain								Denver		
Pacific						San Francisco			Los Angeles	

Three Misfits: Frontier-Urban,
Settled-Rural, and Slave Society

The frontier-rural and metropolitan modes account for the conditions of life of most Americans throughout history, but not all of them. A small minority have lived, often temporarily, in communities at or beyond the edge of settlement, places with odd demographic characteristics which we can call frontier-urban. Much larger numbers have lived in areas that were once frontier-rural but which changed their demographic personalities as they grew older and more densely settled: these are the settled-rural areas, some almost purely farms but others a mix of farms, villages, and small cities. A third mode of life not fitting into the main ones is the slave society of the antebellum South. Some brief account of each of these "misfits" will show how they differed from, and related to, the frontier-rural and metropolitan modes, and what their demographic earmarks were.

Examples of frontier-urban life might begin with colonial seaports, those outposts of Europe on the edge of the wilderness, exercising political, economic, and cultural influence far out of proportion to their size, growing (if they grew at all) from in-migration rather than from natural increase, beset by high death rates and low birth rates in contrast to the frontier-rural regions around them. Frontier-urban cases also include the small villages near the edge of settlement, jumping-off places into frontier areas, the Albanies of 1780 or the Pittsburghs and Cincinnatis of 1810 or the Chicago of 1835.[28] Westport Landing and other outfitting points for the Overland Trail in the 1840s and 1850s are also cases in point.[29] The best examples of frontier-urban life, however, appear only after 1840: mining camps, lumber camps, settlements often connected to extractive industries other than farming and fishing, very often the result of searches for precious and other non-ferrous metals. Those searches required railroads, technology, and power sources not normally available before 1840. The demographic characteristics of such places include a very male-skewed sex ratio—the legendary "frontier town" population where men outnumbered women by two, three, six to one. Families were relatively rare. Single men, from their teens to their thirties, predominated, and so did the behavior one might expect from them. Children were unusual, the birth rate was very low, but so was the death rate in the absence of very many older people. Of the twenty-four towns over 8,000 west of the Missouri Valley in 1880, nearly all were a fourth to a half foreign-born. Except in Kansas, Missouri, and Texas, blacks were fewer than one in twenty in those towns.[30]

Frontier-urban conditions were essentially temporary, and had to be since their demographic regimes were inherently unstable. Some disappeared, when the natural resources which they were established to seek were exhausted; these include many mining towns which became "ghost towns" or something close. Some evolved into the settled-rural nonfarm pattern, as they merged with the aging frontier-rural area around them. Examples of that include Kansas cattle towns such as Abilene or Ellsworth, which ceased to be frontier-urban and started becoming settled-rural nonfarm about ten years after they were founded.[31] Another cattle town, Wichita, however, developed into a regional metropolis. Others continued to grow, from migration and natural increase, and at scarcely definable points became part of the metropolitan mode, receiving people from settled-rural areas. The Chicago of 1835 was frontier-urban; the Chicago of 1875 was metropolitan. The Westport of 1850 was frontier-urban; Kansas City by 1885 was metropolitan. Los Angeles in 1880 was "essentially a real-estate promotion awaiting a boom," but by 1910 it was metropolitan.[32] The reasons some of these places failed or stagnated while others became regional or world metropolises are as different as the places themselves, and would require an enormous digression to explain. In general, the ones that succeeded had developed a stable demographic regime.

Settled-rural areas have included millions of people since their first appearance in the late eighteenth century, and have been demographic opposites of frontier-urban places. They are one-time frontier-rural areas that the frontier has passed by. The best-known studies of colonial Massachusetts towns have noted the crowding of rural areas in the eighteenth century, the declining availability of land, the increasing numbers of poorly-landed young people. Fertility of farm families declined, and as the population's average age rose, a "dramatic rise in mortality" took place.[33]

Lyme, New Hampshire, like other New England towns, was part of the frontier-rural mode from its early settlement around 1780 until its population peaked in 1830. Then it stabilized and declined, donating young people to frontier-rural areas in New York and the Midwest or to the incipient metropolises:

> The hill country could no longer compete in agriculture. Neither did Lyme benefit from the factory epoch: though it was in a region of rapid streams, none of its water powers invited industrial enterprise. . . . Many of Lyme's residents, particularly the younger folk, contributed to the industrial growth of the larger cities of New Hampshire and other states.[34]

By the 1880s, depopulation of rural townships was endemic not just in New England and New York but as far west as the Mississippi Valley. By then people were often going to cities rather than creating new farms.[35] Depopulation was a late feature of settled-rural life, and came several decades after rural populations had become stable. A correspondent of Frederick Jackson Turner's recalled walking along a ridge in the Green Mountains of Vermont in 1920 and seeing no inhabited house within miles, yet he came upon "a bronze tablet stating that Daniel Webster addressed an audience of several thousand people there during the campaign of 1840."[36] The shifts over time were from frontier-rural to settled-rural (donating to western rural places and gradually to eastern urban ones), then finally to depopulation or absorption in the increasingly metropolitan mode of a region such as New England.

The demographic characteristics of settled-rural areas include a drop in fertility, probably in response to land scarcity.[37] The population aged, containing more elderly and fewer children.[38] In at least some places families became more extended as older children remained in their parents' homes and began their families there.[39] As Ohio, for example, shifted from frontier-rural to settled-rural between 1810 and 1860, when its white population was larger than that of any other state except New York and Pennsylvania, its fertility level dropped almost 40 percent, and its rate of population growth dropped from 151 percent in 1810–20 to 18 percent in 1850–60.[40] The picture in Ontario was similar: lower fertility and a drop in birth rate from 61 to 41 per thousand between 1851 and 1871, later age of marriage, out-migration of young men, a sex ratio tending to tilt toward more females than males. The demographic consequence was a push to new lands in the prairie provinces, after passage of the Dominion Lands Act of 1872. The social consequences?

> By 1870 rural society in Ontario had already dealt decisively and effectively with the crisis [of population] that had threatened its future. By means of a dramatic shift in customary patterns of inheritance and consequently the displacement of surplus population, . . . the community had taken steps to protect the integrity of the traditional economic space from which the farm family derived its security, and to maintain the standard of living—the rewards of its labour—historically associated with rural prosperity. In short, radical but nevertheless thoroughly pragmatic adjustments to the size, the structure, and the culture of the farm family by 1867 [when the Canadian Confederation was created] had begun to mitigate the effects of the crisis in rural Canada West.[41]

Analytically distinct from settled-rural farm areas are settled-rural small towns and villages, but the demographic features are not greatly different. These towns and villages had become stable or were declining, would either disappear or become part of the metropolitan mode, were donating young people to frontier-rural areas or to metropolises, and were functionally almost the same as settled-rural farm areas. A case in point is Kingston, New York, the subject of a recent study. Founded in 1658, it had become in 1820, seven generations later, "a distinctly rural town, with some 2,000 farm dwellers surrounding a village whose population had only recently passed 1,000." In the next forty years, after the Delaware and Hudson canal opened and after Irish and German immigrants made it half foreign-born, Kingston had changed from settled-rural to a commercial city, crossing the "urban threshold" to become part of the metropolitan Northeast. Even in 1820 it was not a "traditional" or "peasant" community, but rather agricultural-commercial—yet the pace of life and the occupations of its residents derived from farming. Between 1820 and 1860 "It lost this rural character when most of its people came to reside in densely settled villages, when all but a small proportion of its work force engaged in commerce, manufacturing, and finance, and when local institutions were reoriented to the needs and opportunities of the village population."[42] In small towns and cities in the Northeast, boarding houses proliferated, housing teenagers and persons in their twenties whose farm families were unable to set them up in life. Because these communities were able to attract young people to apprenticeships or factory jobs, they would escape the stagnation of settled-rural life, at least for some generations, and would become part of the metropolitan mode.[43]

The inability of American blacks to participate in the frontier-rural mode before the abolition of slavery has been referred to earlier and needs only a word here. Blacks were brought to the southern frontier as the cotton kingdom expanded. They did not come voluntarily. Indeed the rapid opening of parts of Alabama, Mississippi, and nearby states to large-scale cotton culture contributed to the splitting of slave families, either one parent from the other, or children from parents. For blacks, the frontier meant loss, not gain; deprivation, not opportunity. Free blacks were not encouraged to migrate to the southern frontier and never constituted as much as 1 percent of its population.[44] As nonvoluntary migrants before emancipation, and not property owners, blacks were not part of the frontier-rural mode before emancipation. Even after it, they were not participants except on rare occasions such as the Exoduster migration from Louisiana to Kansas in 1879. The migration of southern blacks, when it finally began in force after 1910, directed them to northern cities rather than to the frontier farms, which by then were no longer available. Slavery formed the boundaries of life for most blacks before 1865, at the very time when the frontier-rural mode was providing the boundaries for the great majority of whites. Not until five decades after emancipation, a period during which their economic and demographic lives changed little from slavery days, did many blacks quit the South. By then their option was limited to the metropolitan mode.

Conjuncture, Early Phase: 1870–1890s

By 1870 the metropolitan mode was securely established. In New England and the Middle Atlantic states, the frontier-rural mode had disappeared, and the absorption of people into metropolitan conditions was pervasive and irreversible, if not yet fully complete. Elsewhere, however, the frontier-rural mode flourished. Historians and economists have often overlooked that fact, spellbound by the rapid rise in manufacturing output, the struggles between labor and capital, the creation of the railroad network, and farmers' declining share of the work force (they fell below 50 percent sometime during the 1870s).

These are undeniable realities. But they divert attention from
the establishing of 600,000 new farms in the 1860s, 1.3 million more in the 1870s, another 550,000 in the 1880s, and still
another 600,000 in the 1890s despite depression. The total
number of farms more than doubled between 1870 and 1900,
as did farm acreage. Farm workers swelled from 5.6 million
persons in 1870 to 9.4 million in 1900. Agriculture grew less
rapidly than manufacturing, but its expansion was still remarkable. Moreover, it expanded in ways continuous with the
pre-1870 frontier-rural pattern of small, family-operated
social-economic units, with young people opening up inexpensive and previously uncultivated land as an alternative to
remaining in land-scarce areas farther east.[45]

Agriculture's economic expansion paralleled the geographic expansion of the settled regions of the country. In 1870 the
westward line of settlement ran westward across Wisconsin
and Minnesota, dropped southward through central Nebraska
and Kansas, skipped the off-limits Indian Territory, and continued south through central Texas to the Rio Grande. West of
it, pockets of settlement—mining and commercial outposts
often of the frontier-urban kind—existed in Colorado,
Nevada, California, and a few other states and territories. San
Francisco was already a thriving commercial city, but the only
one of much consequence west of St. Louis and Chicago. The
Willamette Valley of Oregon, and Mormon Utah, were farming
areas, but isolated ones. Indians were just then being quieted
on the southern Plains and still roamed free on the northern
Plains. Other than the Oregon settlements of the 1840s and
1850s, the Northwest was almost empty, a late frontier. Turner
remarked on this in a draft essay.

When in 1870 James J. Hill, who was to become the "Empire
Builder" of the New Northwest, visited the north western part of
Minnesota with his "grubsack" on a dog train, he passed
through a wilderness where fourteen years later an almost un-
broken wheat field stretched through almost one hundred and

twenty square miles. Between Duluth and the mining camps of the Rocky Mountains were a few military and trading posts. The Indian reservations of Sioux, Arickaree and Gros Ventres, Crow, and Blackfeet occupied vast portions of the zone. Montana and Idaho mining camps contained some thirty-five thousand souls; Wyoming had less than ten thousand; Washington but twenty-four thousand, concentrated about Puget Sound.[46]

Twenty years later these had become states of the Union, and the frontier line was gone. Frontier-rural growth was weakening but not quite dead.

European immigrants, from Germany, Scandinavia, Russia, Ireland, and Bohemia especially, took part in the frontier-rural movement of the 1870s and 1880s, creating the ethnic richness of the rural West North Central states. More often, however, immigrants went to cities of the Northeast and Midwest, and through a combination of immigration and natural increase, cities continued to grow in numbers and population more rapidly than did rural parts of the country, as they had since the 1840s. Between 1870 and 1900, the number of cities of 25,000 or more jumped from 52 to 160, and their number of residents by 338 percent. In those thirty years, rural population—frontier-rural and settled-rural—increased 160 percent: significant, but half the rate of the larger cities.[47]

The demographic earmarks and effects of these parallel patterns of population growth are as follows. As noted in chapter one as part of the long-term observation, the rate of growth of the total population fell abruptly in the 1860s, from the previously normal 33 to 36 percent, to about 26 percent, where it stayed through the 1890s. Then it fell again, to 21 percent in each of the next two decades, thus demarcating the 1870–1920 period as the Conjuncture. The components of this slowing of growth in the 1860s and later are several. The rate of natural increase by the end of the 1870s was probably about half the level at the beginning of the nineteenth century. In 1800 and for some years thereafter, the proportion of total population increase attributable to a surplus of births over deaths in the native-born population, rather than to immigration, was over 90 percent, and therefore the rate of natural increase was probably over 30 percent per decade. That rate declined through the century and from the late 1870s through the mid-1890s hovered around 15 percent. The reasons for the drop are, principally, the encroachment of urban population into the total, which, with the persistently slower natural increase in cities than on farms, reduced the overall rate; and the great increase since the 1840s in immigrants, also a slower-growing group than the native-born rural population. Contraception by various means (interruption, condoms, pessaries, douches), as well as abortion and even infanticide, have been suggested as another reason. But though there is evidence that all of these were practiced, it is by no means clear that they spread or improved in the 1850s and 1860s enough to cause much of the sudden, large drop in aggregate growth that happened just then.

The crude birth rate did decline in the late nineteenth century, but neither it nor the fertility rate among the native-born nor the rate of natural increase in frontier-rural areas—all measures to some extent of the same thing—declined much, once city dwellers and immigrants are removed from the equation. From the 1890s to about 1915, the rates would slow, as the settled-rural, rural-donor pattern spread to many counties in the eastern Midwest and the Gulf-Ohio Valley states, and as they began to depopulate as the New England counties had been doing for several decades. After 1900 the frontier-rural mode was increasingly isolated in shrinking pockets on the Great Plains, notably in Oklahoma. Urban conditions, compounded by immigration from countries where birth rates had been traditionally lower than in frontier-rural America, reduced the crude birth rate and the fertility rate by about one-fourth between the 1860s and the 1890s.[48]

People were beginning to live longer, sustaining the

growth rate. Rural people enjoyed lower death rates than city dwellers did, and whites lower than blacks, but for everyone, it seems, mortality rates started dropping sometime in the 1880s. The death rate for whites in the middle of the nineteenth century through the 1870s was about 22 or 23 per thousand, and was somewhat higher for blacks because of poorer diet and susceptibility to infectious disease. From then on, the white death rate slid to about 17 per thousand in 1900 and to less than 15 in 1915.[49] The reasons for the drop are not entirely clear. Sewage improvements were being introduced, but for the most part had to await the early twentieth century. Infectious diseases declined, especially those hitting infants and children; purer water had some effect, though its main impact was also yet to come.[50] Better access to medical care in cities, better water, pasteurized milk, and higher literacy may have lowered the death rate of urban people in the late nineteenth century, but these are conjectures. Rural mortality continued to be lower than urban.[51]

Immigration in the early Conjuncture contributed to both frontier-rural and metropolitan processes. The immigrants of the 1880s, however, differed in certain important respects from those of the 1840s and 1850s and from those of the late 1860s and the 1870s. Most of the earlier immigrants were permanent migrants, never intending to return to the Ireland or Germany or central Russia or Sweden from which they had come. Finding available land, they joined the frontier-rural crowd. Those who went to New York or Boston or Chicago may have migrated from one of those cities to another,[52] but they seldom recrossed the Atlantic. British and Scandinavians did so in the 1880s more often than before, however. Though they and the Irish and Germans still made up the bulk of the arrivals of the 1880s, post-1880 immigrants came increasingly from Poland, Italy, and other countries of southern and eastern Europe, and increasingly they intended to return after accumulating a measure of wealth in the New World. Of the

large nations of the "newer immigration," only the Jews of
Russia, Poland, Hungary, and elsewhere in eastern Europe
were immigrants in the old sense, fleeing some intolerable
situation (in their case, pogroms or Russian conscription),
never intending to go back. The Italians and Poles responded
to the combination of agricultural backwardness and industrial
opportunity in the middle of the nineteenth century by migrating within Italy or Poland, or at the farthest to Germany or
Austria. But after 1880, railroads leading to Hamburg and
Bremen and steamships sailing regularly from those ports and
from Naples made it easy for Poles and south Italians to get to
the United States or even to Brazil or Argentina. Railroads and
steamships linked the transatlantic economy and added
southern and eastern Europe to it.[53]

If the Mediterranean was the brilliant world of the sixteenth century, as Braudel wrote, the Atlantic was the brilliant
world of the nineteenth. Those who left Europe permanently
after 1880 were many fewer than those who left it for a while,
returning, leaving again, perhaps returning again. The contribution of immigration to total population growth after 1880 in
the United States was smaller than in the wave of 1846 to
1854. Thus, while falling mortality rates sustained the rate of
population growth to some extent, the departure of many
sojourning migrants slowed the rate of growth, combining
with falling birth rates to produce that effect. Thus two of the
three raw determinants of changes in population size, births
and permanent migrants, were moderating from the 1860s
onward, especially in the 1880s and 1890s.

The social, economic, cultural, and political context and
results of these demographic changes would require, if set out
in detail, a massive history of the late nineteenth century.
Once more the temptation to wander from the demographic
boulevard into inviting gardens must be suppressed to nothing more than some teasing possibilities. The changes just
outlined involved rises in the median age of the American

people and rises in the normal age of marriage. Adolescence was becoming defined as a stage of life set apart from childhood and adulthood, more formal schooling was being expected at least among non-manual-laboring families, and the period during which a young person "prepared for life" was lasting longer.[54] Demography, economics, and cultural values combined in such a change. On the other hand, the simultaneous existence of the frontier-rural and metropolitan modes produced unique confusion. A severe depression slowed urban growth from 1873 to 1878 (though not frontier-rural very much), and produced the first truly national conflict of labor and capital, the Great Railway Strike of 1877. With the end of the depression came the highest net immigration since the 1850s, which caused many social tensions yet also was a possible reason why European-style class struggle did not develop in the United States. Or so thought Friedrich Engels, who blamed the cultural and linguistic divisions among immigrant workers for the absence of a workers' political party.[55] The 1879–89 decade, however, was probably the most violent in American history. Both in cities and in frontier-rural areas, whether from the logic of Conjuncture or not, violence erupted in the form of lynchings, labor riots, a presidential assassination, Indian suppression, outlawry and cattle-town shootouts, and vigilantism.[56]

So rapid and confusing were the demographic and economic changes of 1879–93, the years between two depressions, that ideas, values, and institutions could not keep up. Attitudes and folk themes drawn from generations of frontier-rural realities were not appropriate to the metropolitan mode.[57] Social and economic change was rapid and complex, but most Americans persisted in their beliefs in a one-class society, in classic political economy, in the harmony and primacy of the producing classes, and in the moral goodness of exploitative individualism. In the depression of 1893–97, these conventional wisdoms were severely tested. They required replacement or revision. In the later Conjuncture exactly that happened, while—and in part because—the frontier-rural mode then ceased to exist.

Conjuncture, Later Phase: 1890s–1920

The Panic of 1893 and the ensuing four-year depression slowed the growth and ended the euphoria of the 1880s in urban-industrial areas, while much of the South and the frontier-rural parts of the Great Plains already suffered depression. When bad times spread to midwestern and northeastern cities late in 1893, bitterness and disappointment spread with them. Low crop prices and low wages, industrial unemployment in the cities, and forced abandonment of many farms in the Great Plains contrasted sharply with the achievements and promise of the preceding fifteen years. American society seemed to be generating little but violence, poverty, labor conflict, lynchings, vagrancy, alcohol and drug abuse, and corruption in business and government—Malthus's vice and misery, though not because population had outstripped food supply, but because of social and economic problems resting on population changes. With these problems, visible before 1893 but afterwards much more glaring, politicians and parties were unable to cope. William Jennings Bryan's formula of free silver coinage, with which he terrorized the equally unimaginative opposition during the election campaign of 1896, was neither adequate nor acceptable to urban-industrial areas and the settled-rural commercial farms which were functionally part of them by then. The end of the depression restored jobs gradually, but brought no systematic change except a militant campaign by big business magnates, led by J. Pierpont Morgan, to consolidate manufacturing, transportation, and finance into the largest possible units.

The lesson of the depression of the 1890s was that many people were being deprived of the hope or substance of the middle-class dream, a dream not necessarily of wealth or abundance but of opportunity. In frontier-rural America opportunity took the form of ownership of available land. But where were the opportunities under the spreading metropolitan conditions of 1900? This question, in one form or another, tormented perceptive thinkers of the day. If the main outcome of the depression was a more firmly entrenched position for Morgan's and Rockefeller's "supertrusts," then a social revolution impended. Reform, to relieve social and economic problems and to restore opportunity, was needed urgently.

The demographic patterns of the 1880s resumed after the depression. Immigrants arrived (and left) in large numbers, and birth and death rates continued to slide. Frontier-rural growth at 35 percent per decade persisted in Oklahoma and parts of other states until about 1915, but nowhere else; the northern Great Plains states slipped from 45 percent in the 1880s to only about 16 percent in the 1890s, and have been the slowest-growing census division most of the time since. The Mountain states increased rapidly until 1920, and the Pacific states well beyond that, but most of the additions were of the metropolitan variety. Those who were farm dwellers were highly market-oriented. By 1910, farm population reached a plateau at about 32 million, and remained there until the mid-1930s. The peak year was 1916, when the 32.5 million people then on farms constituted 32 percent of the national population. The proportion continued to fall.[58]

Those remaining on farms usually manifested the demographic characteristics of settled-rural people. Mortality, by one estimate, fell among the rural population by about a third between 1870 and 1920, probably because of improvements in diet, in housing (keeping away pneumonia and influenza), and, to a lesser extent, in sanitation.[59] Among farm families, the age of marriage rose. Fertility remained significantly higher than among city women, but it was declining, and urban and rural fertility rates would converge between 1950 and 1975.[60] In the 1920s, farms suffered a net loss of 6.3 million emigrants to urban places. Rural townships on the Great Plains began to lose people, as rural townships farther east had done for almost two hundred years.[61] Productivity rose, and the semisubsistence agriculture typical of much of the frontier-rural period was disappearing. In fact agriculture had always been more market-oriented in the Great Plains than farther east. Tenancy increased, by 1916 including almost 40 percent of farmers nationally and 50 percent of those in the South.[62] Metropolises dotted the Missouri Valley and the Great Plains from Nebraska to Texas, and by 1920 four Texas cities had passed 100,000 and one-third of the state's population was urban.

Immigration from Europe slackened to 200,000 to 300,000 per year during the depression of the 1890s, but resumed in force after that, particularly after 1904. In six of the ten years from 1905 through 1914, over a million migrants entered the United States. Half or more did not stay.[63] Net migration was not as high as in the early 1880s, but did account for about one-third of total population increase from 1900 to 1915.[64] Virtually all of this migration was urban-directed and metropolitan-oriented: those who stayed took up the millions of blue-collar, nonfarming jobs being created by a throbbing economy. A few occupied white-collar jobs, although these were mainly filled by the sons and daughters of the native majority at that time, whether migrants from settled-rural areas or from city families. The children of the immigrants would have to wait a generation or two for their white collars. The sources of immigration had been changing since the 1880s, and after 1900 was largely southern and eastern European. Mexicans began appearing in the Midwest after 1910, as railroad workers and in other urban jobs, resembling frontier-urban settlers at first. Gradually, as the *barrios* became established, they became an immigrant subculture within the metropolis.[65] Migration of rural blacks out of the South started in significant numbers by 1915, but their destinations were northern cities, not western farms. The black migration took people directly from the postslavery, settled-rural South into the metropolitan mode.[66]

Frontier-rural patterns lingered for some time after 1915, like the smell of a large feast already consumed. In the South, technology changed little between 1870 and 1920, and animal power remained important there until the 1950s or 1960s, long after it had become almost quaint on the Plains.[67] Farm women continued into the 1920s or later to perform tasks that city women had been able to avoid since the 1870s or 1880s. Electricity on farms awaited the 1930s and 1940s. Three-fourths of South Dakota farms lacked indoor water in 1935, and a few new sod houses were still going up. Turner grasped for hope of still more frontiers, and thought perhaps Alaska would develop into "our last frontier," "a potential food area at least equal to Finland and Sweden." But he also realized that of the 1,000 counties in the United States that lost population between 1910 and 1920, almost all were rural, and the 2,000 that gained were urban, industrial, and immigrant-receiving.[68]

A last word on Turner. He realized that although the frontier line ended in 1890, frontier conditions persisted in some places beyond that. Yet he also realized that the frontier was gone by 1920. The Malthusian crunch bothered him; he pondered the arguments of the "Nordic alarmists," as he called them, of the 1920s who predicted the exhaustion of oil, minerals, lumber, and food supply within a generation or two unless population were controlled, by immigration restriction and other means. He never joined them, but was worried by the rise in farm tenancy evident in the 1920 census, which might lead, he thought, to an American peasantry. The end of the frontier was at hand, and the postfrontier world with all its unknowns lay ahead. Turner was uncertain about what that world held, did not predict much good from it, and was saved from despair over it more by his natural optimism than by his ideas about it. Had he lived long enough to see post-1920 and post-1930 population patterns as we can see them in the late twentieth century, he might have realized that the metropolitan future had already begun to unfold. Americans were already living in it before the end of the nineteenth century, and the frontier-rural mode, dominant in the eighteenth and nineteenth centuries, had been conjoined through much of his adult life with the metropolitan, the mode dominating the twentieth and perhaps the twenty-first centuries.[69]

Everett Lee in 1961, and David Potter in 1954, attempted to place the significance of the frontier within broader schemes for understanding American history and character. Lee, a demographer, made Turner's frontier a special case of migration, enormously important in America. But Lee added that not all migration was to the frontier; another safety valve was migration to farms well behind the frontier.[70] He might have added rural-to-urban black migration as another example. Potter saw Turner's frontier as a special case of abundance—not only of free land but of many kinds of resources—which had shaped the American character. According to Potter, Turner was quite right in recognizing the force of economic abundance, but saw it only in the rural context, not in the industrial. Potter quoted a statement made by James C. Malin in 1943: "Over-attention to the agricultural context 'diverted attention from the . . . all-important fact that there was still opportunity, created by the fluidity of society based on the industrial revolution.'"[71] Malin was closer to the truth than was Potter. Population has grown throughout American history and will do so until at least 2015, according to the best estimates at the end of the 1970s, and then a fourth phase in American population history may begin. Growth was fastest when land was available, and slowed during the Conjuncture when blue- and white-collar jobs, metropolitan kinds of opportunities, became available. Growth has been slowest in the metropolitan period except for the almost indigestible baby boom, and is slowing even yet. How opportunity will continue to be manifest, and what the demographic causes and effects will be, remain for the next chapter.

The discovery of opportunity—not migration possibilities or abundance—was essential to the passage from frontier-rural dominance to metropolitan dominance. In the Great Conjuncture, that discovery was made gropingly and incompletely before the depression of the 1890s almost ruined everything. But new opportunities appeared increasingly after 1900, when nonfarm jobs, rising real incomes, and consumer goods began to ensure promising futures for large masses of people. In effect, masses of urban dwellers were invited into the middle class, as masses had earlier been invited into the rural middle class. That urban middle class would be a broad, inclusive one, not just the numerically small managers, professionals, and proprietors who made up the directing and middle classes in industrial France,[72] or the slightly larger middle classes of Britain, "that comfortable army of artisans, clerks, shopkeepers, merchants, bankers, and industrialists."[73] Besides such people, the American middle class would include those who wore white collars, and also the farmers who had survived the end of the frontier-rural mode and had adapted to settled-rural and increasingly metropolitan conditions as established landowners and farm operators. Together these groups formed a majority of Americans with a new middle-class consensus. They made it work, though not always without repressive methods. Some were leaders and some were followers; the "new middle class" that historians have often referred to, the new managers and professionals and academics, were not enough. They were only the leadership. Followership had to come from those in the rapidly expanding white-collar occupations, from clerks to executives. The shift from frontier-rural to metropolitan can easily be reduced to a movement of working-class people from farm to city. But that is too simple.

More accurately described, it was a shift in the target of opportunity, a shift from land-hunger to home-ownership-hunger,
money-hunger, or durable-goods-hunger in metropolitan settings. The object of the game did not change, only the shape of
the ball and some of the rules. Most important, almost everybody could play, as in frontier-rural days.

Alexis de Tocqueville remarked in the 1830s on the equality of condition that he found in America, the scarcity of very
poor and very rich, and the presence instead of

> an innumerable multitude of men almost alike who, without
> being exactly either rich or poor, are possessed of sufficient
> property to desire the maintenance of order . . . . They desire,
> with unexampled ardour, to get rich, but the difficulty is to
> know from whom riches can be taken. The same state of society
> which constantly prompts these desires, restrains these desires
> within necessary limits: it gives men more liberty of changing
> and less interest in change.

These were the people he called "people of scanty fortunes,"
and because they wished to keep and if possible increase what
they had, "They love change, but they dread revolutions."[74]
The job of Americans in the early twentieth century was to
take the opportunities of the frontier-rural mode, and the good
chances of their fulfillment, and reimplant them in the metropolitan mode.

The Great Conjuncture of 1870–1920 carried with it many
demographic changes, notably immigration, the start of black
exodus from the South, declines in fertility and mortality with
a rise in the average age of the population, and longer life-
spans. Childhood and adolescence were more clearly limned as
life stages; youth stayed in schools longer, exposed to acceptable values.[75] The nuclear structure of the frontier-rural family
remained. Except that families were started later and birth
rates and fertility rates decreased (in part because of less infant
mortality), the general shape of the family was preserved
rather than altered in the Conjuncture. The young left home

seeking opportunity. That was not new, but the target of opportunity was. As the family was preserved, so was the middle class and "middle-class" ideas, reshaped to fit new social-demographic patterns. The term *embourgeoisement* might be applied to this reshaping; it is handy and suggestive, but if we use it we must do so in the literal sense of movement to towns rather than in the abstract sense of movement from working class to middle class. So many were already middle-class in background, although rural. In that literal sense, however, applied to European rural migrants as well as native-born ones, and rurally-conceived ideas and values, *embourgeoisement* captures much of what happened during the Conjuncture. The "not yet" of Marx and Engels, the expected ripening of the class struggle in America, was postponed indefinitely by the redefining of middle-class opportunity within the metropolitan mode.

The social and demographic characteristics of the reshaped middle class were fairly clear by 1920. We can summarize the main ones as they crystallized in the last ten or fifteen years of the Conjuncture: A large body of people had recently enjoyed a sharp rise in real income and in job opportunities, the economic benefits of World War I. As in other wars since 1860, workers benefited from wartime demand. The ideological fabric contained many frontier-rural threads, but they had become interwoven with a yearning for conscious social controls. Rural black people, men and women, individuals and families, were leaving the South for northern and midwestern cities, changing both areas irreversibly. The prewar crowd of immigrants from Italy, the Balkans, and eastern Europe, stopped by the war, resumed for a few years until powerful pressures for slamming the door on further mass entry could not be stopped.

Despite these infusions from other cultures, the core of American culture was the white, Anglo-Protestant, middle class. For them, and for others anxious and willing to join them, America was close to being what they thought it was: a place where individual liberties and property rights were protected, where government was of laws and not of men. For them, upward mobility beckoned as strongly as it had to earlier generations. The astonishing thing is that opportunity was still there. The urbanized middle class was an accessible class, like the old rural one. If you were nimble you could join it.[76]

Fortunately for social stability, joining the middle class depended not on displacing people already in it but on filling millions of newly created white-collar jobs. Upward mobility for some did not demand downward mobility for others, because the middle class was an expanding universe, not a zero-sum equation. Once more Americans could ignore Malthus—although not with the utter abandon of 1800 or 1820—because the boundaries of opportunity were still flexible. Just when entry into the middle class by the frontier-rural route was closed off from lack of new land, entry opened by the different route of white-collar, urban-located jobs. An increasing number were filled by women, and here a few differences from the older pattern emerged: it was not so essential to be married as it had been for farm formation. Indeed, marriage was sometimes a hindrance. Children were fewer and came later in life. Changes in the labor market, rising participation of women in it, the steady rise in national wealth and income, its fairly wide distribution, and the conformity demanded and taught by the schools and other transmitters of values, aided the rural-to-urban reshaping of the middle class. "A successful ruling class," according to Antonio Gramsci,

> is one that before actually obtaining political power has already established its intellectual and moral leadership. To do this it must have as its core a homogeneous social group that is also capable of attracting support from other groups.

The "hegemony" (his term) of that homogeneous social group, Gramsci wrote, came from the success of that group "in persuading the other classes of society to accept its own moral, political, and cultural values. . . . without force exceeding consensus too much."[77] Something of the sort may have happened in early twentieth-century America, except that the social group with hegemony was a very large one. It excluded most but not all of the blacks, many but not all of the immigrants and their children, and some but not all women. Admission of those groups was going to be gradual. But most others belonged, preserving their dominance more by consensus than by force.

To be sure, examples existed of consensus arrived at by force, either legal or extralegal. Labor-capital conflicts suppurated throughout the Conjuncture, including the bloody year of 1919. Job competition then, among returning veterans, recently migrated blacks, and immigrants, fueled riots which were inextricably racial and economic. Proletarian consciousness provoked hundreds of thousands of votes for Eugene V. Debs and other Socialists, and fired the many thousands who followed the Industrial Workers of the World in 1912–16. The "first Red Scare" in 1920 drove "subversives" underground, but hardly converted them. Legislation more often than force bolstered the hegemony of the middle class, however. Laws prohibited child labor, limited women's hours in factories, and relieved pressure for wholesale socialism by checking the most outrageous (and publicized) forms of exploitation. Tax reforms suggested some redistribution of wealth, and antitrust laws suggested a check on its concentration. Narcotics and alcohol were controlled by new laws. Public education would gradually make native and immigrant children dependably middle-class. The quicker fix, regarding immigrants, was restriction based on literacy tests, and then simply quotas by nationality, to keep out the "low-standard alien invaders" who, despite toiling "willingly and patiently at the hardest tasks set for them in our mines and factories," would inevitably exhaust resources and destroy "the citadel of American prosperity."[78] Professional administrators and bureaucrats were to run governments. The franchise itself was revised to exclude blacks in the South and recent immigrants in the North, and to include white middle-class women.[79] By the end of World War I, a war which Woodrow Wilson correctly predicted would do great things for intolerance, an agenda for hegemony by legislation had been written into the Constitution and the statute books. As Burton Bledstein recently wrote, "The middle class opposed institutions it could not control and favored those it could."[80]

The Great Conjuncture was complete. Demographic indexes had changed in fifty years in favor of less frequent births and deaths and an older population, changes resulting from declining land availability, more city dwelling, immigration, and other reasons both biological and social. But the search for opportunity, and the prevalence of a middle class by then more urban than rural, had survived the collision of the frontier-rural and metropolitan modes. By 1920 the frontier-rural mode had vanished, and a third phase of American population history was beginning.

V

The Metropolitan Period,
1920 — 2020

Early Years: The 1920s to World War II

The Conjuncture ended in 1915 or 1920, the date depending on whether one stresses the statistics of agricultural
stabilization, which favor the former, or the census revelations
of 1920 of another sharp decline in aggregate population
growth in the 1910–20 decade compared to the preceding
several decades. The metropolitan mode continued, unchal-
lenged at last. The visible signs of contemporary, twentieth-
century American society, signs not yet all there in the 1890s,
had finally fallen into place: ethnic diversity, an urban-
dwelling majority,[1] large corporations, millions of white-collar
workers, electric appliances, spreading car ownership, service
stations and paved highways, radio and motion pictures, mass
circulation magazines and newspapers.

The metropolitan mode would change within itself in the
twentieth century, as the frontier-rural mode did in the
eighteenth and nineteenth. It would spread to more recently
settled parts of the country, hastened after the 1930s by rural
electrification, television, and computers as the spread of the
frontier-rural mode was hastened by the railroads in the

nineteenth century. Agriculture, as it mechanized and became ever more capital-intensive, would be subsumed into the metropolitan mode, especially after 1945. The move to suburbs would make the mode metropolitan, and not simply urban, in the geographical sense, and would continue even after the geographical metropolises lost some population in the 1970s. And the mode would exhibit further slowing of population growth, as people became increasingly sensitive to the Malthusian equation, except during the mid-1940s to the late 1950s when the anomalous, infamous baby boom temporarily reversed the trend of two and a half centuries.

In the 1920s the fertility rate for white women dropped by over 13 percent from the preceding decade, almost half again as much as in the previously fastest-dropping decades, the 1840s and 1880s. In 1927, for the first time, the fertility rate fell below 100. The crude birth rate for white women dropped from 27 to 19.5, and for black women it dropped from 36 to 27, between 1920 and 1930. The long-term decline in the number of children that the average woman bore in her lifetime continued, as the population became increasingly urban—though urbanization by no means accounted entirely for the fertility decline. The fertility of farm families also fell over the long term, and in the 1930s, when fertility plummeted, the urban proportion of the population hardly changed at all. Live births fell from an average of about 2.9 million per year in the early 1920s to 2.7 million in the late 1920s, and to 2.3 to 2.4 million in the 1930s. On the other hand, infant mortality was cut in half between the two World Wars, and life expectancy from birth, between 1920 and 1945, increased by a full ten years for whites and black males, and by fifteen years for black women.[2]

Life was definitely lengthening. Early twentieth-century improvements in sanitation, refrigeration, and water purification were reducing deaths not only of infants and children, but of people in all age groups, especially from infectious diseases. The germ theory of disease was finally accepted, and scientific studies of diet and nutrition were wiping out deficiency diseases such as pellagra.[3] The crude death rate continued to slide downward. In the early 1920s it was already at 11 for whites, only half the level of 1880, and it fell slightly further during the 1930s and early 1940s. The greater improvement in the post-1920 period was among blacks, whose overall death rate, 17.7 in 1920, fell to 11.9 in 1945. As for specific causes, fewer deaths were assigned to tuberculosis, intestinal infections, and children's diseases such as diphtheria and whooping cough. On the other hand, the metropolitan period brought more deaths from cancer, heart disease, diabetes, flu, car accidents, and suicide.[4]

Internal and international migration continued, though differently from before. Net numbers of southern blacks migrating to northern cities were almost half a million in 1910–20, 750,000 in 1920–30, and over 400,000 even in the depressed 1930s.[5] That migration overlapped but briefly with the older one of Europeans coming to the United States. The end of World War I and the reopening of shipping lines allowed many Europeans, east European Jews, Poles, Italians, and others in smaller numbers, to make the move that the war had in many cases postponed. The migration was large for a few years—1.3 million from 1921 to 1925—but it included many more women, children, and people over forty than before the war. The golden door was about to close, and many made their choice as to settling *as families* east or west of the Atlantic. From an average of 267,000 per year in the early 1920s, net immigration plunged to 71,000 in the late 1920s as the restriction laws took hold. The legal cutoff in 1929, together with the onset of depression, was followed by actual net out-migration during the 1930s and the early 1940s.[6] Eighty years of mass immigration from Europe ended in the 1920s, as Japanese and Chinese immigration had done twenty or forty years before. Only from Hispanic America were new arrivals to come in numbers at all comparable to certain European groups.

Patterns of family life and formation were more continuous than changing in the 1920s and 1930s. Household size slipped a little, and numbers of divorces increased somewhat (though not the rate, which stood at 1.4 to 1.7 per thousand population per year from 1920 into the 1940s). Women went to work outside the home more often than before, continuing a relatively slow trend since the 1870s. The rise was cumulative, however, so about a fifth of the labor force was female in 1920 but almost a quarter in 1940. Despite that, the median age of first marriage remained quite stable, at twenty-four or slightly older for men, twenty-one or slightly older for women, through the 1920s and 1930s.[7] After 1940, family and marriage patterns would change abruptly. But in the first two decades of the metropolitan period, they continued the trendlines of the Conjuncture.[8]

The resultant of the forces of fertility, mortality, migration, and family size produced aggregate growth of 14.9 percent during the 1910s, 16.1 percent in the 1920s, and but 7.2 percent in the 1930s. All of these rates fell substantially below those of the Conjuncture period, and the only brief time when the growth rate came within five percentage points of even the late Conjuncture was the early 1920s when mass immigration made its final curtain call. The American population was taking on its characteristic twentieth-century shape, which has been urban and middle-class. This middle class continued to include a wide range of occupations, co-opting the so-called lower white-collar people—clerks, salespersons, typists, secretaries, junior accountants, switchboard operators—who were so often young men or young women from rural backgrounds. The middle class, the latter-day people of scanty fortunes, began to include men and women of foreign birth or, more often, of foreign stock. As yet few blacks were included—which was a great blunder from the standpoint of middle-class self-interest—and would not be until the 1960s and 1970s. This reconstituted, now heavily urban, middle class of the 1920s was better educated than the middle class of 1870. Its members were by no means learned or oriented toward liberal knowledge or the arts, but they could cope with the demands of the job market, and had been schooled to look at the world through the same prism of social values. They were eager for respectability, for gain, for enough equality of opportunity to bring within reach a home, a Model T or a Chevrolet, a radio, electric lights, and an electric appliance or two. These things became the common lot of city dwellers during the 1920s.[9] Young middle-class couples enjoyed enough material resources to have children, fewer than their parents or grandparents had had, but children with increasingly good chances of living to adulthood.

New members of the middle class adopted middle-class values too. They complained about government interference, and, like their ancestors who lived on farms and in villages, they wanted to be left alone to do as they pleased. They did not forget their rural origins but brought country ideas to the cities and to business. They adjusted one way or another. The middle-class consensus of the post-1915 metropolitan period thus took peculiarly American forms. The middle class was reconstituted to fit urban and industrial conditions, and remained relatively stable as long as some visible opportunities existed. The only long-lived threat was the Great Depression of 1929–41, and at that time Franklin Roosevelt and his New Dealers talked the people out of radical solutions and into believing that opportunity was only out to lunch. Even in those dark days, despite rises in Socialist and Communist voting and admiration among some people for the Soviet experiment, the mass of people were not ready to throw out the capitalist bourgeois order if it could be made to creak along until better days arrived. Marx and Engels would have been disappointed again.

The transition from frontier-rural to metropolitan was neither simple nor quick. As people became more and more absorbed in the metropolitan mode, they retained attitudes formed in the earlier period. On the plus side, optimism, problem-solving ability, and willingness to change; on the minus side, refusal to recognize scarcity and limits to resources, and a proclivity for quick if jerry-built results. Repression of outgroups and outcasts continued, but moderated over time: manifest in the first Red Scare around 1920, the strength of the Ku Klux Klan in the 1920s, the Scopes trial in 1925, the trial and executions of Sacco and Vanzetti in the 1920s, repression abated in the 1930s and 1940s, when the people shared the binding, leveling experiences of the Depression and World War II. The pressure toward Anglo conformity, however, continued to be very strong. Structural assimilation of immigrant groups was gradual. But by 1930, virtually every group except southern blacks actively participated in the political process, and several large ethnic groups became key parts of the New Deal coalition that kept the Democratic party in the majority nationally without let-up from that day through the 1970s. Americans became comfortable with themselves in many ways during the 1920s, and then they survived the 1930s. When World War II brought the end of the Depression in 1940 and 1941, and jobs were there to be filled once more, and when personal income started rising again, so did the birth rate. A very unexpected and troublesome demographic phenomenon was about to take place.

Baby Boom and Baby Bust

In the context of the Depression immediately preceding it, the Second World War brought abrupt changes in social and demographic behavior. The sudden upturn in demand for labor just when millions of young men were being pulled into the military attracted 2.5 million women into the civilian labor force for the first time, some to heavy industry (the "Rosie the Riveters"), some to office work.[10] Yet the marriage rate among women, at a depression low of 56.0 in 1932 and still only 69.9 in 1938, rose to a wartime high of 93.0 in 1943, and to 118.1 in 1946. The divorce rate also peaked in 1946 at 4.3 but it was nevertheless true that many marriages were lasting, were being contracted at younger ages than before, and were leading to more children. The social and economic behavior of women, entering the job market or entering marriage or both, changed in the early 1940s, with startling historical consequences.[11] Changes evident before the end of World War II continued into the 1950s. The most significant include a lower average age of marriage, a rise in the proportion of women marrying, a rise in the number of women with children, and some increase in families with three or four children. Marrying became the thing to do, job or not, and rising real income of young husbands and wives almost certainly encouraged them to start families young (though it is almost certainly not the only reason).[12] The result was the baby boom, the great and so far only exception to the historic decline in rates of births and population growth in American history.

The baby boom may be dated from 1942, when the fertility rate jumped from 83.4 to 91.5, to 1957, when it peaked at 122.9 and then started to fall. Or it may be extended to 1964, the last year in which the fertility rate was over 100. Numbers of births hit about three million in 1942 and topped four million from 1955 through 1964, and fell thereafter.[13] Since the historic significance of the boom is its reversal of the long-term decline in fertility, it is best dated from the early 1940s to the late 1950s. Having dated it, can we explain it? A number of scholars have tried, but by 1980 they admitted only partial success. We know that it was not confined to the United States: rises in fertility also happened in a few other highly industrial countries, specifically Australia and New Zealand, Britain,

West Germany, and a few of the smaller European countries. Some European countries such as France and Czechoslovakia enjoyed rises in fertility very soon after World War II, as if births were "catching up" on wartime interruptions, but in those countries the rate peaked in the early 1950s and then fell again. In the United States and Canada the peak rates came in the late 1950s, in Australia and New Zealand in 1961, and in Britain and Germany in 1964. By the early 1970s, the fertility rates of most of the baby-boom countries had sunk nearly to the levels of the 1930s, and in Germany, below that level.[14] No comprehensive explanation exists at this point.

Demographers have isolated the strictly arithmetical "causes" of the baby boom, though historians have yet to identify the social causes of those "causes." The boom was not the result of vastly enlarged families, of a fairly constant number of families having, on average, two or three more children and thus reverting to the family size of the early nineteenth century. On the contrary, the numbers of children per family rose only slightly, from roughly two to roughly three. But the numbers of families rose much faster. Most important, women married earlier. Over half of the rise in fertility is assignable to the fact that more women under twenty-five were having children than in the past (or the future).[15] These women also completed their childbearing at a younger age than in the past; there was no reversion to the frontier-rural pattern of continued fertility until a woman was in her forties, and hence, fairly often, had very large numbers of children though they were decimated by infant mortality. The ending of a woman's childbearing in her early or mid-thirties represents a personal decision, reinforced by the availability by the close of the 1950s of steroid pills and other effective contraceptives. Resistance among young Catholics in the 1950s to contraception may have contributed to the boom, since their birth rate was higher than that of the general population; but others were also having children faster than the national average.[16] On the other hand, it is certain that the baby boom hit every group in American society—economic, ethnic, racial, educated or not—with only one or two major exceptions. Whatever the fertility rate of a group before the early 1940s, it rose from then until the late 1950s, and then went down.[17]

But already we are speaking of social, not demographic, causes. Why did women marry earlier? Why did they have children earlier? Why did they do so regardless of income, education, residence, race, or other grouping? The answers are not yet clear. But it is clear that "the baby boom was essentially voluntary and . . . its explanations are necessarily social."[18] Or economic. One prominent economic historian has suggested that the expectation of an income level equal to or better than that of their parents' homes, the level in which they were brought up and which they came to regard as normal, encouraged young people to marry early and have children early. The relative cost of children or ability to pay for them was not the most important economic consideration; the economic level of the young couple during their own formative years was. This idea is attractive, but hard to test. It is possible but not certain.[19] Another possibility is that fertility was forced down in the 1930s by adverse economics, and as soon as employment and income rose in World War II it began to "catch up." The trouble with that explanation is that any catching up should have been accomplished long before the late 1950s; it does not explain why the boom lasted so long. Also, prosperity does not always bring high fertility. Fertility dropped in the late 1920s and in the late 1960s and the 1970s, which were all relatively prosperous times. Contraceptive technology was a contributing factor to the end of the boom, but not its cause; steroids and other devices only became widely available and legal after the fertility rate started dropping. Contraception, and legalized abortion after 1973, facilitated decisions not to give birth made on other grounds, very likely grounds of social and moral values.[20]

However unclear the boom's causes, its effects are evident. As one pair of demographers put it, "the postwar fertility swings represent unprecedented and sweeping social change. The societal consequences of these fluctuations in period fertility rates are enormous and affect virtually every major social institution."[21] Schools, the job market, consumer patterns, future demographic behavior, have all been and will continue to be affected until the boom babies' abnormally large cohort disappears from the population by the 2020s and 2030s. The boom caused a drop in the median age in the 1950s and 1960s, a rise in household and family size, and in numbers of children. But these all fell after the late 1950s, bringing return to historic patterns of slower aggregate growth.[22]

The boom babies, whether products of postwar American exuberance or consumer choice or family-oriented values, are very much alive and present, and are now lurching into early adulthood (see figure 3). The boom was part of the self-comfort and self-satisfaction that marked the American mood in the 1940s and 1950s and into the early 1960s. Americans felt they could still ignore Malthus; opportunities were there. They saw few limits to their ideological, economic, political, or biological capabilities. They could export democracy, double the GNP every ten or twelve years, and resume the birth rates of the 1910s and 1920s on a much larger population base. The harsh realities of the Depression made no comeback after 1945 despite the fears of many economists. With sporadic exceptions, employment and personal income remained comparatively high. Seldom were middle-class expectations easier to achieve. Into the middle class crowded the children and grandchildren of immigrants, their drive to higher status lubricated by high school, college, and professional educations. Even the long-submerged blacks began to join. The gap in income and other important matters between whites and blacks remained large even after twenty-five years of integration, but absolute levels of income and education among blacks rose in real terms. After bitter struggles, but in the historic view very quickly, the Jim Crow system fell apart in the South, where race relations changed radically from the late 1950s to the 1970s. Changes were easy after it became clear that desegregation meant no profound threat to social order. The benefits of these changes to the South have been great, not least the fact that the out-migration of blacks to northern cities slowed, stopped, and then to a small extent reversed in the late 1960s and early 1970s.

The economy may never have been healthier than it was in the early 1960s, when the longest uninterrupted growth period in American economic history took place, yet with inflation at only 1 or 2 percent a year. The birth rate had already peaked, but numbers of births remained high. It was a time of headlong expansion: new colleges and universities, ever more students to fill them, new interstate highways, two and three-tone cars to run on them, the first color televisions, a secure leadership in world affairs, and reduction in Cold War tensions after the 1962 Cuban missile crisis and the 1963 treaty to end atmospheric nuclear testing. Resources and possibilities never seemed more limitless. Between 1950 and 1960 the birth rate touched 25, the death rate slipped below 9, and the population increased by 28 million, the largest increase in any decade. The per-decade growth rate of 19 percent was the highest since the days of mass immigration and improving medical care in 1900–10.

Such was the first half-century of the metropolitan period, from the arrival at a recognizably contemporary society by 1915 or 1920, through an unscheduled halt to expansion during the 1930s, through the gaudy years of wartime and postwar society and the baby boom, ending in the mid-1960s.

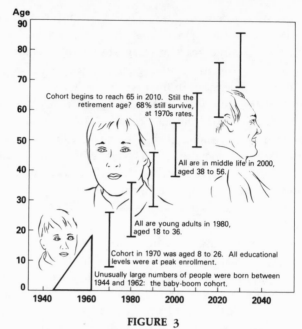

Age

Cohort begins to reach 65 in 2010. Still the
retirement age? 68% still survive,
at 1970s rates.

All are in middle life in 2000,
aged 38 to 56.

All are young adults in 1980,
aged 18 to 36.

Cohort in 1970 was aged 8 to 26. All educational
levels were at peak enrollment.

Unusually large numbers of people were born between
1944 and 1962: the baby-boom cohort.

1940   1960   1980   2000   2020   2040

FIGURE 3

The life cycle of the boom babies

In those postwar years agriculture became definitively agribus-
iness, corporate and capital-intensive. The United States did
not have farms, according to the German novelist Hans Egon
Holthusen after a stay in Indiana in the late 1960s, but "agricultural installations."[23] Turner wrote in 1925 that

> We shall need food producing sections and certain great regions
> will be more suitable for agriculture than for manufactures.
> Whether the relationship will be that of a partnership between
> industrial and agricultural life or whether industrial society will
> give the dominant tone to America, only the future can tell.[24]

The future, as it unfolded by the 1960s, told that agriculture
would become an industry. Except for a slight upturn at the
end of World War II, farm population declined steadily from
about 25 million in 1946 to under 10 million in 1970 and 6.5

million by 1980, as people continued to migrate away (see table 4).[25] Immense increases in productivity allowed one farm worker, who fed 10.7 people in 1940, to feed 22.8 in 1957 and 45.3 in 1969 and yet more by 1980: a silent revolution, in the words of historian John Shover. By 1980 only 2.3 million farms fed most Americans and many millions of others.[26] Mass consumption became general, and a country that first included an urban majority in 1919 had a suburban majority by 1969. The infrastructure of the metropolitan mode changed in important ways after 1915, but it remained the pervasive mode nonetheless.

For many reasons the mood and the reality of American life changed for the worse in the mid-1960s, as what may become the second fifty years of the metropolitan period began. On a lovely July day in 1964, fires and rioting began to rage in New York's Harlem. They marked a new era, continued by four more summers of urban violence, from Harlem out to the Watts neighborhood of Los Angeles and back again, with stops in between, an era of disturbances which also shut down universities, saw political leaders murdered, and brought rising inflation. Other events, listed at the outset of this book, created a mood in the late 1960s and through the 1970s far different from that of the twenty years following the end of World War II. These problems are well known and have made Americans untypically doleful.

Another source of the sour national mood, less obvious, is demographic. The life course of the boom babies has not helped. Age-related antisocial behavior has been prominent. "Juvenile deliquency" and "crime in the streets" occurred more often if for no other reason than that more people were alive of the ages when people usually do those things. Presumably, prosocial behavior has also increased but has received little applause. The supply-and-demand pressures, however, stemming from the swollen size of the baby-boom cohort, have reduced its chances for success. The rise in di-

vorce and suicide, unemployment and inflation, and nonpar-
ticipation in politics despite the eighteen-year-old voting age
being ratified in 1971, are accompaniments of the arrival of the
cohort into the teens and twenties.[27] In the 1980s the cohort
will arrive at young adulthood, the usual time for family formation, home ownership, and increasingly steep climbs
toward success. Many will be disappointed. The good news
will be for society, not for them, as a much smaller teens-and-
twenties cohort takes their place. At the close of the 1970s, the
parents of the boom babies were paying (literally) for their
sins as they met the costs of putting one or two or more children through college at the same time, the problem for the
middle-aged known as "college age sib[ling] squeeze."[28] The
boom babies themselves, then in their twenties or a little
older, were jostling each other for jobs, finding no places or
else places beneath their expectations and training. At that
very time, moreover, when employable young adults were in
unprecedented oversupply, the employment market was
further saturated by the entry into it of millions of women
who, had they done as their mothers did in the baby-boom
years, would have opted for early marriage and family. Instead, by the close of the 1970s, just under 50 percent of the
women in the United States were working, compared to 38
percent in 1960. Half of the wives were working outside the
home. The young man who had the bad judgment to be born
between the early 1940s and early 1960s was doubly unfortu-
nate demographically: he competed with many more males his
own age, and also with the even more numerous females.

By 1979, the birth rate stood at 15.4, the death rate at 8.6,
and thus natural increase at 6.8, lower than during the Depression of the 1930s. The marriage rate stood at 10.4—low
considering the great numbers of people of normally marrying
age—but the divorce rate was 5.2, the highest ever.[29] Between
1970 and 1978 the proportion of women between twenty-five
and thirty-four who had never married rose 111 percent, and

the proportion divorced rose 170 percent. Completed fertility, at 3.8 children per woman under forty-four in 1957, fell to 1.8 in 1978, guaranteeing a decline in total population in about thirty years if that rate continued.[30]

The Specious Present and the Near Future: From Pyramid to Cylinder

It remains now to note recent changes in the age structure of the American population. These changes appear to be permanent, similar to those in some other advanced industrial countries, and very consequential over the next thirty to fifty years.[31] If we visualize a geometric structure with a broad base, narrowing as it ascends to a point at the top, we will see how people have been distributed according to age in most societies throughout world history, including the United States from the late seventeenth century until the 1950s. If we divide the population into five-year cohorts, beginning with infants younger than five years at the base, then children five to nine, and so forth, until we reach the oldest five-year cohort at the top, after which everyone has ascended into heaven, we will have depicted the American age structure as it was through the frontier-rural period, the Conjuncture, and the first forty years of the metropolitan period (see figure 4). The pyramid rose more steeply than usual during the years of massive foreign immigration, since immigrants before 1915 were disproportionately adults. But that elongation ceased in the 1920s, first because wives, children, and parents were a large part of the immigration of 1919–24, and then because immigration was cut off by law. Conversely, the base of the pyramid widened as infant and child mortality diminished. Population growth continued to decelerate.[32] Farther-reaching changes affected the pyramid after 1940.

By 1970 its sides were bulging in strange places. At the top, the over-sixty-five cohorts had swelled to over 20 million

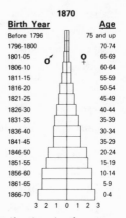

1870

Birth Year		Age
Before 1796		75 and up
1796-1800		70-74
1801-05	♂ ♀	65-69
1806-10		60-64
1811-15		55-59
1816-20		50-54
1821-25		45-49
1826-30		40-44
1831-35		35-39
1836-40		30-34
1841-45		35-29
1846-50		20-24
1851-55		15-19
1856-60		10-14
1861-65		5-9
1866-70		0-4

3 2 1 0 1 2 3

The 1870 distribution is close to a classic pyramid and is typical of the frontier-rural period.

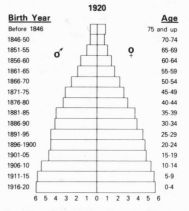

1920

Birth Year		Age
Before 1846		75 and up
1846-50		70-74
1851-55	♂ ♀	65-69
1856-60		60-64
1861-65		55-59
1866-70		50-54
1871-75		45-49
1876-80		40-44
1881-85		35-39
1886-90		30-34
1891-95		25-29
1896-1900		20-24
1901-05		15-19
1906-10		10-14
1911-15		5-9
1916-20		0-4

6 5 4 3 2 1 0 1 2 3 4 5 6

In 1920 the distribution is "normal" except for an excess of males who were 25–29 in 1920, the result of rapid prewar migration. Immigration is also responsible for the excess of men over women in ages 30 to 65. World War I made almost no impact, nor did the influenza epidemic of 1918–19, which was spread among several cohorts.

FIGURE 4

Pyramids: U.S. age structure in 1870, 1920, 1950

Figure 4 continued

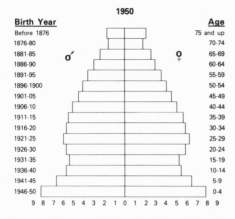

The "normal" pyramid is evident in cohorts born up
to 1920–25, but then abnormalities creep in: 1) a
smaller cohort in the late 1920s than in the early
1920s, perhaps because of "consumer" choices; 2)
many fewer births during the depression years of
the 1930s, especially the first half; 3) the start of the
baby boom, evident in the very large 1946–50
cohort.

people, or about 10 percent of the whole, while in 1920 they
had numbered 5 million and were less than 5 percent of the
whole. The pyramid thus flattened at the top, as the over-
sixty-fives took their time about ascending into heaven. Near
the bottom, the baby boom made another difference. Aged
about ten to twenty-five in 1970, that group bloated the
pyramid almost out of recognition at a point ten years above
the base. The 1980 census will show the same bulge, but ten
years farther up from the base, aged twenty to thirty-five. It
will eke its way upward until it disappears out the top sometime in the second quarter of the twenty-first century. It is a
very large group, but probably uniquely so. Contrary to some
expectations, no echo of the baby boom has yet appeared, no

new outsized cohort resulting from the great numbers of
female boom babies reaching childbearing age in the 1970s
and 1980s. On the contrary, their reluctance to create echoes
seems persistent.[33]

Given these two changes in the traditional pyramid, and
given the smaller-than-normal cohorts born in the 1930s and
since the late 1960s, the pyramid itself is becoming obsolete.
By 1970 the American age structure began to resemble not so
much a pyramid as a cylinder (see figure 5). That shape will
become increasingly obvious in the censuses of 1990 and
2000. Instead of a pyramid, the age structure will have nearly
vertical sides, and a flattish top not much narrower than the
base. Already the cylinder better describes the age structure of
Sweden, West Germany, and a few other European countries
with very low birth rates and sometimes negative rates of
natural increase.[34] The British population up to age seventy
was almost cylindrical in 1976. The French birth rate was so
low in the late 1970s that if it continued until 2030, the population would drop from the existing 53 million to 14 million.
The West German Statistical Office noted that German population was already shrinking and would fall from 57 million in
1977 to 52 million by 2000.[35] These trends are unprecedented,
"as stunning demographically as nuclear weaponry is militar-
ily."[36] In each of these countries, and in the United States and
Canada where the same phenomena are now taking shape, the
main worry is the "dependency ratio"—the ratio of the growing dependent elderly to the stable or shrinking productive
adults who maintain them through social security and its
equivalents. Other worries will no doubt occur to demographers and policy makers in the decades ahead. (Recall that
the simple question of food supply worried Malthus.)

Americans will soon share these concerns. Their per capita
incomes are not as high now as those in several other
countries—not, however, because of declining wealth but
rather because of an excess at the moment of youthful per-

FIGURE 5

Cylinders: U.S. age structure in 1976 and 2000

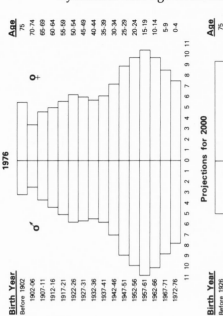

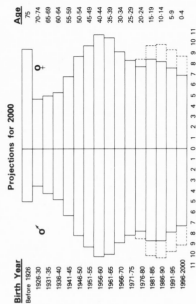

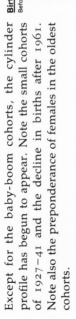

Except for the baby-boom cohorts, the cylinder profile has begun to appear. Note the small cohorts of 1927–41 and the decline in births after 1961. Note also the preponderance of females in the oldest cohorts.

The Census Bureau's projections, made in 1977, of the age structure in 2000. Solid lines represent a reasonable low-side projection (called series III), while the dotted lines represent a middling projection (series II). In either case the pyramid has given way to the cylinder. The depression cohort of the 1930's has climbed nearly to the top, and the boom babies have reached middle age. Among the over-seventy-fives, women outnumber men almost two to one.

Source: U.S. Census Bureau, *Current Population Reports* (series P-25, no. 704, July 1977: "Projections of the Population of the United States, 1977 to 2050"), pp. 28, 60, 71.

capitas. In any case, the cylinder is already a reality in the United States, though its shape is not yet perfect. The graying of America is already well under way. Median age rose from 27.9 years in 1970 to almost 30 by 1979. Before 1990 it will pass 30, making the median age just twice that of 1790. While the entire population has multiplied nine times since 1850, the number over age sixty-five has multiplied by forty.[37]

The shift from pyramids to cylinders may be as symptomatic of very broad social changes as declining growth rates have been since the eighteenth century. The full implications are not yet clear. Stable or declining populations in highly industrial countries are phenomena new in the history of the world. The most reasonable estimate of the late 1970s was that U.S. population may reach 253 million in 2015, and stabilize or decline after that.[38] Natural increase slowed to about 0.8 per thousand per year in the 1970s, down a third from the rate of the mid-1960s.[39] By the end of the 1970s, as a national average, women were having 1.8 children in their lifetimes, a level of completed fertility well below the 2.1 needed for eventual stability of the total population. Growth in the 1970s was only slightly faster than during the depressed 1930s, if we do not consider unregistered immigrants.[40] Estimates of future population are error-prone because no one can predict with certainty people's attitudes and behavior concerning reproduction and families. But the predictions may be correct this time.[41] The wholesale entry of women into the labor force appears to be permanent and rising; it reduces constantly the national pool of woman-years of potential childbearing. Contraception is cheap, safe, and nearly certain. Birth rates are ungovernable in the literal sense—they cannot be legislated—but court decisions on abortion have undoubtedly depressed the birth rate. About 1.37 million abortions were carried out in 1978, terminating almost 29 percent of pregnancies. Three-fourths were among unmarried women, one-third among teenagers, a sign of a sharp drop in the age at

TABLE 4

The stabilizing of American agriculture: Some major indicators

	People living on farms (millions)	Percent of the U.S. population	Number of farms (millions)	Average acreage	Value of total net farm output (in billions of 1967 dollars)	Horsepower produced by work animals (millions of HP)
1890	24.7	42.3	4.6	137	—	16.0
1900	29.9	41.9	5.7	147	13.0	18.7
1910	32.1	34.9	6.4	139	14.6	21.5
1915	32.5	32.0	6.4	143	—	—
1920	32.0	30.1	6.5	149	16.8	22.4
1925	31.2	27.0	6.4	145	—	—
1930	30.5	24.9	6.3	157	18.4	17.7
1935	32.2	25.3	6.8	155	—	—
1940	30.5	23.2	6.1	175	20.8	12.5
1945	24.4	17.5	5.9	195	—	—
1950	23.0	15.3	5.4	216	24.9	7.0
1955	19.1	11.6	4.7	258	—	—
1960	15.6	8.7	4.0	297	30.8	2.8
1965	12.4	6.4	3.4	340	—	—
1970	9.7	4.7	3.0	373	35.6	1.5
1975	8.9	4.2	2.8	387	—	—
1978	6.5	3.0	2.3	440	—	—

Source: *Historical Statistics 1975*, series K1, K2, K4, K7, K392, S4; *Statistical Abstract of the United States 1976*; *World Almanac 1980*.

which many women began sexual activity, despite the rise in age of marriage.[42] If all, or many, of these pregnancies had resulted in births, the rate would have approached that of the 1960s.

For whatever set of reasons, and despite uncertainties about predictions, the cylinder will probably depict the age structure for the next forty years or more. Median age should continue to rise, aided by low birth rates, the bubbling-up the cylinder of the great crowd of boom babies, and the expansion of over-sixty-fives. Fertility among minority women will probably converge with the rates for whites.[43] The middle-aged and elderly will not be as outnumbered by adolescents as they were in the 1960s, or by young adults as in the 1970s. Old may come to outnumber young. Now at 24 million, the over-sixty-fives will number almost 60 million in 2030, and will be not 10 percent of the whole but over 20 percent.[44] The trend to longer life apparent between 1920 and 1970 may continue. The burden of old-age pensions will obviously be greater. But it may be offset by raising the normal age of retirement, and by increased productivity among older people, especially older women. By 2010, far more than in 1980, a greater proportion of then-older women will have spent lives gainfully employed in positions demanding substantial skill. By 2010 large numbers of women over seventy will be alive, many more than men if women continue to outlive men as they have been doing, but because of a lifetime of work careers they will be better equipped to make a greater social and economic contribution than women over seventy could do in 1980, on the average.

It is even possible that age structure will come to resemble a cone rather than a cylinder, with more people at the top than at the bottom, at least until the boom babies disappear by the 2030s. It may also be that, if population stabilizes and begins to decline in 2015 or 2020, the end of the post-1915 metropolitan period in American history will be at hand, and a fourth period, whose shape I would not dare to predict, will appear.

The metropolitan period of 1920–2020 will have had certain demographic unities: for one thing, low immigration, compared to the seventy-five years (1845–1920) preceding it; a continuing decline in fertility, except for the aberration of the baby boom, after which fertility became low enough to stabilize or shrink the population. Mortality, especially infant and child, dropped swiftly in the early years of the period but has stabilized around 9 per thousand. (It was slightly below that in the 1970s, but that was because of the great numbers of young people. By 2000 or 2010, when the boom babies hit late middle age, mortality will rise because of the disproportionate number of older people. But age-specific mortality has not changed much since the early years of the metropolitan period.) Finally, the age structure has changed gradually from the traditional pyramid in the early metropolitan period to a cylinder. Within this demographic regime have come changes in the occupational structure, the position of minority groups, and values. The history of women, with regard to labor, the family, and fertility has been eventful, especially since the 1940s. If population growth ceases in about 2020, after four hundred years of demographic history, and after a hundred years of the metropolitan period, a new phase, with its own problems and possibilities (not solely the dependency ratio) should begin. It may already be starting in Germany and a few other countries. If a new phase does begin then, the *longue durée* periods become *Vorzeit,* to around 1720; I) frontier-rural period, 1720–1870; II) Conjuncture, 1870–1920; III) metropolitan period, 1920–2020; IV) period of stable population, 2020–?

As for the middle-class consensus developed so laboriously in the early twentieth century, is it still there, and will it continue through the remaining decades of the metropolitan period? Is it still the combination of property-owning and property-anticipating groups that it was during the first fifty or sixty years of the period? The answer is depressing if we allow ourselves to focus too closely on the short-term demographic and economic abnormalities resulting from the baby-boom cohort. Their difficulties in entering the labor force, buying a home, or accumulating a middle-class net worth have been referred to. These are real problems and will continue to trouble that unlucky cohort, which will have, from cradle to grave, unusual problems because of its unusual size. On the other hand, the much smaller cohorts born in the 1960s and 1970s should have a much easier time joining the middle class, as did those born in the late 1920s and the 1930s. The decline in fertility after 1958 bred fewer people and also bred a hidden stability.[45] In the nineteenth century and early in the twentieth, stability followed upon the frontier and then upon the expansion of urban-located jobs, especially white-collar ones. Instability and discontent followed lack of opportunity, and still does. Though some observers saw mobility and opportunity decreasing in the 1960s and 1970s,[46] others stressed that the combination of demographic pressure and job demands was "extraordinary," and that the economic-demographic realities should improve.[47]

In the perspective of the past three hundred years of population history, or just the metropolitan period alone, the United States does not appear to be in a uniquely dangerous crisis, although it suffers the problems stemming from the unique exception to the secular decline in growth rates. The late twentieth century ought to be an easier time than the late nineteenth century. In the 1940s and 1950s Americans ignored Malthus again, and the results are still being visited on their children. If they ignore him no more, and resume their semirational, semiconscious understanding of the relation of population to opportunity in a frontierless age, which put brakes on population growth, their future should be brightly bourgeois again.

The question remains whether opportunity still exists, and whether (as one historian of the frontier put it) Americans still "have a roughly *equal* opportunity to become *unequal*."[48] For it has not been abundance but opportunity that has been the key to the middle-class order, whether frontier-rural or metropolitan. No one has predicted, around 1980, a new host of opportunities of the magnitude of the available land in the eighteenth and nineteenth centuries or the expansion of urban-located jobs in the nineteenth and twentieth. But as long as demand for opportunity does not exceed supply, the middle-class consensus of the metropolitan period should hold. Supply exceeded demand for many of the boom babies, and that is the source of their discontent, which they expressed as teenagers, then as the college-age and Vietnam generation, and lately as young adults. Soon they will express discontent appropriate to the middle-aged, perhaps regarding underemployment, tax inflation, and medical care. The free-wheeling population growth of the eighteenth and nineteenth century frontier-rural mode owed much to the availability of land and to the widespread fact of land ownership among Tocqueville's "people of scanty fortunes." Because of them, Americans would ignore Malthus for a long time. Population growth in the early metropolitan period was much reduced, but was still considerable. It was coeval with dwindling rural opportunities, but also with rapidly rising ruban ones. Demand did not outrun supply. The supply-demand ratio got out of kilter in the late 1960s and the 1970s, when the boom babies reached the employment market just when more and more women regarded that same market as an attractive target of their own. The dysfunction is serious but short-term. As the age structure becomes more perfectly cylindrical, pressure will diminish.

Women as workers, in the middle if not the short run, should have a stabilizing effect not only on the fertility rate, but on the middle-class consensus. Many now seek opportunity, which makes them part of the problem, but as they find it they will become part of the solution. As the average level of skills inevitably increases, output will rise, and the lowered productivity of the 1970s, the result of a labor force temporarily under-skilled, will turn upward. The economy should become more vigorous, in turn creating more opportunities for the job-seeking cohorts. For these reasons, and out of bourgeois self-interest, women and minorities should be co-opted into middle-class economic opportunities as rapidly as possible. Downtrends in productivity and per-capita income may continue, but only briefly. As in the past, they will disappear when the middle class becomes more inclusive. Thus the sooner the population of career and job-seeking women participates fully in the labor market, on a level of equality with white males in skills, responsibilities, and compensation, the better for the stability of the entire society. The same argument holds, of course, for black, Hispanic, and other minorities.

The American past bears many continuities, and thus great relevance, to the present and future. If the United States, moreover, together with a few other advanced industrial countries, finds its population becoming stable amid high levels of personal income, its population history may be relevant to other societies where stable population size may be further off. America may yet be a case in point of a cosmopolitan theory of social change, better able to accommodate unusual histories than modernization theory has been.

Whether that happens, it seems evident that changes in population growth, the results of millions of essentially independent, individual decisions, accidents, and events, have made differences in American civilization, and that, as Braudel asked, we have been able "to see correlations, regular patterns, and general trends where at first sight there appear only incoherence, anarchy, a series of unrelated happenings."[49] Although the United States in the late twentieth century is very different from what it was in its frontier-rural mode and the early decades of the metropolitan mode, its history is continuous, not marked by a radical break in the 1960s or 1970s. If we extrapolate from the population already at hand, it will not be so marked in the next four decades either.

NOTES

Note citations of books and articles will provide the (principal) author(s), year of publication, short title if helpful, and page number(s) if any. For full citations, consult the list of works cited.

CHAPTER ONE

1. (London) *Economist,* 10 June 1978. See the graph depicting inflation from 1668 to 1977. In the United States, very high inflation took place during the Revolutionary and Civil wars and a few other times, but postwar contractions receded at least somewhat from those peaks. The 1970s–1980s inflation threatens to be more permanent.

2. *New York Times,* 8 September 1977.

3. *New York Times,* 30 September 1977. The writer was Peter H. Balbert of Wells College, Aurora, New York. The other rejoinder was from Edward L. Keenan, like Donald a professor of history at Harvard. Donald's article and Keenan's rejoinder were reprinted, together with a letter from historian Blanche Wiesen Cook, in the American Historical Association's *AHA Newsletter* for December 1977, 3–6.

4. Terms arising from the work of French historian Fernand Braudel. I will discuss them later in this chapter.

5. The reader who has gone through modernization theory and come out the other side, as some historians have done, will please bear with me. That reader, who may have attended conferences held in recent years at which historians have sifted modernization theories and found little, or who may have written for or read scholarly journals such as the *American Behavioral Scientist* for November-December 1977, is in an enlightened state, but also in a minority. Quite a few historians are presently intrigued with the possiblities of modernization theory for historical analysis, and many others are aware of it dimly if at all.

6. Lipset 1963, *First New Nation.*

7. The full title of his 1798 essay was *An Essay on the Principle of Population, as it affects The Future Improvement of Society, with remarks on the speculations of Mr. Godwin, M. Condorcet, and other writers.* Malthus published revised and extended editions in 1803 and later.

8. The markings which Beethoven gave to the movements of his Sixth Symphony, the "Pastoral," were (1) Erwachen heiterer

148   *Notes for Pages 4 –9*

Empfindungen bei den Ankunft auf dem Lande, (2) Szene am Bach,
(3) Lustiges Zusammensein der Landleute, (4) Gewitter, Sturm, (5)
Frohe, dankbare Gefühle nach den Sturm.
  9. For easy access to Gramsci, see Joll 1978, *Gramsci*. A reevalua-
tion of Tönnies's relevance for American history, as well as a strong
criticism of modernization theory as recently practiced, is Bender
1978, *Community and Social Change*, especially chapter two.
  10. It appeared in the leading periodical in American history in
1979: Cassity 1979, "Modernization and social crisis." Other recent
appearances include Kaelble et al. 1978, *Probleme der Modernisierung
in Deutschland*; T. L. Smith 1978, "Religion and ethnicity in
America"; Appleby 1978, "Modernization theory and the formation
of modern social theories"; Jensen 1978, *Illinois*.
  11. Goldscheider 1971, *Population, Modernization, and Social
Structure*; Berger, Berger, and Kellner 1973, *Homeless Mind*; Inkeles
and Smith 1974, *Becoming Modern*. The Inkeles-Smith volume is unusually suffused with confidence in progress, the belief that economic
development will transform human nature for the better (289).
  12. Eisenstadt 1973, *Tradition, Change, and Modernity*.
  13. Eisenstadt 1973, 10.
  14. Inkeles and Smith 1974, 284–85, 290.
  15. E. Weber 1976, *Peasants into Frenchmen*.
  16. Deane 1965, *First Industrial Revolution*, 2.
  17. Eisenstadt 1973, *Tradition* . . . , and 1977, "Convergence and
divergence," especially 7–8.
  18. Several scholars have raised this problem, for example Cassity 1979, 42.
  19. The classic statement of the demographic transition was by
Kingsley Davis, 1945, "The world demographic transition," 1–11
(esp. 4–5), an article not without subtlety but by 1980 startling in the
ease with which it built a world-historical theory on slender evidence, and in its ability to influence demographers since its publication. For methodological criticisms see Goldscheider 1971, 14; Drake
1974, *Historical Demography*, 18. For its application to France and to
Europe generally, see Guillaume and Poussou 1970, *Démographie historique*, 119–20, 159, 169 (a text based on the lengthier *Histoire
générale de la population mondiale* (1968) by Reinhardt, Armengaud,
and Dupâquier. For a well-documented conclusion that the transition
did not occur in French Canada, see Henripin and Péron 1972, "The
Demographic Transition in Quebec."
  20. In *American Behavioral Scientist*, 21 (November-December
1977), 289–310.
  21. Grew 1977, 289, 301, 305, 308. Other criticisms or considerations include Luraghi 1972, "Civil War and modernization," which
finds ideological conflict between political classes more useful for un-

derstanding the South; Warden 1970, "L'urbanization américaine avant 1800," which finds American modernization to have proceeded very differently from European; Seward 1978, *American Family*, chapter one and page 179, finds no evidence for the eighteenth and nineteenth centuries that family size changed from extended to nuclear, a variable usually regarded as important evidence of modernization by its theorists.

22. Bodnar 1976, "Immigration and modernization," 45, 60; Bender 1978, *Community and Social Change*, 27–43 and elsewhere.

23. Bender 1978, 35, 40, 62, 47, 51. Fischer 1977, *Growing Old*, 25, also complains of imprecise timing of modernization applications. Transition theory, insofar as it demands unilinear progress, was found to be flawed from the standpoint of symbolic logic in Loschky and Wilcox 1974. By extension, modernization theory must be similarly flawed.

24. See the section on *Vorzeit* in chapter two.

25. A sure sign of the modern man, wrote Inkeles and Smith 1974, 284–85.

26. Henretta 1973, *Evolution of American Society*, 8.

27. Quoted in Lipset 1963, *First New Nation*, 114.

28. Chevalier 1839, *Society, Manners and Politics*, 207, 284.

29. Tocqueville 1840, *Democracy in America*, 234, 168.

30. Gutman 1973, "Work, culture and society," and Rodgers 1978, *Work Ethic*, document this in various ways.

31. See the final section in chapter three.

32. See for example MacDonagh 1976, "Irish famine emigration," 360–66.

33. Hansen is quoted in Taylor 1971, *Distant Magnet*, 279. On Poles and Italians and the difference between migrants and immigrants, see Golab 1977, *Immigrant Destinations*, chapter four. For the syncretism of Slavic peasant cultures with American industrial-urban conditions to form a working-class culture, see Bodnar 1976, 44–71.

34. See D. S. Smith 1970, "American elite composition," 372, on changing "sociological catergories" in America from 1650 to 1950. For a theory of change in fundamental social structures, see Braudel 1958, "Longue durée."

35. Appleby 1978, "Modernization theory," 285.

36. The 1893 essay was reprinted in Turner 1920, *Frontier in American History.* Quotations are from 1, 11, 37, 38.

37. Williams 1966 [1961], *Contours*, 183.

38. Marx and Engels 1953, *Letters*, 45 (Marx to Joseph Weydemeyer, 5 March 1852), 157–58 (Engels to Mrs. [Florence Kelley] Wischnewetsky, 3 June 1886), 239 (Engels to Sorge, 6 January 1892). The term "safety valve" does not appear in Turner's writings that were published, but it does in some of his manuscripts at the

Huntington Library. For a discussion of the frontier as a safety valve for German emigration, and the mention of Sombart, see Moltmann 1978, "Nordamerikanische 'Frontier'."

39. Turner to Isaiah Bowman, 9 January 1931, in Turner mss. See also Billington 1971b, "Turner and the Closing of the Frontier," 46–54; Billington 1971a, *Genesis of the Frontier Thesis*, 445, quoting Turner in 1931: "The moving West having given way as the dominant force in American history, the way is open for capitalistic, socialistic, progressive, and all kinds of proposals to take its place in the new era"—in other words, anything could happen once the moorings of the frontier had been slipped.

40. Billington 1971b, "Closing," 54–55; "Alarmist Arguments" folder, Turner mss.

41. Arieli 1966, *Future-Directed Character*, 9, 20–21.

42. Turner 1920, *Frontier*, 37–38.

43. See Glacken 1967, *Rhodian Shore*, 625–32, 646–49; Aldridge 1949, "Franklin as Demographer," 25; Spengler 1935, "Malthusianism," 691.

44. Malthus 1798, *Essay*, 11–12, 13–14. Malthus continued, "This implies a strong and constantly operating check on population from the difficulty of subsistence. This difficulty must fall some where; and must necessarily be severely felt by a large portion of mankind [14] . . . No fancied equality, no agrarian regulations in their utmost extent, could remove the pressure of it [the law of population] even for a single century. And it appears, therefore, to be decisive against the possible existence of a society, all the members of which, should live in ease, happiness, and comparative leisure; and feel no anxiety about providing the means of subsistence for themselves and families. Consequently, if the premises are just, the argument is conclusive against the perfectibility of the mass of mankind" [16–17].

45. *Dictionary of National Biography*, 1893, XXXVI:3.

46. Malthus 1798, *Essay*, 17, 37–38.

47. The idea of a "preventive check" which was voluntary was implied in the 1798 edition, where Malthus reflected that in Europe population doubled very slowly if ever, much slower than it might have (1798, 62–63). But the term "moral restraint" was not explicit until the 1803 edition. Concerning it, Malthus's conclusion was that "On the whole, therefore, though our future prospects respecting the mitigation of the evils arising from the principle of population, may not be so bright as we could wish, yet they are far from being entirely disheartening, and by no means preclude that gradual and progressive improvement in human society, which, before the late wild speculations on the subject, was the object of rational expectation" [1803, 603–04].

48. Malthus 1803, *Essay*, 387–89.
49. Senior 1928 [1840s], *Pressure of Population*, 305, 330–31, 337–40. For Ireland, where the population rose to about eight million by the mid-1840s, just before the potato famine produced starvation and emigration (and whose present population is less than half that), see Connell 1950, *Population of Ireland*, early chapters; MacDonagh 1976, "Irish famine emigration." Extremely high birth rates in a population with abundant resources is understandable. It was the American experience in the eighteenth and nineteenth centuries. Extremely high birth rates among populations without resources or much hope is also understandable for quite different reasons. That was the Irish pre-famine experience. As Nassau Senior remarked, people as poor as that need not be prudent, for they had no hope of accumulating anything.

It has also been the pattern in the refugee camp of Gaza, where birth rates were extremely high and children ubiquitous in the late 1970s. The pattern was apparently set during 1948–67, when the refugees could not leave the camp, but it has persisted in the post-1967 years despite the fact that they may (and some do) acquire housing in Gaza City from the government, commute to jobs in Israel proper (at least 35,000 did in 1979), attend Cairo University (several thousand), etc.

50. Malthus 1798, 101–02, 341–42. Did Turner read Malthus?
51. Malthus 1798, 20–21. The 1803 edition has almost the same wording, page 4.
52. Malthus 1803, 4. His source was Richard Price's *Observations on Reversionary Payments* of 1771; Price cited Stiles's "Discourse on the Christian Union" of 1760.
53. McInnis 1977, "Childbearing and Land Availability."
54. R. White 1978, "Winning of the West," 329–30.
55. Malthus 1798, 342–43.
56. Taylor 1971, *Distant Magnet*, 87.
57. Bowen 1976, *Economics and Demography*, 78.
58. John Adams was unkind and not really accurate when he commented, "That the first want of man is his dinner, and the second his girl, were truths well known to every democrat and aristocrat, long before the great philosopher Malthus arose, to think he enlightened the world by the discovery." Quoted in Aldridge 1949, "Franklin as demographer," 25.
59. Ricardo 1815, "Essay on . . . price of corn," especially 11, 15, 20–21.
60. Malthus 1798, 32.
61. The name of the journal was then changed to, and remains, *Annales: Économies, Societés, Civilisations*. For a succinct analysis of the *Annales* school and its doyen for much of the postwar period,

152 *Notes for Pages 22–28*

Fernand Braudel, see the special issue of the *Journal of Modern History* for December 1972, and especially the essay by Hexter, "Fernand Braudel and the *Monde Braudellien*."

62. A fact noted by J. Potter 1976, review of R. Wells. Potter was almost a voice crying in a wilderness when in 1965 his long essay on American population history before 1860 appeared ("Growth of Population").

63. Turner mss., TU Box 15C.

64. D. S. Smith 1979, "Estimates of early American . . . demographers," 34.

65. Parke 1979, "Population changes," 7 and *passim*.

66. Quoted in Deane 1965, *First Industrial Revolution*, 34.

67. Braudel 1972 [1966], *Mediterranean*, I:403.

68. Sharlin 1977, "Historical demography," 252.

69. The clearest treatment of the *longue durée*, where history and social science meet, is Braudel 1958, 727–31, 751. The best discussion in English of Braudel's scheme is Hexter 1972. It includes a valid criticism: Why only three *durées*? Why not many more? (505–06) Braudel accepted the criticism, but it does not invalidate the structure-conjuncture-event scheme for his purposes or ours. Antonio Gramsci, by the way, made a somewhat similar distinction between what he called "organic" movements (like Braudel's *longue durée)* and "conjunctural" movements, "which appear as occasional, immediate, almost accidental," in his attempts to separate world-historical patterns such as Marx's from practical politics (Joll 1978, *Gramsci*, 113–14). But Braudel's three-level scheme is clearer yet. For critical discussions of Marxism by two leading *Annalistes*, see Braudel 1958, "*Longue durée*," 752, and Le Roy Ladurie, 1978, "Haute-Normandie."

70. These are not precise uses of Braudel's terms but a close adaptation of them to the American experience.

71. Braudel 1972, *Mediterranean*, II:737. Another leading *Annaliste*, Pierre Goubert, concluded his *Beauvais et le Beauvaisis* (1960, I:624), another of the monuments of the school, with a hymn to social history which should inspire anyone attracted to the field.

72. *Hist. Stats.* 1975, series A2, Z1–Z19. A recent study of colonial censuses, Wells 1975, *Population of the British Colonies*, is also very illuminating and helpful.

73. Which was of course not the case with respect to the history of first settlement, Puritanism, the Quakers, the beginnings of slavery, and other critical events of the first century of English colonization in North America. But by 1670 or 1700 not enough people lived there to allow stable, enduring social and demographic patterns to have formed.

74. Even the Civil War, with its rivers of blood and its death from battle and disease, affected population growth only slightly.

Fertility dropped sharply and recovered only slightly, remaining at lower levels in the 1870s than in the 1850s (Coale and Zelnick 1963, *New Estimates,* 38). Also, 600,000 dead, though a staggering number, is only 1.9 percent of 31 million. The demographic damage was much less than that done by World War I to France, Britain, Russia, Austria, or Germany.

75. Reps 1979, *Cities of the American West,* cites many examples of western town-building but they largely date from after 1850. Also, for some time after that and certainly before, the mass of people experienced rural, not urban (or even village), conditions.

76. What the Census termed Type II (6 to 18) and Type III (18 to 45) regions according to people per square mile.

77. Phase breaks in the early 1860s and at about 1915 unfortunately coincide with the Civil War and World War I (although the United States was not a belligerent until 1917). But neither of those wars had much direct impact on demographic patterns in the United States, certainly no obvious causal impact. It may even be that those wars were somehow results, not causes, of changes in *longue durée* structures.

78. Why, and what relation or impact the two have on each other, is a matter of concern and debate among historical demographers.

79. A recent paper (Easterlin, Wachter, and Wachter 1978, "Changing impact of population swings," especially 119–22) states that changes in the rate of population growth from 1870 to 1930 were due "almost entirely" and "overwhelmingly" to migration rather than to changes in birth rates, which they find were the overriding cause of changes in rates from 1940 on. The main thrust of the paper is to warn policy makers to fine-tune their responses to unemployment and inflation by paying closer attention to demographic patterns, especially shifting sizes of age cohorts—the point being that aggregate demand responds to the size of cohorts born twenty or more years ago. That point is persuasive and its intent laudable. But the historical part of the paper, the contention that rates of change responded to aggregate demand by means of in-migration up to the 1920s, is not especially necessary for proving the main point, and presents other problems. The 1870–1920 period did witness much growth from migration, but "almost entirely" is overstating it. Further difficulties: starting with 1870 emphasizes heavy immigration, while starting with 1800 or even 1840 would not have. Also, the contention does not account for secularly diminishing growth, even when immigration was heaviest, as in 1880–90 and 1905–14; nor does it leave room for drops in fertility in the 1880s and 1890s (by the authors' table, fertility dropped 2.0 percent from early to late 1870s, 1.9 percent from late 1870s to early 1880s, 2.7 percent from early to late

1880s, 2.1 percent from 1905–10 to 1910–15); nor does it consider drops in death rates. In short, so much stress is placed on immigration that changes in vital rates momentarily disappear. As one of the leading economic demographer-historians now active, Easterlin is aware of demographic complexities in this and other periods. But this 1978 paper seems to simplify the 1870–1920 period, albeit in a good cause. (For estimates of population growth separated into natural increase and immigration, concluding that immigration played a "small part" in most decades up to 1930, see Thompson and Whelpton 1933, *Population Trends*, 303.)

80. D. S. Smith 1979, "Estimates of early American historical demographers."

81. Chaunu 1973, "Nouveau champ," is a good theoretical discussion. For an American application, see Henretta 1978a, "Families and farms."

82. His papers contain many notes and calculations on the results of the 1920 census. I found no such attention, in fact none, to the 1930 census, however. Other concerns pressed upon his failing strength in the last months of his life, and he drew no conclusions about the 1930 census even on occasions when, in earlier years, he probably would have; e.g. Turner to Frederick Merk, 15 May 1931 (TU Box 45), on revising a syllabus they wrote in 1922 for the frontier course at Harvard. Also, typescript memoir by M. H. Crissey, TU Box 57, Turner mss.

83. "Notes for Shop Club Lecture," 17 November 1923, TU Box 15C.

84. Speech to meeting of Association of American Geographers at Madison, Wisconsin, 1926, in TU Box 14D. Also, notes on farm tenancy in Boxes 10A, 15C.

85. The items in the Turner papers which best document these statements are Turner to Isaiah Bowman, Pasadena, 24 December 1931 (Box 46); Bowman to Turner, New York, 5 January 1932 (Box 47); notes for three lectures, "Shop Club" 1923 (Box 15C), at U.C.L.A. April 1927 (Box 15A), and in Pasadena February 1928 (Box 14B); folder, "Sequence to end of frontier," Box L2.

CHAPTER TWO

1. Braudel 1972, *Mediterranean*, I:404.

2. Braudel 1972, I:370, II:826.

3. Though most French Caribbean colonies and outposts of New France were established in the seventeenth century, Jacques Cartier explored the St. Lawrence in 1534.

4. The number is not precisely known, but the range seems certain.

5. McNeill 1976, *Plagues and Peoples*, 115, 224. Crosby 1976, "Virgin soil epidemics," finds no support for the hypothesis that the Indians, isolated for tens of thousands of years from Europeans and Asians, were genetically non-immune. He believes the "virgin soil" argument sufficient—that these diseases simply struck a fresh population territory in which no one possessed immunity built up from endemic contact. He points out that American soldiers in the Civil War died from smallpox at about the same rate as did the Aztecs in 1520, if one corrects for vaccination and childhood exposure, which the Aztecs lacked (292–95).

6. Jacobs 1974, "Tip of an iceberg," 128. Also, McNeill 1976, 203–08. On population estimates and specific diseases see Borah 1976, "Renaissance Europe and the population of America," 47–61, the writings of Henry Dobyns and Sherburne Cook, and the essays in Denevan 1976, *Native Population*. Estimates of aboriginal population in 1500 have been as low as 5 million, but the debate by the late 1970s centered on 50 million to 100 million for the entire New World. Since both figures result from estimates based on archaeological evidence, not on censuses, uncertainty will probably continue, but in that range. Braudel thought that the highest estimates (80 million to 100 million) were "romantic inventiveness" and "fanciful," but agreed "that the European Conquest brought a colossal biological slump to America" (Braudel 1973 [1967] *Capitalism and Material Life*, 5–6). McEvedy and Jones 1978, *Atlas*, also take a cautious approach (289–91). A good recent analysis is Ubelaker 1976, "Prehistoric . . . population size." For a single tribe, the Mandans, over four centuries, see Glassner 1974.

7. Rutman and Rutman 1976, "Of agues and fevers," 40–46, find that Europeans brought malaria to Maryland, and their African slaves brought a more virulent form of it, but some other tropical and subtropical diseases were not the killers in the future United States that they were farther south.

8. Driver 1969, *Indians*, 63.

9. Ubelaker 1976, 664, table 2. The largest clusters were in the future North Atlantic states (157,000), the Gulf states (474,000), the Mississippi Valley (168,000), the Great Plains (404,000), and California (310,000). See also J. Potter 1976, review of Wells. Another recent estimate gives 4.4 million in 1500 in the future United States, Canada, Alaska, and Greenland (Denevan 1976, *Native Population*, 291). My thanks to Wilbur Jacobs for making me aware of Denevan's book. See also the discussion by Calvin Martin 1978, *Keepers of the Game*, 43–47. Martin (47–54) argues ingeniously that European disease destroyed not only Indians but their culture and religion as well. Taboos against overhunting disappeared with the loss of their beliefs in nature and spirits.

10. Driver 1969, map 6 (no page; at rear of book). Ten per square mile equals about four per square kilometer.

11. Driver 1969, 302.

12. Driver 1969, 486; *Hist. Stats.* series A148.

13. Crosby 1976 enumerates many of these, and although he warns that because of unreliable sources "skepticism is eminently justified" about numbers, he is worth quoting at length:

"Even so, the surviving records for North America do contain references—brief, vague, but plentiful—to deadly epidemics among the Indians, of which we shall cite a few of the allegedly worst. In 1616–1619 an epidemic, possibly of bubonic or pneumonic plague, swept coastal New England from Cape Cod to Maine, killing as many as nine out of every ten it touched. During the 1630s and into the next decade, smallpox, the most fatal of all the recurrent Indian killers, whipsawed back and forth through the St. Lawrence–Great Lakes region, eliminating half the people of the Huron and Iroquois confederations. In 1738 smallpox destroyed half the Cherokees, and in 1759 nearly half the Catawbas. During the American Revolution it attacked the Piegan tribe and killed half its members. It ravaged the plains tribes shortly after they were taken under United States jurisdiction by the Louisiana Purchase, killing two-thirds of the Omahas and perhaps half the population between the Missouri River and New Mexico. In the 1820s fever devastated the people of the Columbia River area, erasing perhaps four-fifths of them. In 1837 smallpox returned to the plains and destroyed about half of the aborigines there."

14. Kalm 1937 [1770, 1750], *Travels*, 258–59. He added contradictorily that "brandy is said to have killed most of the Indians."

15. Cited in Cassedy 1969, *Demography in Early America*, 90, 90n. Also R. White 1978, "Winning of the West," 342–43.

16. Guillaume and Poussou 1970, *Démographie historique*, 115, 118.

17. Braudel, 1973, *Capitalism . . .* , 53. Defoe (1722, 287) wrote, "I shall conclude the Account of this calamitous Year therefore with a coarse but sincere Stanza of my own, which I plac'd at the End of my ordinary Memorandums, the same Year they were written:

A dreadful Plague in London was,
In the year Sixty Five,
Which swept an Hundred Thousand Souls
Away; yet I alive!"

18. Notestein 1954, *English People on the Eve*, 245–46, 256.

19. The list given by Cassedy 1969, 149.

20. Morgan 1971, "Labor problem at Jamestown," 595–96, 602–03.

21. Communities certainly existed but at the cost of expelling dissenters such as Roger Williams, Anne Hutchinson, and others less celebrated.

22. Hofstadter 1971, *America at 1750*, xii. Incidentally, I call this period *Vorzeit* rather than *prehistory* not out of linguistic obscurantism but in order to avoid the connotations of the English word and its even more pejorative adjective, *prehistoric*. It was not prehistoric. It simply preceded the long-term structures.

23. Respectively 578,000, 406,000, and 267,000 in the late 1970s (*World Almanac* 1980).

24. Boorstin 1964 [1958], *The Americans: Colonial Experience*, book one, "The Vision and the Reality," 1 –143, explores the corrosive effect of American realities in the seventeenth and eighteenth centuries on the cleverly drawn plans of various Englishmen.

25. Fogel et al. 1978, "Economics of mortality," 75 –76; D. S. Smith 1979, "Estimates of . . . demographers," 30 –31.

26. Carr and Walsh 1977, "Planter's wife," 542 –45, 552 –53; Walsh and Menard 1974, "Death in the Chesapeake," 219 –22; Rutman and Rutman 1976, "Of agues and fevers," 31.

27. Menard 1975, "Maryland Slave Population," 32 –42. It seems unlikely that the sex ratio of whites was more male-skewed than among slaves; perhaps future research will clarify that.

28. Carr and Walsh 1977, 543 –44, 550 –54; Menard 1975, 42; Rutman and Rutman 1976, 49.

29. Walsh and Menard 1974, 227.

30. Menard 1975, 48, 53 –54; Carr and Walsh 1977, 565, 567.

31. Lockridge 1970, *New England Town*, 66 –67; D. S. Smith 1972, "Demographic history of colonial New England," 171 –73; Demos 1970, *Little Commonwealth*, 193; Greven 1970, *Four Generations*, 183, 195, 200 –01; Rutman and Rutman 1976, 49; Morgan 1944, *Puritan Family*, 22, 39, 44, 71.

32. Lockridge 1970, 140.

33. Feinstein 1976, *Stamford*, 1, 5.

34. Isaac 1971, review essay, 729.

35. Bidwell and Falconer 1925, *History of Agriculture . . . Northern U.S.*, 59, 65 –66; Lockridge 1970, 71, 74 –75; Greven 1970, 241; Henretta 1973, *Evolution*, 29 –30; Feinstein 1976, 98.

36. Lockridge 1968, "Land, population," 68 –69; Henretta 1973, 29 –30; Greven 1970, 227 –30.

37. Lockridge 1970, *New England Town*, 93 –94.

38. Greven 1970, 177 –78, 183, 200 –01; Lockridge 1970, 93 –94.

39. As elsewhere in this book, we can only mention changes in values, stratification, social control, *mentalités*, and other fascinating avenues as we pass them by. On the decline of occult beliefs after the

seventeenth century (and thus *Vorzeit*), see Butler 1979, "Magic, astrology, and the early American religious heritage."

40. Stiles 1799 [1760], "Discourse on the Christian Union," 63–64.

41. Lockridge 1968, "Land, population," 62; *Hist. Stats.* 1975, Z6, Z8; Feinstein 1976, 96. In the middle colonies, including Pennsylvania and New York, neither the New England community pattern nor the Chesapeake's indentured-servant and planter pattern prevailed. Proprietors granted large tracts to individuals, and the *Vorzeit* was a less distinct phase in those colonies for that reason and because those colonies were not effectively founded until late in the seventeenth century. The *Vorzeit* ended as those large land parcels were broken up into small-farmer holdings. Bidwell and Falconer 1925, 65–66.

42. Guillaume and Poussou 1970, *Dém. hist.*, 119.

43. McNeill 1976, *Plagues and Peoples*, 223–24, points out that no new disease strains appeared in Europe after 1500; previously epidemic diseases declined in virulence to become, sometimes, endemic "children's diseases"; killers like plague and malaria shrank in geographic range.

44. Franklin 1755 [1751], "Observations," 12.

45. Franklin to Peter Collinson, in L. W. Labaree 1962, *Papers of Benjamin Franklin*, V:158–59, cited in Cassedy 1969, 168. In his "Observations" (1755, 14) Franklin's racism showed when he argued against any immigration except English, and among Germans only the Saxons, since those groups are "the Principal Body of White People on the Face of the Earth" while the Spanish, French, Swedes, and Russians [!] are "swarthy."

46. Henretta 1973, 12.

47. Vinovskis 1971, "1789 Life Table," 589; Vinovskis 1972, "Mortality rates . . . in Massachusetts," 197–98.

48. McNeill 1976, 245, 251; Cassedy 1969, 133–42.

49. Cassedy 1969, 270–71.

50. J. Potter 1965, "The Growth of Population in America," 640, 643, 662.

51. Braudel writes, "There is always a correlation between the patterns of births and deaths. Under the *ancien régime* the two coefficients were both at around the same figure: 40 per 1000. What life added, death took away." (1973, *Capitalism . . .* , 37.)

52. The role of declining mortality is stressed by McKeown 1976, *Modern Rise of Population*, 34–35, 41, 43; D. S. Smith, 1972, "Demographic history of colonial New England," 171–74. Fogel et al. 1978, 75–76, notes stability in rural New England mortality for two centuries.

53. D. S. Smith and Hindus 1975, "Premarital pregnancy," 538,

559, attempt to relate long-term cycles in premarital pregnancy to social continuity and change.

54. Cassedy 1969, 148.

55. Franklin 1755, 4. He also suggested the reason: "Land being thus plenty in America, and so cheap as that a labouring Man, that understands Husbandry, can in a short Time save Money enough to purchase a Piece of new Land sufficient for a Plantation, whereon he may subsist a Family; such are not afraid to marry; for if they even look far enough forward to consider how their Children when grown up are to be provided for, they see that more Land is to be had at Rates equally easy, all Circumstances considered" (3).

56. Stiles 1799 [1760], 138.

57. Cassedy 1969, 186.

58. Quoted in Cassedy 1969, 187.

59. Cassedy 1969, 198–99; Henretta 1973, 166.

60. Jefferson 1782, *Notes on . . . Virginia*, 153.

61. Belknap 1792, *New Hampshire*, III:235.

62. Kalm 1937 [1750], *Travels*, 211.

63. Belknap 1792, III:237. Thomas Cooper (*Some Information Respecting America*, Dublin 1794), in a passage given me by (and for which I thank) Professor Charlotte Erickson, remarked on the absence of anxiety about the future success of one's family as the greatest advantage of emigration. In England, Cooper wrote, the young unmarried man "flies to prostitution, for fear of the expense of a family establishment," while the "married man . . . doubts whether each child be not a misfortune." In America these worries were groundless.

CHAPTER THREE

1. And it was a period of scattered, limited demographic data; the principal sources were cited in chapter two. Much has been learned since Potter's essay of 1965 and Greven's review of it (Greven 1967, 445), yet the sources for aggregate trends improve by 1790 and 1800. Much of what follows is based on aggregate census data. I am aware that there are "difficulties associated with inferring the behavior of individuals from aggregate data, known under the 'ecological fallacy' rubric" (Shortridge 1976, "Frontier's Influence on Voter Turnout," 452; Selwyn Troen also made the point forcefully to me, 1979). Individual behavior certainly differed from the statistical averages of births, family size, age of marriage or death, and other demographic indicators. A figure for life expectancy means very different things depending on whether infant mortality is excluded. It still seems sensible to me to employ aggregate census data to describe general trends over long periods, since those data afford comparisons.

Individual behavior does cluster around means, although the range
may be wide or narrow. It is very unlikely that populations behaved
wholly bimodally and that means and medians are entirely statistical
fictions rather than rough generalizations about reality.

2. The average for whites nationally. The figure for blacks or for
people in fresh settlements is not known but may have been higher.
Thompson and Whelpton 1933, *Population Trends*, 306; J. Potter 1965,
"Growth of Population," 672; Forster and Tucker 1972, *Economic Opportunity and . . . Fertility*, ix and ff., 40.

In this book I follow the normal practice of population studies in
expressing rates: birth rates as the number of live births per thousand
people (male and female, all ages) in a year; death rates as the number
of deaths per thousand per year; fertility rates as the number of live
births per thousand women of child-bearing age (usually counted as
15 to 44) per year.

3. Wells 1971, "Demographic Change and the Life Cycle," 85;
Easterlin 1976b, "Decline of farm family fertility," 603–04; Grabill,
Kiser, and Whelpton 1973 [1958], "A Long View," 383, show the
national average fertility rate (children under 5 years old per 1,000
women aged 20–44) at 1,300 to 1,400 in 1800. In comparison the
U.S. birth rate in the late 1970s was around 15, and in western
Europe in 1974 it ranged from 10 to 16 (Bowen 1976, *Economics and
Demography*, 142–50). For Jewish Israelis in 1977 it was 23.6, for
Christian Israelis (mostly Arabs) 25, and for Muslim Israelis 45
(*Statistical Abstract of Israel* 1978, 75, 77).

4. McInnis 1977, "Childbearing and Land Availability," 202;
Henripin and Péron 1972, "Demographic Transition in Quebec,"
218–23. This is pure speculation, but it may be that Ontario's fertility
rates in the early and mid-nineteenth century were even higher than
Ohio's in part because Ontario contained more Irish and Scotch-Irish
who had recently emigrated; and though demographic factors in Ireland and Ontario were quite different, the Irish cultural pattern of
large families may have persisted for a generation or more. Inter-
rupted by the potato famine and the migration experience, the Irish
and Scotch-Irish Canadians may have reasserted the large-family cus-
tom, and indeed may have intensified it by a desire to retrieve fertility opportunities postponed by those events.

5. Thompson and Whelpton 1933, 306.

6. The Census Bureau did not keep mortality statistics until
1900, and then only for states and cities requiring death registration—the so-called registration area. By 1929 the area included
forty-six of the forty-eight states. Massachusetts was the first to require death registration, in 1841. Between then and 1900 the registration area was limited to New England and parts of the Middle Atlantic and East North Central states. For other areas, statements about

morality have to rest on scattered evidence. (Thompson and Whelpton 1933, 228–29; Yasuba 1962, *Birth Rates* 100–01.) A large-scale effort to build a data base for the study of morality since 1650 has been announced by Robert Fogel and associates (Fogel et al. 1978, "Economics of mortality," 79–89).

7. Rutman and Rutman 1976, "Of agues and fevers," 48–49, 52; Fogel et al. 1978, 77.

8. Vinovskis 1972, "Morality rates," 204, 212.

9. Thompson and Whelpton 1933, 231; Vinovskis 1972, 202–12; Eblen 1974, "New estimates of the vital rates," 301.

10. Fischer 1977, *Growing Old*, 228, gives the mean age of death as 56 (male and female) in 1800, and 61 (female) or 62 (male) in 1850, but his figure for 1800 "is a linear interpolation between 1750 and 1850," while "Mortality in 1750 was assumed to be the same as 1700": hence the change could have taken place any time between 1700 and 1850, if we credit the 1700 and 1850 figures as being representative of the whole population; both assumptions are large ones. Vinovskis 1972, 207, gives life expectancies by decade from 1820 through 1860, but the figures are only for Salem, Massachusetts, a settled-rural place by then.

11. D. S. Smith 1979, "Estimates of early American demographers,"31.

12. McKeown 1976 *Modern Rise of Population*, 39; Thompson and Whelpton 1933, 243, 252; Eblen 1974, 301.

13. Experts differ on this point; see the summary of positions in Leet 1976, "Determinants of the fertility transition," 360n4. A few see mortality declining fairly steadily after 1850, but I am impressed by Meeker 1972, "Improving health of the United States," 354–58, which points to the 1880s.

14. Kalm 1937 [1750], *Travels*, 32.

15. McKeown 1976, 72, 153; Fogel et al. 1978, 78; J. Potter 1965, 677.

16. *Hist. Stats.* series A119–A134. The precise figures are, for 1800, 34.7 percent for males, 34.1 percent for females. In 1870, 26.5 percent for males, 26.4 percent for females. In 1850 or 1851, the proportion under age ten in England was 24.9 percent, in Sweden 23.3 percent, and in France 18.7 percent (J. Potter 1965, 670). The American population was converging with those of some other industrializing countries in age structure, but all exhibited the normal pyramid shape.

17. Fischer 1977, 228.

18. Morgan 1952, *Virginians at Home*, 47.

19. J. Potter 1965, 633. Kett 1971b, "Growing up," 106–08.

20. Which implies some incidence of prenuptial fertility. J. Davis 1977, *Frontier America*, 107–08. Davis also writes that southern mi-

grants were, on average, even younger than northern ones (103).

21. Forster and Tucker 1972, 42, 49–50, confirming Yasukichi Yasuba 1962, *Birth Rates*. . . . Also, Goldscheider 1971, *Population, Modernization, and Social Structure*, 302; Wishart 1973, "Nebraska frontier," 107–19.

22. Fischer 1977, 228.

23. Aldridge 1949, "Franklin as demographer," 34; Rindfuss and Sweet 1977, *Postwar Fertility Trends*, 3; J. Davis 1977, 35. Davis cites the case of one William Gregory, born Pittsylvania County, Virginia, in 1776, and died on his fourth or fifth homestead near Burlington, Iowa, in 1858, aged 82: with his first wife he had ten children, every two years from 1796 to 1814, when she died in childbirth. With his second wife, who had three children from a former marriage, he had eight, every two years from 1815 to 1831 (and stillborn twins in 1823). With a third wife, who had eight from a previous marriage, he had none; they divorced. With his fourth wife, who had two children earlier, he had three, in 1841, 1842, and 1843. Thus the total between Gregory and wives one, two, and four was twenty-one children, not counting the thirteen from the four wives' earlier marriages. In direct or close lateral lines within my own family between 1800 and 1900 there were several cases of nine to fifteen children per set of parents, the largest families occuring in frontier-rural settings.

24. Kett 1971, "Growing up," 10.

25. J. Davis 1977, 20–21, 56–57, 66–67, 99. Seward 1978, *American Family*, 53–55, 77–93, 102, 128–34.

26. Gray 1933, *Agriculture in the Southern U.S.*, 439.

27. Quoted in Bidwell and Falconer 1925, *Agriculture in the Northern U.S.* 163. They continue,". . . the farmer did most of the work himself with the help of one or two big boys. His wife, and perhaps an older daughter, was called on for help in planting and hoeing corn and to rake grain and hay at harvest time. . . . In addition to occasional field work, the farm women regularly cared for the vegetable garden and the poultry, and carried on besides a great variety of industrial pursuits indoors, spinning, knitting, weaving, and making clothing both for themselves and for the men-folks. As a rule, the women did the milking and made the butter. . . . The children of poor families were sometimes 'bound out' or apprenticed at farm work, and occasionally a farmer might employ one of the poorer emigrants while the latter was earning money to buy land. These were few, and with the prevailing high rate of wages and cheapness of land they did not long remain hired hands."

28. Ryan 1975, *Womanhood in America*, 63–64: "The agrarian frontier economy kept the sexual division of labor simple and primitive, while the household system of social organization precluded the isolation of women in a private and undervalued sphere. These fac-

tors in turn inhibited the cultural gestation of sexual stereotypes."

29. R. H. Brown 1943, *Mirror for Americans*, 31, 32.

30. MacDonagh 1976, "Irish famine emigration," 393. The Irish famine migrants included a minority—10 percent?—of Protestants.

31. For immigration figures see *Hist. Stats.* series C1 and ff. A useful computation of net immigration versus natural increase is in Gibson 1975, "Contribution of immigration," 157–77.

32. Napoleon sold it readily for a demographic reason, McNeill tells us: it was to have supplied the food for the French army in Haiti, but when yellow fever wiped out the army, the logistical necessity for Louisiana disappeared. McNeill 1976, *Plagues and Peoples*, 266.

33. R. White 1978, "Winning of the West," 325–33 on nineteenth-century smallpox epidemics, and 339–43 on intertribal warfare, presenting a *realpolitisch* explanation of wars among the Plains Indians and how the whites benefited.

34. J. Davis 1977, *Frontier America*, 20, cites the resistance that faced the French in Algeria, the Russians in Siberia, and others, and suggests that "the relative ease with which Indians were overcome or dispersed did much to nourish national confidence," which is "possibly the prime prerequisite for democracy"—a point reminiscent of Turner's belief in the frontier as the cause of American democracy. But Turner did not specify conquest of the Indians as the root.

35. Freudenberger and Cummins 1976, "Health, work and leisure," 1–2, 9–10.

36. Taylor 1971, *The Distant Magnet*, 87.

37. Chevalier 1839, *Society, Manners and Politics*, 108. Drink was abundant, more so in the early nineteenth century than ever. Spirits distilled from grain and fruit, including gin and rum, averaged three gallons per person per year in about 1810, and in 1806 and 1807 over 9.5 million gallons of foreign spirits were imported. To this add beer, malt liquor, cider, and fruit liquors. R. H. Brown 1943, *Mirror for Americans*, 82. See also Rorabaugh 1979, *Alcoholic Republic*.

38. Bivans 1969, "Diary of Luna Warner," 276–311 and 411–42.

39. Garland 1891, *Main-Travelled Roads*, 7–10.

40. Johnson 1977, "Rough was the road," 79.

41. Langer 1975, "America's foods and Europe's population growth."

42. R. H. Brown 1943, chapter 4, or see any U.S. Census of Manufactures for the period.

43. Hofstadter 1971, *America at 1750*, 135; see also 158, 163, 164, 169.

44. Morgan 1952, *Virginians at Home*, 22– 23.

45. Main 1971, "Trends in wealth concentration," 446.

46. Cassedy 1969, *Demography in Early America*, 208, writes that by 1790 fewer than 10,000 Indians remained east of the Alleghenies,

and in New York and Pennsylvania they were on reservations.

47. Henretta 1973, *Evolution of American Society*, 22: Outlying fields were given over to sheep and cattle-raising for market by the 1760s, and small in-lying fields to domestic foods. "Because it was convenient for each farmer to have direct access to his pasture lands, this mode of production discouraged settlement in the large nucleated villages favored by the first colonists. It acted instead like a centrifugal force, pushing individual families outward on to their own lands and making dispersed autonomous farmsteads the most common form of settlement."

48. Billington 1974, *Westward Expansion*, 104: "Between 1760 and 1776 seventy-four new towns were settled in Vermont, one hundred in New Hampshire and ninety-four in Maine, many of them peopled by restless migrants making their second or third move toward the frontier." Also, Stilwell 1937, "Migration from Vermont," 75–77.

49. Clark 1970, *Eastern Frontier*, 359, 354.

50. Laslett 1965, *World We Have Lost*, 52, writes of a "one-class society" in seventeenth- and eighteenth-century England, though it was not based on abundant land and the prospect of quick ownership.

51. Obviously not everyone moved to the new region. Those who stayed behind, and others who stayed behind in rural areas at other times and places, constituted a "settled-rural" type. That will be discussed in chapter four.

52. American inheritance practices, North or South, eighteenth or nineteenth century, are not yet clearly understood and demand the attention of historians in the near future. The facts are not known about inheritance, yet the subject touches on many important questions, such as the push of young people away from ancestral areas toward the frontier—the topic of these pages; also, parental values about children and child-rearing, the law of property, changes in labor markets and occupations, distribution of property and other wealth, all deserve study. Several patterns of land inheritance were probably used in nineteenth-century America, but the extent of each is not yet known. See McInnis (1976) reply to Gagan 1976. "Indivisibility of land"; Easterlin 1976a, "Population change and farm settlement," 74–75; Bogue, comments following Easterlin, same place, 78.

53. Easterlin 1976a, 69. Henretta 1973, 29.

54. Lockridge 1968, "Land, population," 70. Fischer 1977, 98.

55. Gray 1933, *Agriculture in Southern U.S.*, 620.

56. Easterlin 1976a, "Population change," proposes a "bequest model" which says that farm family fertility in settled areas was distinctly lower than in newly settled areas (a fact not at issue) because

farm parents feared they would not be able to provide good life changes for very many children. In a comment, Bogue (78) questions whether enough evidence exists to support what he calls Easterlin's "clairvoyant countryman" model—that farmers limited their fertility because they predicted stability or decline in the values of their farms twenty years later when the children would come of age. One can add also that it seems doubtful whether reproductive behavior is quite as rational as Easterlin suggests. Further, plenty of cases will show that for many farm children, younger siblings and females, inheritance might as well have been nonpartible, because they received nothing.

57. Gagan 1976, "Indivisibility of land," 128–40; McInnis reply, 144–46. Gagan 1978, "Land, population, and social change," 297–302.

58. The term used by Lockridge 1968, 71. Also, Rutman and Rutman 1976, 56–57. Yasuba 1962 found land availability to correlate with high fertility much more strongly than did industrialization-urbanization, higher income, or immigration (22, 187, and chapter five *passim*).

59. R. H. Brown 1943, *Mirror for Americans*, 31–32.

60. Easterlin 1976a, "Population change," 71. Easterlin, Alter, and Condran 1978, "Farms and Farm Families . . . in 1860," 62, 69–73. Henretta 1978b, review of Hareven, 1322–23. Lindert 1978, *Fertility and Scarcity*, 137. J. Davis 1977, *Frontier America*, 164.

61. Vinovskis 1976, "Socioeconomic determinants," 384–86, 392–96, finds illiteracy to have been more determinant of fertility than land availability, but he is alone in this view. See the review by Leet 1978, 344. Also, Leet 1976, "Determinants of fertility," 372–78, and Leet 1977, "Interrelations . . . and fertility," 388–89. Leet stated the demographic problem clearly in 1975, "Human Fertility," 145: "The general hypothesis is that in a virgin area land will be plentiful relative to the number of potential young farmers in the county and thus early marriage and high marital fertility will be the rule. With great supplies of land, a large family conceived as rapidly as possible would be an economic asset. On the other hand, as the land becomes settled the amount of unused virgin land necessarily decreases. The farmers, and especially the prospective new farmers, of any given county will necessarily find it more difficult to enlarge their present farmstead or to obtain a virgin farmsite. This increasing scarcity of land with respect to demanders will, theoretically, produce a delay in the age at marriage and possibly promote intramarital fertility restriction. Both a rise in the age at marriage and the increased use of abortion or contraception would reduce the fertility rate." He finds the model confirmed, 156.

62. As Danhof 1969, *Change in Agriculture*, 116, wrote of the midwestern frontier.

63. Grabill, Kiser, and Whelpton 1973, "A Long View," 379–80.
Stilwell 1937, "Migration from Vermont," 69 (on stumps and clearings: "In Vermont it took one man a month to clear three acres"); 73
(on Indians); 97 (on vital increase); 82, 99–101, 105–06 (on
semisubsistence farming; wheat, flour, potash, and hogs were marketed in Canada or down the Connecticut River).
64. Easterlin 1976b, "Farm family fertility," 612–14.
65. McInnis 1977, "Childbearing and Land Availability,"
202–03.
66. Gallaway and Vedder 1971a, "Mobility of Native Americans," 628–37. Swedes emigrating later in the nineteenth century
also came, usually, from areas of high density and scarce land, from
"small farms, crofters' holdings, and squatters' plots" (Runblom and
Norman 1976, *From Sweden to America,* 143).
67. Joseph Schafer to F. J. Turner, Madison, 23 September 1931,
in TU Box 46, Turner mss. On ages, Stilwell 1937, 66: "Migration
[into and] from Vermont was in a very real sense a 'youth Movement.'" The median age rose sharply after emigration began. The dis-
appearance of the young may have had something to do with the
steep decline in the number of distilleries. Stilwell wrote that two
hundred distilleries were "turning out 50 gallons of liquor a day or
600 barrels a year [in 1800]. . . . The multitude of mixed drinks at the
roadside taverns — flip, punch, sling, toddy and eggnog — fills a
modern reader with envy or disgust. Only a life of strenuous, outdoor
exercise . . . could have resisted the moral and physical strain of such
ubiquitous tippling; and one is tempted to inquire whether many of
the rashnesses of the early Vermont leaders may not have been per-
petrated in their cups." By 1840, after so many young people had left,
only two distilleries were operating. (Stilwell 1937, 109, 178.) Vermont passed a prohibition statute in the 1840s, but by then little was
left to prohibit.
68. Easterlin 1976a, "Population change," 54. Speaking of the
Midwest a few years later, he says that when farmland reached
twenty dollars per acre, out-migration began.
69. Billington 1974, *Westward Expansion,* 248. Land near Lake
Champlain that sold for two dollars an acre in 1790 was already
bringing seven dollars by 1807 (P. White 1979, *Beekmantown, New
York,* 56).
70. Forster and Tucker 1972, *Economic Opportunity,* 18.
71. Billington 1974, 252.
72. Quotes are from R. H. Brown 1948, *Historical Geography,*
178, 180; Bidwell and Falconer 1925, *Agriculture in the Northern U.S.,*
75.
73. Stilwell 1937, 123–24 (emigration 1790–1810); 125–32
(emigration 1808–16). On 1816, see Stommel and Stommel 1979,

"The year without a summer," and for a description of that "meteorologically . . . fantastic year" in Germany, see Walker 1964, *Germany and the Emigration*, 5-7. Also, Stilwell 1937, 82 (diet), 98, 152 (soil exhaustion and "bankrupt" resources), 211 (young women in the 1840s leaving for factories). So many women left that, oddly enough, Vermont's sex ratio in the 1840s was skewed toward males. (Immigrants from Ireland and Canada, the majority male, probably contributed to that as well.)

A recent study of Vermont agriculture at about 1840 reveals that the young emigrants were not really "surplus labor," since they could have found work at home, but opportunities elsewhere, whether in western farms or eastern industries, were superior. Farmers continued to specialize in dairying or wool. A vicious circle resulted: "Unlike the Midwest where farmers could adopt labor-saving machinery, these hill farmers had no such technological alternative to counteract the high price and scarcity of farm labor. Instead, they adopted the less promising tactic of staying with wool. As wool prices declined, farm values stagnated and local farming became less attractive, increasing the likelihood of continued outmigration, lessened immigration, and the continued shortage of needed farm labor." (Barron 1980, "Rural depopulation," 335.)

74. J. Potter 1965, "Growth of Population in America," 635-36. Vedder and Gallaway 1975, "Migration and the Old Northwest," 162-63. Bowden 1971, "Great American Desert," made the point convincingly that the idea of a "great American desert" on the trans-Missouri Plains was never widely held and did not discourage migration and settlement.

75. J. Davis 1977, *Frontier America*, 60-61. Modell 1971, "Family and Fertility," 615, 620.

76. Danhof 1969, *Change in Agriculture*, 77, 88, 107.

77. Ankli 1974, "Farm-making costs in the 1850s," 70, and reply by Klein, 74.

78. Bidwell and Falconer 1925, 156, 273.

79. R. H. Brown 1948, *Historical Geography*, 347. By the 1880s Canadians were leaving Ontario for Manitoba or the Great Plains of the United States (Gagan 1978, "Land, population," 315).

80. "Kuznets-Thomas" 1964, *Population . . . and Economic Growth*, III:4-6. Kansas City and Omaha reached 100,000 by 1890, Dallas and Fort Worth by 1920, thirty to forty years after the first substantial agricultural settlements nearby.

81. Wishart 1973, "Nebraska frontier," 111. J. Davis 1977, 116.

82. Cott 1977, *Bonds of Womanhood*, 3, 92, 197, discusses the development of ideals of domesticity and recent schools of historical interpretation of women's experience. Also, Welter 1966, "Cult of true womanhood," 152. For fertility rates, which at times approached

2,000 children under 5 years of age per 1,000 women aged 20 to 44, see Grabill, Kiser, and Whelpton 1973 [1958], 383–84; *Hist. Stats.* series B67–B68.

83. Cooper 1823, *The Pioneers*, 2–3. Like his contemporaries he believed the Malthusian reckoning was a long way off.

84. Garland 1891, *Main-Travelled Roads*, 119, 152.

85. Hollon 1974, *Frontier Violence*, 196, described frontier days in Oklahoma and Texas: "I once interviewed dozens of elderly people who had participated in the settlement of Oklahoma Territory in the late 1880s and early 1890s. When I asked them what they remembered most about the recent frontier, the answer that a great majority gave was the wretched loneliness and almost total lack of excitement in their lives. [U.S. House Speaker] Sam Rayburn once reminisced about his experiences in growing up on the frontier of northeastern Texas. He recalled the boredom that he could never escape. Even though he worked in the fields all week, from sunup to sundown, the worst time of all was Sunday afternoon, when he had nothing to do. There were no newspapers to be read and no books other than the family Bible, there was no one his age to talk with, and the nearest store was miles away. He usually passed the entire afternoon sitting on the wooden fence in front of the unpainted family house, gazing down the country road in the hope that someone would ride by on horseback, or, even more exciting, in a buggy."

86. Hargreaves 1976, "Women in the agricultural settlement of the Great Plains," 182. She describes the normal tasks of farm women, 184–85: "Women in rural areas everywhere in the early years of the twentieth century [on the Great Plains] continued to perform tasks from which urban women had begun to break away in the 1870s [earlier yet in New England]. Farmers' wives kept the chickens, milked the cows, planted and tended the gardens, churned the butter, baked the bread, salted the meat, brined the kraut and corn, canned and preserved the fruit and vegetables, sewed the women's clothing and much of the men's, cooked the meals, washed and ironed, cleaned and decorated the house, and occasionally helped in the fields. On the plains women did all these chores and more—they served as midwifes and nurses for ailing neighbors, circulated petitions to get schools established, and provided lodging and means for transients. . . ." In a footnote, Hargreaves wrote that women "rarely engaged in field work, but . . . Scandinavian women in Dakota frequently helped out at harvest," which corroborates Garland's story.

While Rølvaag focussed on one character, Willa Cather's novel *My Antonia* (1961 [1918]) subtly portrays the childhood and young adulthood of several women in early Nebraska. Their responses to life ranged widely.

87. Garland 1891, 123, 126.

88. Already the "family farm" was becoming dubious as an economic enterprise in some places. See Nugent 1966, "Some parameters," 269.

89. The title of a popular account by Baldwin, 1853.

90. From 1.044 million to 1.025 million.

91. Gray 1933, *Agriculture in the Southern U.S.,* 907.

92. J. Davis 1977, *Frontier America,* 149. Huffman 1977, "Town and Country in the South," 367.

93. Leet 1976, "Determinants of the fertility transition," 371. J. Davis 1977, 79–93.

94. Atherton 1949, *Southern Country Store,* 3. A few large holdings, farmed by tenants, existed in the North but they were rare.

95. Spahr 1896, . . . *Distribution of Wealth,* 31. Atherton 1949, 10, 38. Gray 1933, 480.

96. Atherton 1949, 14–15. Gray 1933, 443–44, 452, 456–57, 880–81.

97. J. Davis 1977, 125, 132. Bidwell and Falconer 1925, 163.

98. Meeker 1976, "Mortality trends of southern blacks," 36–37. J. Davis 1977, 133, reflected on the absence of blacks from the frontier movement: "The consequences of this monumental act of exclusion are impossible to determine precisely and fully, but the undeniable fact that relatively few blacks settled on the frontier (and few of these did so of their own volition) vigorously suggests that fresh western soil—for hundreds of thousands of eager whites the instrument by which astounding economic success and social advancement were obtained—was of little direct consequence in the lives of the vast majority of black people."

99. Jefferson 1782, *Notes on the State of Virginia,* 161–62.

100. And in certain parts of Europe. See the papers by Berkner on Saxony, and Hermalin-van de Walle on France, in Lee 1977, *Population Patterns.*

101. Bidwell and Falconer 1925, 162–65, 449–52.

102. J. Davis 1977, 68.

103. Tocqueville 1840, *Democracy in America,* 168. J. Davis 1977, 151, supports this point and adds that semisubsistence farmers also did a lot of bartering.

104. J. Davis 1977, 137, 139.

105. Bivans 1969, "The diary of Luna Warner"; author's personal knowledge of Oklahoma farm families; Bieder 1973, "Kinship and migration."

106. The "new rural history" now spreading among social historians in the United States may soon answer questions like this one.

107. Guither 1972, *Heritage of Plenty,* 45, lists several important technological devices, among them Eli Whitney's cotton gin, 1793; Jethro Wood's improved cast iron moldboard plow, 1818; John

Deere's steel share and wrought iron plow, 1837; the reaper, by Hussey in 1833 and McCormick in 1834; Hiram and John Pitt's threshing machine, 1836; Rockwell's horse-drawn corn planter, 1839; Pennock's grain drill, 1841; Ketchum's hay mower, 1844; Page's revolving disc harrow, 1847. By the time of the Civil War, horse-powered threshers, mills, corn shocker-loaders, gang plows, planters, drills, and other implements were available (82–83).

108. Runblom and Norman 1976, *From Sweden to America,* photos from the Emigranteninstitutet, Växjö, following 176.

109. Farm horse population peaked in 1915 at 21.4 million, and over 10 million were around in 1941. Mules peaked in 1925 at 5.9 million, and in 1945 there were still over 3 million. *Hist. Stats.* series K570, K572.

110. Danhof 1969, 2. Danhof wanted to emphasize that the proportion going to markets doubled in fifty years, which is certainly significant, but I am emphasizing the obverse, that 60 percent did not, even as late as 1870.

111. Quoted in Danhof 1969, 115–16.

112. Danhof 1969, 183.

113. Herndon, interview with G. A. Miles, in Ward Lamon mss., Huntington Library (Herndon Papers LN 2408, vol. II, 234–35). I am grateful to Professor Paul Zall for giving me the reference.

114. J. Davis 1977, 98.

115. Cogswell 1975, *Tenure, Nativity, and Age,* also review by Winters 1976, 656. Lockridge 1968, "Land, population," 76, notes the decline of middle-class opportunities in Connecticut and Massachusetts in the late eighteenth century. Davis 1977, 161–62, writes of temporary hiring-out in the 1830s and 1840s of people on their way to joining the property-owning middle class.

116. Nugent 1966; Higgs 1970, "Railroad rates and the Populist uprising."

117. Lindert 1977, "Fertility Patterns," 260, on the decline of farm fertility.

118. Berthoff 1971, *Unsettled People.* Lockridge 1968, 76, sees middle-class opportunities closing off in the late eighteenth century. The section on modernization in chapter one refers to this idea and the problems historians have had in dating it.

119. Hays 1973, "Social Structure in the New Urban History," makes the connection between age structure and migration, and disagrees, as I do, with the notion of a social collapse in the nineteenth century.

CHAPTER FOUR

1. Bridenbaugh 1938, *Cities in the Wilderness,* and 1955, *Cities in*

Revolt; Nash 1980, *Urban Crucible.* Hofstadter 1971, *America at 1750,* 135, stressed the "basic rural theme" in American life in 1750, noting five exceptions: the five coastal towns of Boston, Newport, New York, Philadelphia, and Charleston; New England villages; Hudson River estates; "Chesapeake society"; and the planters of South Carolina. Combined, they formed a small minority in numbers compared to the backcountry mass.

    2. A. F. Weber 1899, *Growth of Cities,* 241–42, 283.

    3. Bender 1975, *Toward an Urban Vision,* 29: "The traditional village was not severely disrupted by the massing of population or by the development of unusually large work groups. The social system in Slater's factory villages clearly represented an extension of the existing mill-handicraft-farm complex of Jeffersonian America and was not the first step in the creation of an urban-industrial social order."

    4. Bender 1975, 32: "The Boston Manufacturing Company was the first factory in the country, maybe in the world, in which all the processes of the manufacture of cotton cloth, from the opening of the bale to the finishing of the fabric, were performed under a single roof by machinery." The cultural implications of the Waltham-Lowell factory system are explored in Bender's book, especially chapters two and five.

    5. Dublin 1979, *Women at Work,* 40 (quotation), 23, 28, 31–33, 51–52.

    6. Dublin 1979, 52.

    7. Another discussion is in Ryan 1975, *Womanhood in America,* chapter two. Cott 1977, *Bonds of Womanhood,* discusses the emergence by 1830 or so of a "woman's sphere" among wealthier New England women, for whom "The canon of domesticity expressed the dominance of what may be designated a middle-class ideal, a cultural preference for domestic retirement and conjugal-family intimacy over both the 'vain' and fashionable sociability of the rich and the promiscuous sociability of the poor" (92, 200, and *passim*). Only gradually did this "middle-class ideal"—which was upper-middle—spread from a restricted group to the wider, property-owning middle class of urban households.

    8. DeBow 1854, *Statistical view,* 192–93. The four were Boston (93,000), Cincinnati (46,000), Brooklyn (36,000), and Albany (34,000). Eight more fell between 20,000 and 30,000 (Lowell, Providence, and Rochester in the Northeast, Pittsburgh and Louisville in the Ohio Valley, Washington, Richmond, and Charleston in the South). Fourteen more were between 10,000 and 20,000, nine in the Northeast, four in the South, and St. Louis in the Midwest.

    9. *Hist. Stats.* series A195, A202.

    10. DeBow 1854, 192–93; Census of 1870, I:380.

    11. J. Davis 1977, *Frontier America,* 110n. Thompson and

Whelpton 1933, *Population Trends*, 306, give birth rates per 1,000 white women aged 15–44 as follows (the number is the average of the years within the given decade, to which I add the computed percentage decline from one decade to the next):

	Rate	% Drop		Rate	% Drop
1800s	276	—	1870s	161	8.5
1810s	267	3.3	1880s	146	9.3
1820s	250	6.6	1890s	134	8.2
1830s	231	7.6	1900s	124	7.5
1840s	208	9.96	1910s	115	7.3
1850s	189	9.1	1920s	100	13.0
1860s	176	6.9			

Limited statistics make it very difficult to make some potentially interesting distinctions, such as between the fertility of rural women and urban women (to say nothing of between settled-rural and frontier-rural), or native-born and immigrant. The changes in the white fertility rate, given in the table, are more useful than changes in crude birth rate, aside from the fact that the c.b.r. series of Thompson and Whelpton and the series of Yasuba and of Forster and Tucker vary sufficiently within the 1800–1860 period to counsel silence on drawing any large conclusions from them.

As for changes in population increase attributable to the native-born and to immigrants, we can separate net natural increase from total increase and then compare decades to see how fast or slowly the natural increase declined. Gibson 1975, "The contribution of immigration," provides a table of net immigration per decade. Subtracting this from total population increase per decade as given in *Hist. Stats.* series A2 yields net natural increase per decade. This is given in the following table, column A. As column B implies, the largest decline in natural increase as a percent of total population in the nineteenth century was in the 1860s (24.1 to 19.1 = drop of 20.7 percent), less in the 1880s (20.3 to 16.5 = 18.7 percent), and still less in the 1830s (31.4 to 26.7 = 15.0 percent drop).

Natural Increase as a Proportion of All Increase

Column A = Net natural increase of the native-born population per decade, in millions[1]

Column B = How much the population grew without immigration: net natural increase as a percent of the entire population at the start of each decade[2]

Column C = Proportion of total population growth in each decade attributable to native-born only[3]

% Change = How much the growth attributable to the native-born
          changed from decade to decade

Decade	A	B	C	% Change in C
1750s	1,329	33.8	96.4	—
1800s	1,862	35.1	96.4	0.0
1810s	2,284	31.5	95.2	−1.2
1820s	3,024	31.4	93.7	−1.6
1830s	3,441	26.7	81.9	−12.6
1840s	4,524	26.5	73.9	-9.8
1850s	5,588	24.1	67.7	−8.4
1860s	6,019	19.1	71.9	+5.8
1870s	8,069	20.3	78.1	+8.6
1880s	8,300	16.5	64.9	−19.5
1890s	10,515	16.7	80.6	+24.2
1900s	10,692	14.1	66.9	−17.0
1910s	10,542	11.5	76.7	+14.6
1920s	13,979	13.2	81.9	+6.8
1930s	8,790	7.2	98.8	+20.6
1940s	17,509	13.3	92.0	−6.9
1950s	26,167	17.4	91.4	−0.7
1960s	21,171	11.8	88.5	−3.3

[1]Source: Gibson 1975 has a table showing net immigration per decade. I have subtracted that from total population increase per decade, derived from the census figures in *Hist. Stats.* 1975, series A2. The result is natural increase per decade.

[2]Column A divided by total population in series A2.

[3]Column A divided by total increase in each decade, from A2.

In sum, if the data are close to being accurate, the fertility of white women, given in the first table above, dropped unusually fast in the 1840s and 1850s, and again in the 1880s and 1920s. These were all decades of rapid urbanization; perhaps there was a connection between the two trends. The rate of natural increase among the native-born, as shown in the second table, slowed in the 1830s and 1880s but most of all in the 1860s. Large influxes of immigrants from 1846 through most of the 1850s helped keep total population growth high, but also depressed the fertility rate of white women, since immigrant women were included in those statistics—and for various reasons their fertility was lower, on average, than that of native-born women.

12. Water power did continue to be used widely into the next century, however.

13. Quoted in Bidwell and Falconer 1925, *Agriculture in the Northern U.S.*, 252.

14. *Hist. Stats.* series P1, P5.

15. *Hist. Stats.* series Q321.

16. Computed from *Hist. Stats.* series A7 and C89.

17. MacDonagh 1976, "Irish famine emigration," 361, 369, 405–06, 410, 426–30.

18. MacDonagh 1976, 410, 427–29, 432–33.

19. From 1846 to 1860 inclusive, German immigrants numbered 1,280,000 and Irish 1,508,000, though many more Irish also entered by way of British North America and were not counted.

20. Forster and Tucker 1972, *Economic opportunity . . . and Fertility*, 78, 114n.

21. Wade 1972, "Violence in the Cities," 479.

22. R. H. Brown 1948, *Historical Geography*, 357, listed the fifteen leading American industries as of 1870. Most were of consumer perishables or semidurables. Beginning with the largest, the list included lumber and woodworking, flour and gristmills, clothing, iron and steel, foundries and machine shop products, printing and publishing, cotton textiles, boots and shoes, woolens, railroad cars, tobacco products, leather, bakery goods, sugar and molasses, carriages and wagons.

23. Golab 1977, *Immigrant Destinations*, 4. Weber 1899, 304–09.

24. Sennett 1970, *Families Against the City*.

25. Furstenberg, Hershberg, and Modell 1975, "Origins of the female-headed black family," 213–14, provide a table showing that the two-parent pattern appeared in Philadelphia in 1850 among 71.5 percent of the black families, 79.4 percent of the Irish, 82.6 percent of native whites, and 93.5 percent of German. In 1880 the figures were: black 68.8, Irish 79.8, native white 80.2, German 86.5.

26. Perhaps, suggests Ryan 1979, "Reproduction in American history," 321, because abortion was widespread in cities, terminating as many as one in three pregnancies among native-born married women. Goldscheider 1971, *Population, Modernization, and Social Structure*, 262–64. Sallume and Notestein 1932, "Trends in the size of families," 398, 408.

27. Paullin 1932, *Atlas*, plate 138A-E.

28. Wade 1959, *Urban Frontier*.

29. Glaab 1962, *Kansas City*; Unruh 1979, *Plains Across*.

30. Larsen 1978, *Urban West*, 24; also xii, 8, 116.

31. Dykstra 1968, *Cattle Towns*. Reps 1979, *Cities of the American West*, ix-x, reiterates that cities often began frontier development rather than emerging as the final stage of it. True, but that does not reduce the centrality of the frontier-*rural* mode, which involved vastly more people.

32. Larsen 1978, xii.
33. Lockridge 1968, "Land, population," 62–63, and (citing Charles Grant's study of Kent, Connecticut) 69. Isaac 1971, review article, 731, citing Greven on Andover. Easterlin, Alter, and Condran 1978, "Farms and Farm Families," 68–69.
34. R. H. Brown 1948, *Historical Geography*, 159–60.
35. Golab 1977, 221n3, citing Glaab and Brown 1976 [1967], *History of Urban America*, and Ward 1971, *Cities and Immigrants*.
36. R. M. Harper to Turner, University, Alabama, 15 December 1931, in Turner mss. Also, Harper to Turner, 5 November 1931. Turner argued with O. E. Baker (senior economist at the U.S. Department of Agriculture) about stabilization and decline in rural New England: did it happen as early as 1830, or did it come later? Baker pointed out that cultivated acreage did not begin to drop until after 1880, but Turner replied that "While the acreage . . . did not decrease so early as 1830, I suppose it would take some time after exodus set in, for the phenomenon to reveal its full meaning. Lands would be sold to the 'stayers' and occupied also by relatives even after it was unprofitable until the manufacturing centers, city milk demand etc. brought changed conditions." Turner to Baker, San Marino, 2 September 1931. The rest of the exchange is Baker to Turner, Washington, 20 August 1931 and 6 October 1931, and Turner to Baker, 20 October 1931.
37. Easterlin 1976a, "Population change," 46.
38. J. Davis 1977, *Frontier America*, 177. Fischer 1977, *Growing old in America*, 104.
39. Seward 1978, *The American Family*, 105–06.
40. Leet 1975, "Human Fertility," 142–43. Hist. Stats. series A195.
41. Gagan 1978, "Land, population," 308, 313–14. The work of Gagan and McInnis on Ontario rural demography makes that area better understood at the close of the 1970s than the states of the United States.
42. Blumin 1976, *Urban Threshold*, xii, 2–3, 9, 49, 73, 80. Much of Kingston's trade was in farm or farm-derived products. In settled-rural areas, such as Kingston in the early nineteenth century, or rural Vermont and New Hampshire as already described, farming usually had a commercial aspect. At the moment, however, we do not know enough to say whether that aspect outweighed the subsistence aspect, or whether farmers in settled-rural areas were more or less commercial than farmers in frontier-rural areas.
43. Boarding houses, with the age, sex, and occupation of their residents, appear in (for example) the U.S. manuscript census of 1850 for Watertown, New York, a place then changing from a frontier-rural entrepôt to a mill town.

44. J. Davis 1977, 125, 132.
45. *Hist. Stats.* series K4, K5, D16.
46. TU box 15E, Turner mss.
47. *Hist. Stats.* series A58–A63, A69.
48. *Hist. Stats.* series B6 gives white crude birth rate as 38.3 in 1870, 30.1 in 1900. Thompson and Whelpton 1933, 306, give fertility rate (births per 1,000 white women aged 15–44) as 176 in the 1860s, 134 in the 1890s, a drop of 23.9 percent. On contraception in the nineteenth century, see the review essay on the subject, and on some recent books, by Ryan 1979.
49. Higgs 1973, "Mortality in rural America, " 182–83. Meeker 1972, "Improving health of the U.S. 1850–1915," 361–62. Fogel et al. 1978, "Economics of mortality," 78–79. Easterlin, Wachter, and Wachter 1978, "Changing impact of population swings," 121. Meeker 1976, "Mortality trends of southern blacks," 36–37. These authors differ in some respects as to the precise level of the death rate in given years, but the trend seems clear enough.
50. On the other hand, if Higgs 1979, "Cycles and trends of mortality," 382–86, 401–02, is correct, immigrants may have contributed to death rates, not among themselves because they were not in the most vulnerable age groups, but because they may have carried infectious diseases which struck the urban populations into which they came.
51. Larsen 1978, 65, 68. Meeker 1972, 364–73. Condran and Crimmins 1979, ". . . Mortality data in the federal census," 16–20.
52. Thernstrom and Knights 1970, "Men in motion."
53. An excellent discussion of the "Atlantic economy" idea, developed earlier by Frank Thistlethwaite and Brinley Thomas, and extended in this case to the Poles especially, is Golab 1977, 5, 20, 224n., and *passim.*
54. Kett 1977, *Rites of Passage: Adolescence in America*, 171–72.
55. Engels to Friedrich Adolph Sorge, London, 2 December 1893, in Marx-Engels 1953, 257–58. Engels gave three reasons why "American conditions involve very great and peculiar difficulties for a steady development of a workers' party." First, the two-party system, which makes an American reluctant to "throw his vote away" on a third party; "and more especially, immigration, which divides the workers into two groups: the native-born and the foreigners, and the latter in turn into (1) the Irish, (2) the Germans, (3) the many small groups, each of which understands only itself: Czechs, Poles, Italians, Scandinavians, etc. And then the Negroes. To form a single party out of these requires quite unusually powerful incentives. Often there is a sudden violent *elan* [in 1886 the Haymarket riot and Gould strikes] but the bourgeois need only wait passively, and the dissimilar elements of the working class fall apart again." Third was worker pros-

perity from the protective tariff and large domestic market.

56. Richard Maxwell Brown, "Historical Patterns of Violence in America," 45–84, and Sheldon G. Levy, "A 150-Year Study of Political Violence in the United States," 84-100, both in Graham and Gurr 1969, *The History of Violence in America.*

57. An idea explored further in Nugent 1977, *Centennial to World War,* chapter two.

58. *Hist. Stats.* series K1.

59. Higgs 1973, "Mortality in rural America," 178, 185–94. Better medicine and health-care delivery were probably not important at that time, though they would be later in the century. Sewer systems and clean water lowered the urban death rate but not, as yet, the rural.

60. Rindfuss and Sweet 1977, *Postwar Fertility Trends . . . in the U.S.,* 3, 170. Lindert 1977, "American Fertility Patterns since the Civil War," 259–60.

61. *Hist. Stats.* series C78.

62. Seventy-five percent of black farmers. *Hist Stats.* series K109, K113, K124, K128.

63. Approximate. *Hist. Stats.* series C301 from 1908, and extrapolation backward from that series.

64. Easterlin, Wachter, and Wachter 1978, 121, give rate of total increase in 1900–05, 1905–10, and 1910–15 as 18.5 per 1,000, 19.8 per 1,000, and 17.5 per 1,000. Net migration rates for the three periods were 6.0, 6.9, and 5.3.

65. Laird 1975 describes the process in Kansas City, Kansas.

66. Histories of the beginnings of the black migration are numerous and increasing. See Henri 1975, *Black Migration.* On aspects of it see Cohen 1976, "Negro involuntary servitude in the South," Thomas 1973, *Migration and Economic Growth,* Higgs 1976, "The boll weevil . . . ," and Meeker and Kau 1977, "Racial discrimination and occupational attainment."

67. Fite 1979, "Southern agriculture," 15, 18.

68. Hargreaves 1976, "Women in the agricultural settlement of the Great Plains," 184–89. Lebergott 1976, *The American Economy,* 280. Turner, notes on article and speech of 1926, TU Boxes 14B, 14D, Turner mss.

69. On Turner and the close of the frontier, see Billington 1971b, ". . . Closing of the Frontier." Also TU Boxes 10, L2 in Turner mss. For an assessment of Turner's contribution, see Billington 1973, *Turner,* 464–65: "Modern Americans living in urban-industrial complexes, to whom the rural past is only a near-forgotten memory, are inclined to forget that somehow the continent was settled, and that this settlement generated social stresses certain to influence those enduring them. No nation could spill a sizable portion of its population into a

wilderness for two centuries without being affected by the experience. No people who realized that opportunity for self-advancement beckoned beyond the western horizon could escape changes in mental attitudes and social traits. Such experiences defy historical analysis, but their significance cannot be ignored."

70. Lee 1961, "Turner thesis re-examined," 78, 80.

71. D. Potter 1954, *People of Plenty*, 144–45, 147.

72. Codaccioni 1976, on "les classes dirigentes et moyennes." Also, remarks by Professor Edward Gargan at a session of the Social Science History Association, Philadelphia, October 1976. Stearns 1978, *Paths to Authority*.

73. Deane 1965, *The First Industrial Revolution*, 200. She describes the early nineteenth century, but the middle class was not much more inclusive, if at all, in the early twentieth.

74. Tocqueville 1840, *Democracy in America*, 269, 271–72.

75. Kett 1977, 243. Dann 1978, "'Little Citizens': working class and immigrant childhood . . . ," 214–15. Landes and Solmon 1972, "Compulsory schooling legislation," 86–87.

76. Spahr 1896, . . . *Wealth in the United States*, King 1915, *Wealth and Income*, and other writers among the progressives of the early twentieth century pointed out great inequalities in the distribution of wealth and income in the United States. They did not prove that the range and extent of inequality had changed much since mid-nineteenth century, and recent writers such as Lee Soltow and Edward Pessen have shown that inequality existed in the 1830–1870 period. At any time, however, opportunity existed, and the need in the early twentieth century was to be sure that that was still true. Progressives sought that assurance through social legislation. Then and in the nineteenth century, the evil was not inequality but inequity.

77. Joll 1978, *Gramsci*, 129–30.

78. King 1915, 175–76, 254–55.

79. Kousser 1974, *Shaping of Southern Politics;* Aylsworth 1931, "Passing of Alien Suffrage."

80. Bledstein 1976, *Culture of Professionalism*, 122. For the middle-class agenda, Nugent 1977, chapter seven.

CHAPTER FIVE

1. Technically. The census of 1920 showed 51 percent living in places of 2,500 or more.

2. On fertility rates, see Thompson and Whelpton 1933, *Population Trends*, 306. Also, *Hist. Stats.* 1975, series B6, B7 (birth rate), B1 (live births), B143, B144 (infant mortality), B111–112, B114–115 (life expectancy). Also D. S. Smith 1979, "Estimates of early . . . demographers," 31.

3. Etheridge 1972, *Butterfly Caste*, relates the tracking-down of pellagra, a deficiency disease, and the efforts to change public thinking and policy to effectuate the scientific findings.

4. *Hist. Stats.* series B168, B171 (death rates), B149–B166 (incidence of fatal diseases).

5. *Hist. Stats.* series C25–C62. Between 1870 and 1910, net migration of blacks from the South to other regions was 472,000; between 1910 and 1970 it was 6,162,000.

6. *Hist. Stats.* series C89, C301. Subtracting arriving immigrants from departing aliens (not perfectly comparable series, but indicative) gives out-migration of 804,000 in 1931–35, 573,000 in 1936–40, and 108,000 in 1941–45.

7. *Hist. Stats.* series A291 (household size), B4, B216 (divorce), D36 (women in the work force), A158–A159 (age at marriage).

8. Modell, Furstenberg, and Strong 1978, "Timing of Marriage," 143.

9. Not universal, but common. Lebergott 1976, *American Economy,* for tables.

10. Chafe 1972, *American Woman,* 140–42. D. Campbell 1979, "Wives, workers and womanhood," *passim.*

11. *Hist. Stats.* series B215, B216: marriage rates are for unmarried females, divorce rates are per thousand of the entire population.

12. *Hist. Stats.* series A353–A358, on family size. Also, on the suddenness of the drop in marriage age and its ambiguous relation to economic productivity, see Modell, Furstenberg, and Strong 1978, 125, 129.

13. *Hist. Stats.* series B1, B8.

14. A. Campbell 1974, "Beyond the demographic transition," 550.

15. A. Campbell 1974, 552, 555–57. Cutright and Shorter 1979, "The effects of health on . . . fertility," 191, 206, 208, make a strong case that participation of black women in the baby boom resulted from major improvements in their health, diet, natal care, and living conditions after 1940, so that they were physically able to have a baby boom for the first time, whether desired or not. They believe that blacks were victims of a "fifty year 'epidemic'" of disease and debility in the decades following emancipation.

16. T. White 1978, *In Search of History,* 480, citing a study by Donald Barrett which reported that in the 1950s, Catholic population increased 35.8 percent but general population 16.6 percent.

17. Rindfuss and Sweet 1977, *Postwar Fertility Trends,* ix, 6–7, and *passim.* The only exceptions were "older [30–44] rural women with only a grade school education . . . [or] who attended but did not complete high school" (160).

18. Rindfuss and Sweet 1977, 41.

19. Easterlin, Wachter, and Wachter 1978, "Impact of population swings," Also Eversley 1977 review of Lee 1977, 542; Leet 1979, review of Lindert 1978, 361–62.

20. The U.S. Supreme Court struck down anti-abortion statutes in *Roe* v. *Wade* and related cases in 1973.

21. Rindfuss and Sweet 1977, 185.

22. Seward 1978, *The American Family*, 163–71. Fischer 1977, *Growing Old in America*, 103.

23. Holthusen 1969, *Indiana Campus*, 5.

24. TU Box 14C, Turner mss.

25. Guither 1972, *Heritage of Plenty*, 168.

26. Shover 1976, *First Majority–Last Minority*, xiii, 117. *World Almanac* 1980, 113–38.

27. Easterlin, Wachter, and Wachter, 1978, *passim*.

28. Parke 1979, "Population changes," 4.

29. Also, of course, partly due to the large numbers of people of divorceable age. Compare the divorce rate in 1970, which was 3.5, and in the 1950s, 2.1 to 2.5. *Hist. Stats.* series B216. *World Almanac* 1980, 951.

30. U.S. Census Bureau report, "Statistical Portrait of Women in the United States—1978," reported in *Los Angeles Times*, 21 March 1980. Also, Census Report (P-25, 802) of May 1979, 1.

31. For the connection between change in cohort sizes and economic output see Kelley 1969, "Demographic cycles and economic growth," and the Kuznets and Easterlin items in the bibliography.

32. For reasons not fully understood either in rural or urban situations; in the United States both slowed through the nineteenth and twentieth centuries, but a comprehensive theoretical explanation remains elusive. See also Sharlin 1977, "Historical demography as history and demography," 251.

33. Unless the "Easterlin thesis" of a new baby boom in response to widening opportunities among young, post-baby-boom young adults in the 1980s and 1990s comes true (see p. 134 above).

34. Westoff 1978, "Marriage and fertility," 36.

35. (London) *Economist*, 24 December 1977, 3 February 1979. (Paris) *International Herald-Tribune*, 29 January 1979. United Nations, 1979, World Population Trends, 19, 25. Lawrence Veysey 1979, "The autonomy of American history reconsidered," argues, on a range of nondemographic evidence, a kind of convergence of the United States and other industrially advanced societies. He maintains that "The real trend of American history—no less so for usually being unacknowledged—is toward a loss of whatever distinctiveness the society once possessed. It is a trend that gives scant comfort either to mainstream nationalists or to leftists (who commonly have their own strongly held alternative ideal 'America,' replete with its sense of an influential

mission to perform in the world). But for over a hundred years, and in some respects for much longer, the merger of America into a common pattern of modern life has been the great underlying tendency" (477). Similarities between the United States and much of Europe may be getting stronger with regard to age structures and vital rates.

36. Address by Professor George Stolnitz, Indiana University, 5 November 1979.

37. Louisville *Courier-Journal*, 14 May, 7 June, 1978.

38. Westoff 1978, 35. Predictions can be wildly wrong. Men as prudent as Thompson and Whelpton in 1933 predicted a maximum of 205 million in the United States in 1980, and thought 155 million more likely (*Population Trends in the United States*, 318–19). They extrapolated from too short a base when birth rates were falling unusually rapidly, and like everyone else they had no inkling of the baby boom ten or twenty years ahead.

39. U.S. Census Bureau report cited in (Paris) *International Herald-Tribune*, 21 November 1978.

40. The number was possibly six to eight million. Louisville *Courier-Journal*, 22 October 1978. Other industrial-urban countries with low fertility attract surplus labor from elsewhere. The *Gastarbeiter* of Germany and Switzerland are the most prominent examples at present, but such migrant labor goes at least as far back as the mid-nineteenth century in Europe.

41. Lindert 1977, "American Fertility Patterns since the Civil War," 271–72, supports this view from an explanatory model of fertility patterns. Also, Westoff 1978, 35–38, explains why fertility should remain low.

42. Guttmacher Institute survey, cited in *Los Angeles Times*, 6 January 1980. Also, Census Bureau *Pocket Data Book* 1976, tables 41, 47.

43. Or at least it has before. Rindfuss and Sweet 1977, 116.

44. From remarks by Joseph A. Califano (Secretary of Health, Education, and Welfare), Jerusalem, November 1978. My thanks to the librarian of the American Cultural Center, Jerusalem, for giving me a transcript.

45. A very good summary prognosis, including a consideration of the "Easterlin thesis" and suggestions for federal policy in the 1980s, is Greider 1978, "Warning: Good Times Ahead." He concluded, ". . . the nation has to get over the gloom from the past, the conventional wisdom that nothing works. The demographic cycles described by Easterlin and others suggest to me that a major re-evaluation ought to be undertaken of the Great Society's alleged failures, one that takes account of the burgeoning age-shift which confronted those social programs. I suspect, if academics began making those comparisons, they would find that the Great Society youth

programs did not fail in relative terms—they were overwhelmed by the unlucky cohort."

46. For example, Thernstrom 1973, *Other Bostonians,* 260.
47. Parke 1979, 5.
48. J. Davis 1977, *Frontier America,* 183.
49. Braudel 1972, *Mediterranean,* II:737.

WORKS CITED

Aldridge, Alfred. 1949. "Franklin as demographer." *Journal of Economic History*, 9 (May), 25–44.

Ankli, Robert E. 1974. "Farm-making costs in the 1850s." *Agricultural History*, 48 (January), 51–70.

Appleby, Joyce. 1978. "Modernization theory and the formation of modern social theories in England and America." *Comparative Studies in Society and History*, 20 (April), 259–85.

Arieli, Yehoshua. 1966. *The Future-Directed Character of the American Experience*. Jerusalem: The Magnes Press of the Hebrew University.

Atherton, Lewis E. 1949. *The Southern Country Store, 1800–1860*. Baton Rouge: Louisiana State University Press.

Aylsworth, Leon E. 1931. "The passing of alien suffrage." *American Political Science Review*, 25 (February), 114–16.

Baldwin, Joseph G. 1853. *The Flush Times of Alabama and Mississippi*. New York: D. Appleton & Co.

Barron, Hal Seth. 1980. "The impact of rural depopulation on the local economy: Chelsea, Vermont, 1840–1900." *Agricultural History*, 54 (April), 318–35.

Bateman, Fred, and James D. Foust. 1974. "A sample of rural households selected from the 1860 manuscript censuses." *Agricultural History*, 48 (January), 75–93.

Belknap, Jeremy. 1792. *The History of New-Hampshire*. 3 vols. Boston: Re-printed for the author.

Bender, Thomas. 1975. *Toward an Urban Vision: Ideas and Institutions in Nineteenth-Century America*. Lexington: The University Press of Kentucky.

———. 1978. *Community and Social Change in America*. Clarke A. Sanford—Armand G. Erpf Lecture Series on Local Government and Community Life. New Brunswick: Rutgers University Press.

Berger, Peter L., Brigitte Berger, and Hansfried Kellner. 1973. *The Homeless Mind: Modernization and Consciousness*. New York: Random House.

Berthoff, Rowland. 1971. *An Unsettled People: Social Order and Disorder in American History*. New York: Harper & Row.

Bezucha, Robert J. 1978. Review of Félix-Paul Codaccioni 1976, *Inégalité sociale dans . . . Lille (q.v.)*. In *American Historical Review*, 83 (June), 739.

Bidwell, Percy Wells, and John T. Falconer. 1925. *History of Agriculture in the Northern United States, 1620–1860*. Washington: Carnegie Institution.

Bieder, Robert E. 1973. "Kinship as a factor in migration." *Journal of Marriage and the Family*, 35 (August), 429–39.

Billington, Ray Allen. 1970. *"Dear Lady": The Letters of Frederick Jackson Turner and Alice Forbes Perkins Hooper, 1910–1932*. "With the collaboration of Walter Muir Whitehill." San Marino: The Huntington Library.

————. 1971a. *The Genesis of the Frontier Thesis: A Study in Historical Creativity*. San Marino: The Huntington Library.

————. 1971b. "Frederick Jackson Turner and the Closing of the Frontier." Pages 45–56 in Roger Daniels (editor) 1971, *Essays in Western History in Honor of T. A. Larson*. University of Wyoming Publications, 37, no. 4.

————. 1973. *Frederick Jackson Turner: Historian, Scholar, Teacher*. New York: Oxford University Press.

————. 1974. *Westward Expansion: A History of the American Frontier*. Fourth Edition. New York: Macmillan Publishing Company.

Bivans, Venola Lewis. 1969. "The diary of Luna E. Warner, a Kansas teenager of the early 1870s." *Kansas Historical Quarterly*, 35 (autumn), 276–311, and (winter), 411–42.

Bledstein, Burton. 1976. *The Culture of Professionalism: The Middle Class and the Development of Higher Education in America*. New York: W. W. Norton & Company.

Blumin, Stuart M. 1976. *The Urban Threshold: Growth and Change in a Nineteenth-Century American Community*. Chicago: University of Chicago Press.

Bodnar, John. 1976. "Immigration and modernization: The case of Slavic peasants in industrial America." *Journal of Social History*, 10 (fall), 44–71.

Bogue, Allen. 1976. Comments on paper by Richard A. Easterlin. *Journal of Economic History*, 36 (March), 76–80.

Bonazzi, Tiziano. 1978. "Some problems concerning the process of growth and modernization of the English colonies. . ." *Annali dell'Istituto italo-germanico in Trento*, IV (1978), 273-93. Bologna: Il Mulino.

Boorstin, Daniel J. 1964 [1958]. *The Americans: The Colonial Experience*. New York: Vintage Books.

Borah, Woodrow. 1976. "Renaissance Europe and the population of America." *Revista de Historia* [Sao Paulo], 53: 47–61.

Bowden, Martyn J. 1971. "The Great American Desert and the American Frontier, 1800–1882: Popular Images of the Plains." Pages 48–79 in Tamara Hareven (editor) 1971, *Anonymous Americans*. Englewood Cliffs, N.J.: Prentice-Hall.

Bowen, Ian. 1976. *Economics and Demography*. London: George Allen & Unwin.

Braudel, Fernand. 1958. "Histoire et sciences sociales: La longue durée." *Annales E.S.C.*, 13 (October-December), 725–53.

———. 1972 [1966]. *The Mediterranean and the Mediterranean World in the Age of Philip II*. Translated from the [second] French [edition] by Siân Reynolds. New York: Harper & Row . (See also: *La Méditerranée et le monde méditerranéen à l'époque de Philippe II*. Third edition. Paris: Librairie Armand Colin, 1976.)

———. 1973 [1967]. *Capitalism and Material Life*. Translated from the French by Miriam Kochan. New York: Harper & Row. [First French edition, 1967.]

Bridenbaugh, Carl. 1938. *Cities in the Wilderness: The First Century of Urban Life in America, 1625–1742*. New York: Ronald Press.

———. 1955. *Cities in Revolt: Urban Life in America 1743–1776*. New York: Alfred A. Knopf.

Brown, Ralph H. 1943. *Mirror for Americans: Likeness of the Eastern Seaboard, 1910*. New York: American Geographical Society.

———. 1948. *Historical Geography of the United States*. New York: Harcourt, Brace, and Company.

Brown, Richard D. 1976. *Modernization: The Transformation of American Life, 1600–1865*. New York: Hill and Wang.

Brown, Richard Maxwell. 1969. "Historical Patterns of Violence in America." Pages 45–84 in Graham and Gurr 1969, *Violence in America (q.v.)*.

Butler, Jon. 1979. "Magic, astrology, and the early American religious heritage." *American Historical Review*, 84 (April), 317–46.

Campbell, Arthur A. 1974. "Beyond the demographic transition." *Demography*, 11 (November), 549–61.

Campbell, D'Ann. 1979. "Wives, workers and womanhood: America during World War II." Unpublished Ph.D. diss., University of North Carolina.

Canada. Manuscript censuses for 1851, 1861, 1871. Canadian National Archives/Archives Nationales du Canada, Ottawa.

Carr, Lois Green, and Lorena S. Walsh. 1977. "The planter's wife: The experience of white women in seventeenth-century Maryland." *William and Mary Quarterly*, 34 (October), 542–71.

Cassedy, James H. 1969. *Demography in Early America: Beginnings of the Statistical Mind, 1600–1800*. Cambridge: Harvard University Press.

Cassity, Michael J. 1979. "Modernization and social crisis: The Knights of Labor and a Midwest community, 1885–1886." *Journal of American History*, 66 (June), 41–61.

Chafe, William Henry. 1972. *The American Woman: Her Changing So-*

cial, Economic, and Political Roles, 1920–1970. New York: Oxford
University Press.

Chaunu, Pierre. 1973. "Un nouveau champ pour l'histoire sérielle? Le
quantitatif au troisième niveau." In [anon.] *Mélanges en l'honneur de
Fernand Braudel.* Vol. 2, Méthodologie de l'Histoire et des Sciences
Humaines. Toulouse: Edouard Privat.

Chevalier, Michael [Michel]. 1839. *Society, Manners and Politics in the
United States: Being a series of letters on North America.* "Translated
from the third Paris edition." Boston: Weeks, Jordan and Company.

Clark, Charles E. 1970. *The Eastern Frontier: The Settlement of Northern
New England, 1610–1763.* New York: Alfred A. Knopf.

Coale, Ansley, and Melvin Zelnik. 1963. *New Estimates of Fertility and
Population in the United States.* Princeton: Princeton University
Press.

Codaccioni, Félix-Paul. 1976. *De l'inégalité sociale dans une grande ville
industrielle: Le drame de Lille de 1850 à 1914.* Lille: Université de Lille
III. Review by Robert J. Bezucha (*q.v.*).

Cogswell, Seddie. 1975. *Tenure, Nativity and Age as Factors in Iowa
Agriculture, 1850–1880.* Ames: Iowa State University Press. Review
by Donald Winters (*q.v.*).

Cohen, William. 1976. "Negro involuntary servitude in the South,
1865–1940: A preliminary analysis." *Journal of Southern History*, 42
(February), 31–60.

Condran, Gretchen A., and Eileen Crimmins. 1979. "A description
and evaluation of mortality data in the federal census: 1850–1900."
Historical Methods, 12 (winter), 1–23.

Connell, K. C. 1950. *The Population of Ireland, 1750–1845.* Oxford:
Clarendon Press.

Cooper, James Fenimore. 1823. *The Pioneers, or the Sources of the Sus-
quehanna; a descriptive tale.* Two volumes. New York: Published by
Charles Wiley. E.B. Clayton, printer.

Cott, Nancy F. 1977. *The Bonds of Womanhood: "Woman's Sphere" in
New England, 1780–1835.* New Haven: Yale University Press.

Crosby, Alfred W. 1976. "Virgin soil epidemics as a factor in aboriginal depopulation in America." *William and Mary Quarterly*, 33
(April), 289–99.

Curtin, Philip D. 1969. *The Atlantic Slave Trade: A Census.* Madison:
University of Wisconsin Press.

Cutright, Phillips, and Edward Shorter. 1979. "The effects of health
on the completed fertility of nonwhite and white U.S. women born
from 1867 through 1935." *Journal of Social History*, 13 (winter),
191–217.

Danhof, Clarence H. 1969. *Change in Agriculture: The Northern United
States, 1820–1870.* Cambridge: Harvard University Press.

Dann, Martin. 1978. "'Little Citizens'": Working class and immigrant childhood in New York City, 1890–1915." Unpublished Ph.D. diss., City University of New York.

Davis, James E. 1977. *Frontier America, 1800–1840: A Comparative Demographic Analysis of the Settlement Process.* Glendale: Arthur H. Clark.

Davis, Kingsley. 1945. "The world demographic transition." *Annals of the American Academy of Political and Social Science,* 237 (January), 1–11.

Deane, Phyllis. 1965. *The First Industrial Revolution.* Cambridge: At the University Press.

DeBow, J. D. B. 1854. *Statistical view of the United States. . . . and being a compendium of the seventh Census.* Washington: Beverley Tucker, State Printer.

Defoe, Daniel. 1722. *A Journal of the Plague Year: being Observations or Memorials, of the most Remarkable Occurrences, as well Publick as Private, which happened in London during the last Great Visitation in 1665.* London: Printed for E. Nutt at the Royal Exchange. . . .

Demos, John. 1970. *A Little Commonwealth: Family Life in Plymouth Colony.* New York: Oxford University Press.

Denevan, William M., editor. 1976. *The Native Population of the Americas in 1492.* Madison: University of Wisconsin Press.

Drake, Michael. 1974. *Historical Demography.* Milton Keynes: Open University.

Driver, Harold E. 1969 [1961]. *Indians of North America.* Second edition, revised. Chicago: University of Chicago Press.

Dublin, Thomas, 1979. *Women at Work: The Transformation of Work and Community in Lowell, Massachusetts, 1826–1860.* New York: Columbia University Press.

Dykstra, Robert R. 1968. *The Cattle Towns.* New York: Alfred A. Knopf.

Easterlin, Richard A. 1976a. "Population change and farm settlement in the northern United States." *Journal of Economic History,* 36 (March), 45–75. With comments by A. Bogue.

———. 1976b. "Factors in the decline of farm family fertility in the United States: Some preliminary research results." *Journal of American History.* 63 (December), 600–14.

———. 1978. "What will 1984 be like? Socioeconomic implications of recent twists in age structure." *Demography,* 15 (November), 397–432.

Easterlin, Richard A., George Alter, and Gretchen A. Condran. 1978. "Farms and Farm Families in Old and New Areas: The Northern States in 1860." Pages 22–84 in Tamara K. Hareven and Maris A. Vinovskis 1978, *Family and Population in Nineteenth-Century America.* Princeton: Princeton University Press.

Easterlin, Richard A., Michael L. Wachter, and Susan M. Wachter.
1978. "The changing impact of population swings on the American
economy." *Proceedings of the American Philosophical Society*, 122
(June), 119–30.
Eblen, Jack E. 1965. "An analysis of nineteenth-century frontier
populations." *Demography*, 2: 399–413.
——— 1974. "New estimates of the vital rates of the United States
black population during the nineteenth century." *Demography*, 11
(May), 301–19.
Economist (London). 3 February 1979. "Rock-a-bye baby, one is
enough" [on German population]; 24 December 1977; 10 June
1978.
Eisenstadt, S. N. 1973. *Tradition, Change, and Modernity*. New York:
John Wiley & Sons.
———. 1977. "Convergence and divergence of modern and modernizing societies." *International Journal of Middle East Studies*, 8: 1–27.
Eldridge, Hope T. 1964. "A cohort approach to the analysis of migration differentials." *Demography*, 1: 212–19.
Etheridge, Elizabeth. 1972. *The Butterfly Caste: A Social History of Pellagra in the South*. Westport: Greenwood Publishing Company.
Eversley, D. E. C. 1977. Review of R. D. Lee 1977, *Population Patterns
in the Past (q.v.)*. In *Demography*, 14 (November), 542.

Farrell, James J. 1978. Review of R. D. Brown 1976, *Modernization
(q.v.)*. In *Journal of Social History*, 11 (summer), 580–82.
Feinstein, Estelle S. 1976. *Stamford from Puritan to Patriot: The Shaping
of a Connecticut Community 1641–1774*. Stamford: Stamford Bicentennial Corporation.
Fischer, David Hackett. 1977. *Growing Old in America*. New York: Oxford University Press.
Fite, Gilbert C. 1979. "Southern agriculture since the Civil War: An
overview." *Agricultural History*, 53 (January), 3–21.
Fogel, Robert W., Stanley L. Engerman, James Trussell, Roderick
Floud, Clayne L. Pope, and Larry T. Wimmer. 1978. "The econom-
ics of mortality in North America, 1650–1910: A description of a
research project." *Historical Methods*, 11 (spring), 75–108.
Forster, Colin, and G.S.L. Tucker. 1972. *Economic Opportunity and
White American Fertility Ratios, 1800–1860*. With the assistance of
Helen Bridge. New Haven: Yale University Press.
[Franklin, Benjamin.] 1755. *Observations concerning the Increase of
Mankind, Peopling of Countries, &c*. Bound with William Clarke, *Ob-
servations on the late and present conduct of the French. . . .* Boston:
Printed and sold by S. Kneeland in Queen-street.
Freudenberger, Herman, and Gaylord Cummins. 1976. "Health,

work and leisure before the Industrial Revolution." *Explorations in Economic History*, 13 (January), 1–12.

Furstenberg, Frank F., Jr., Theodore Hershberg, and John Modell. 1975. "The origins of the female-headed black family: The impact of the urban experience." *Journal of Interdisciplinary History*, 6 (autumn), 211–34.

Gagan, David P. 1976. "The indivisibility of land: A microanalysis of the system of inheritance in nineteenth-century Ontario." *Journal of Economic History*, 36 (March), 126–41. Followed by comments of Marvin McInnis, 142–46.

———. 1978. "Land, population, and social change: The 'critical years' in rural Canada West." *Canadian Historical Review*, 59 (September), 293–318.

Gallaway, Lowell E., and Richard K. Vedder. 1971a. "Mobility of Native Americans." *Journal of Economic History*, 31 (September), 613–49.

———. 1971b. "Emigration from the United Kingdom to the United States, 1860–1913." *Journal of Economic History*, 31 (December), 885–97.

Garland, Hamlin. 1891. *Main-Travelled Roads: Six Mississippi Valley Stories*. Boston: Arena Publishing Company.

Gibson, Campbell. 1975. "The contribution of immigration to the United States population growth: 1790–1970." *International Migration Review*, 9 (summer), 157–77.

Glaab, Charles N. 1962. *Kansas City and the Railroads: Community Policy in the Growth of a Regional Metropolis*. Madison: State Historical Society of Wisconsin.

Glaab, Charles N., and A. Theodore Brown. 1976 [1967]. *A History of Urban America*. New York: Macmillan Publishing Co.

Glacken, Clarence J. 1967. *Traces on the Rhodian Shore: Nature and Culture in Western Thought from Ancient Times to the End of the Eighteenth Century*. Berkeley: University of California Press.

Glass, D. C., and D. E. C. Eversley, editors. 1965. *Population in History: Essays in Historical Demography*. London: Edward Arnold Ltd.

Glass, D. C., and Roger Revelle, editors. 1972. *Population and Social Change*. London: Edward Arnold Ltd.

Glassner, Martin Ira. 1974. "Population figures for Mandan Indians." *The Indian Historian*, 7 (spring), 41–46.

Golab, Caroline. 1977. *Immigrant Destinations*. Philadelphia: Temple University Press.

Goldscheider, Calvin. 1971. *Population, Modernization, and Social Structure*. Boston: Little, Brown and Company.

Goubert, Pierre. 1960. *Beauvais et le Beauvaisis de 1600 à 1730*. Contri-

bution à l'histoire sociale de la France du XVIIe siècle. Two volumes. Paris: S.E.V.P.E.N.

Grabill, Wilson H., Clyde V. Kiser, and Pascal K. Whelpton. 1973. "A Long View." Pages 374–94 in Michael Gordon (editor) 1973, *The American Family in Social-Historical Perspective.* New York: St. Martin's Press.

Graham, Hugh Davis, and Ted Robert Gurr, editors. 1969. *The History of Violence in America: Historical and Comparative Perspective.* New York: Frederick A. Praeger.

Gray, Lewis Cecil. 1933. *History of Agriculture in the Southern United States to 1860.* Assisted by Esther Katherine Thompson. Two volumes. Washington: Carnegie Institution.

Grieder, William. 1978. "Warning: Good Times Ahead." *Washington Post,* 13 October 1978.

Greven, Philip J., Jr. 1967. "Historical demography and Colonial America." *William and Mary Quarterly,* 24 (July), 438–54.

——. 1970. *Four Generations: Population, Land, and Family in Colonial Andover, Massachusetts.* Ithaca: Cornell University Press.

Grew, Raymond. 1977. "Modernization and its discontents." *American Behavioral Scientist,* 21 (November-December), 289–310.

Guillaume, Pierre, and Jean-Pierre Poussou. 1970. *Démographie historique.* Paris: Librairie Armand Colin.

Guither, Harold D. 1972. *Heritage of Plenty: A Guide to the Economic History and Development of U.S. Agriculture.* Danville, Ill.: The Interstate Printers and Publishers, Inc.

Gutman, Herbert G. 1973. "Work, culture and society in industrializing America, 1815–1919." *American Historical Review,* 78 (June), 531–88.

Hargreaves, Mary W. M. 1976. "Women in the agricultural settlement of the Great Plains." *Agricultural History,* 50 (January), 179–89.

Hays, Samuel P. 1973. "Social Structure in the New Urban History." Unpublished paper delivered at York University, January 1973.

Henretta, James A. 1973. *The Evolution of American Society, 1700–1815.* Lexington, Mass.: D. C. Heath.

——. 1978a. "Families and farms: *Mentalité* in pre-industrial America." *William and Mary Quarterly,* 35 (January), 3–32.

——. 1978b. Review of T. Hareven 1977, *Family and Kin in Urban Communities* (New York: New Viewpoints). In *American Historical Review,* 84 (December), 1322–23.

Henri, Florette. 1975. *Black Migration.* Garden City, N.Y.: Anchor/ Doubleday.

Henripin, Jacques, and Yves Péron. 1972. "The Demographic Transition in Quebec." Pages 213–32 in Glass and Revelle 1972, *Population and Social Change (q.v.).*

Hexter, J. H. 1972. "Fernand Braudel and the *monde braudellien.*" *Journal of Modern History,* 44 (December), 480–539.

Higgs, Robert. 1970. "Railroad rates and the Populist uprising." *Agricultural History*, 44 (July), 291–97.

———. 1971. "Race, skills and earnings: American immigrants in 1909." *Journal of Economic History*, 31 (June), 420–28.

———. 1973. "Mortality in rural America, 1870–1920: Estimates and conjectures." *Explorations in Economic History*, 10 (winter), 177–95.

———. 1976. "The boll weevil, the cotton economy, and black migration, 1910–1930." *Agricultural History*, 50 (April), 335–50.

———. 1979. "Cycles and trends of mortality in eighteen large American cities, 1871–1900." *Explorations in Economic History*, 16 (October), 381–408.

Hist. Stats. See United States Bureau of the Census, *Historical Statistics*.

Hofstadter, Richard. 1971. *America at 1750: A Social Portrait*. New York: Alfred A. Knopf.

Hollon, W. Eugene. 1974. *Frontier Violence: Another Look*. New York: Oxford University Press.

Holthusen, Hans Egon. 1969. *Indiana Campus: Ein amerikanisches Tagebuch*. Munich: R. Piper.

Huffman, Frank J., Jr. 1977. "Town and country in the South, 1850–1880: A comparison of urban and rural social structures." *South Atlantic Quarterly*, 76 (summer), 366–81.

Inkeles, Alex, and David H. Smith. 1970. "The fate of personal adjustment in the process of modernization." *International Journal of Comparative Sociology*, 11 (June), 81–114.

———. 1974. *Becoming Modern: Individual Change in Six Developing Countries*. Cambridge: Harvard University Press.

International Herald-Tribune (Paris). 29 January 1979.

Isaac, Rhys. 1971. Review article of books by Demos, Greven, Lockridge, and Zuckerman. *American Historical Review*, 76 (June), 728–37.

Israel. Statistical Abstract of Israel for 1978. Jerusalem: Central Statistical Office, 1979.

Jacobs, Wilbur R. 1974. "The tip of an iceberg: Pre-Columbian Indian demography and some implications for revisionism." *William and Mary Quarterly*, 31 (January), 123–32.

———. 1968. *The Historical World of Frederick Jackson Turner, with Selections from His Correspondence*. New Haven: Yale University Press.

Jefferson, Thomas. 1782. *Notes on the State of Virginia; written in the year 1781, somewhat corrected and enlarged in the winter of 1782* . . . [n.p. Proof copy].

Jensen, Richard. 1978. *Illinois: A Bicentennial History*. New York: W. W. Norton.

Johnson, Anna (Dockal). 1977. "Rough was the road they journeyed." *Palimpsest*, 58 (May-June), 66–83.

Joll, James. 1978. *Antonio Gramsci*. New York: Penguin Books.

Kaelble, Hartmut, et al. 1978. *Probleme der Modernisierung in Deutschland: Sozialhistorische Studien zum 19. und 20. Jahrhundert*. Wiesbaden: Westdeutscher Verlag.

Kalm, Peter. 1937 [1770]. *The America of 1750: Peter Kalm's Travels in North America*. The English Version of 1770, revised from the original Swedish. Adolph B. Benson, editor. New York: Wilson-Erickson Inc. Two volumes.

Kelley, Allen C. 1969. "Demographic cycles and economic growth: The long swing reconsidered." *Journal of Economic History*, 29 (December), 633–56.

Kett, Joseph F. 1971a. "Adolescence and Youth in Nineteenth-Century America." Pages 95–110 in Rabb and Rotberg 1971, *The Family in History (q.v.)*.

———. 1971b. "Growing up in Rural New England, 1800–1840." Pages 1–16 in Tamara K. Hareven, editor, 1971. *Anonymous Americans: Explorations in Nineteenth-Century Social History*. Englewood Cliffs, N.J.: Prentice-Hall.

———. 1977. *Rites of Passage: Adolescence in America, 1790 to the Present*. New York: Basic Books.

Keyfitz, Nathan, and Wilhelm Flieger. 1968. *World Population*. Chicago: University of Chicago Press.

King, Willford Isbell. 1915. *The Wealth and Income of the People of the United States*. New York: The Macmillan Company.

Klingaman, David C., and Richard K. Vedder, editors, 1975. *Essays in Nineteenth Century Economic History: The Old Northwest*. Athens: Ohio University Press.

Kousser, J. Morgan. 1974. *The Shaping of Southern Politics*. New Haven: Yale University Press.

Kuznets, Simon. 1958. "Long swings in the growth of population and in related economic variables." *Proceedings of the American Philosophical Society*, 102 (February), 25–52.

"Kuznets-Thomas." 1957, 1960, 1964. *Population Redistribution and Economic Growth, United States 1870–1950*. "Prepared under the direction of Simon Kuznets and Dorothy Swaine Thomas." Vol. I: *Methodological Considerations and Reference Tables*, by Everett S. Lee, Ann Ratner Miller, Carol P. Brainerd, and Richard A. Easterlin. Vol. II: *Analyses of Economic Change*, by Simon Kuznets, Ann Ratner Miller, and Richard A. Easterlin. Vol. III: *Demographic Analyses and Interrelations*, by Hope T. Eldridge and Dorothy Swaine Thomas. Philadelphia: American Philosophical Society.

Ladurie, Emmanuel Le Roy. 1978. "En Haute-Normandie: Malthus ou Marx (note critique)." *Annales E.S.C.*, 33 (Jan.-Feb.), 115–24.

Laird, Judith. 1975. "The Argentine, Kansas, Barrio, 1910–1960." Unpublished Ph.D. diss., University of Kansas.

Landes, William M., and Lewis C. Solmon. 1972. "Compulsory schooling legislation: An economic analysis of law and social change in the nineteenth century." *Journal of Economic History*, 32 (March), 54–91.

Langer, William L. 1975. "America's foods and Europe's population growth, 1750–1850." *Journal of Social History*, 8 (winter), 51–66.

Lantz, Herman, Martin Schultz, and Mary O'Hara. 1977. "The changing American family from the preindustrial to the industrial period: A final report." *American Sociological Review*, 42 (June), 406–21.

Larsen, Lawrence H. 1978. *The Urban West at the End of the Frontier.* Lawrence: The Regents Press of Kansas.

Laslett, Peter. 1965. *The World We Have Lost.* New York: Charles Scribner's Sons.

Lebergott, Stanley, 1976. *The American Economy: Income, Wealth, and Want.* Princeton: Princeton University Press.

Lee, Everett S. 1961. "The Turner thesis re-examined." *American Quarterly*, 13 (spring), 77–83.

Lee, Ronald Demos, editor. 1977. *Population Patterns in the Past.* New York: Academic Press.

Leet, Don R. 1975. "Human Fertility and Agricultural Opportunities in Ohio Counties: From Frontier to Maturity, 1810–60." Pages 138–58 in Klingaman and Vedder 1975, *Essays in Nineteenth Century Economic History (q.v.).*

———. 1976. "The determinants of the fertility transition in antebellum Ohio." *Journal of Economic History*, 36 (June), 359–78.

———. 1977. "Interrelations of population density, urbanization, literacy, and fertility." *Explorations in Economic History*, 14 (October), 388–401.

———. 1978. Review of Maris A. Vinovskis, 1976, *Demographic History and the World Population Crisis* (Worcester: Clark University Press). In *Journal of Interdisciplinary History*, 9 (autumn) 342–44.

———. 1979. Review of Peter H. Lindert, 1978, *Fertility and Scarcity in America (q.v.).* In *Journal of Interdisciplinary History*, 10 (autumn), 360–63.

Levy, Sheldon. 1969. "A 150-Year Study of Political Violence in the United States." Pages 84–100 in Graham and Gurr 1969, *Violence in America (q.v.).*

Lindert, Peter H. 1977. "American Fertility Patterns since the Civil War." Pages 229–76 in Ronald D. Lee 1977, *Population Patterns in the Past (q.v.).*

―――. 1978. *Fertility and Scarcity in America*. Princeton: Princeton University Press.

Lipset, Seymour Martin. 1963. *The First New Nation: The United States in Historical and Comparative Perspective*. New York: Basic Books.

Lockridge, Kenneth. 1968. "Land, population and the evolution of New England society, 1620–1790." *Past and Present*, 39 (April), 62–80.

―――. 1970. *A New England Town: The First Hundred Years*. New York: W. W. Norton.

Los Angeles Times. 21 March 1980.

Loschky, David J., and William C. Wilcox. 1974. "Demographic transition: A forcing model." *Demography*, 11 (May), 215–25.

Louisville Courier-Journal. 22 October 1978.

Luraghi, Raimondo. 1972. "The Civil War and the modernization of American society: Social structure and industrial revolution in the Old South before and during the war." *Civil War History*, 18 (September), 230–50.

MacDonagh, Oliver. 1976. "The Irish famine emigration to the United States." *Perspectives in American History*, 10:357–446.

McEvedy, Colin, and Richard Jones. 1978. *Atlas of World Population History*. Harmondsworth: Penguin Books.

McInnis, R. M. 1976. Comments on paper by David P. Gagan. *Journal of Economic History*, 36 (March), 142–46.

―――. 1977. "Childbearing and Land Availability: Some Evidence from Individual Household Data." Pages 201–27 in Ronald D. Lee 1977, *Population Patterns in the Past* (q.v.).

McKeown, Thomas. 1976. *The Modern Rise of Population*. London: Edward Arnold.

McNeill, William H. 1976. *Plagues and Peoples*. Garden City, N.Y.: Anchor Press/Doubleday.

Main, Jackson Turner. 1971. "Note: Trends in wealth concentration before 1860." *Journal of Economic History*, 36 (June), 445–47.

Malthus, Thomas Robert. 1798. *An Essay on the Principle of Population, as it affects the future improvement of society, with remarks on the speculations of Mr. Godwin, M. Condorcet, and other writers*. London: Printed for J. Johnson, in St. Paul's Church-Yard.

―――. 1803. *An Essay on the Principle of Population; or, a view of its past and present effects on human happiness; with an inquiry into our prospects respecting the future removal or mitigation of the evils which it occasions*. A new edition, very much enlarged. London: Printed for J. Johnson, in St. Paul's Churchyard.

Martin, Calvin. 1978. *Keepers of the Game: Indian-Animal Relationships and the Fur Trade*. Berkeley: University of California Press.

Marx, Karl, and Frederick Engels. 1953. *Letters to Americans, 1848–1895: A Selection*. New York: International Publishers.

Mayer, Arno J. 1975. "The lower middle class as historical problem." *Journal of Modern History*, 47 (September), 409–36.

Meeker, Edward. 1972. "The improving health of the United States, 1850–1915." *Explorations in Economic History*, 9 (summer), 353–73.

———. 1976. "Mortality trends of southern blacks, 1850–1910: Some preliminary findings." *Explorations in Economic History*, 13 (January), 13–42.

Meeker, Edward, and James Kau. 1977. "Racial discrimination and occupational attainment at the turn of the century." *Explorations in Economic History*, 14 (July), 250–76.

Menard, Russell R. 1975. "The Maryland slave population, 1658 to 1730: A demographic profile of blacks in four counties." *William and Mary Quarterly*, 32 (January), 29–54.

Modell, John. 1971. "Family and fertility on the Indiana frontier, 1820." *American Quarterly*, 23 (December), 615–34.

Modell, John, Frank F. Furstenberg, Jr., and Douglas Strong. 1978. "The Timing of Marriage in the Transition to Adulthood: Continuity and Change, 1860–1975." Pages 120–50 in John Demos and Sarane Spence Boocock, editors, 1978, *Turning Points: Historical and Sociological Essays on the Family (American Journal of Sociology,* 84, Supplement). Chicago: University of Chicago Press.

Moltmann, Günter. 1978. "Nordamerikanische 'Frontier' und deutsche Auswanderung—soziale 'Sicherheitsventile' im 19. Jahrhundert?" Pages 279–96 in Dirk Stegmann, Bernd-Jürgen Wendt, and Peter-Christian Witt 1978, *Industrielle Gesellschaft und politisches System: Beiträge zur politischen Sozialgeschichte.* Festschrift für Fritz Fischer zum 70. Geburtstag. Bonn: Verlag Neue Gesellschaft.

Morgan, Edmund S. 1944. *The Puritan Family: Essays on Religion and Domestic Relations in Seventeenth-Century New England.* Boston: Trustees of the Public Library.

———. 1952. *Virginians at Home: Family Life in the Eighteenth Century.* Williamsburg: Colonial Williamsburg.

———. 1971. "The labor problem at Jamestown, 1607–18." *American Historical Review*, 76 (June), 595–611.

Nash, Gary B. 1980. *The Urban Crucible: Social Change, Political Consciousness, and the Origin of the American Revolution.* Cambridge: Harvard University Press.

New York. Census of the State of New York, 1855. Manuscript microfilm.

New York Times. 8 September 1977; 30 September 1977.

Notestein, Wallace. 1954. *The English People on the Eve of Colonization.* New York: Harper and Brothers Publishers.

Nugent, Walter. 1966. "Some parameters of populism." *Agricultural History*, 40 (October), 255–70.

————. 1977. *From Centennial to World War: American Society 1876–1917*. Indianapolis: Bobbs-Merrill.

Parke, Robert. 1979. "Population changes that affect federal policy: Some suggestions for research." [Social Science Research Council] *Items*, 33 (March), 3–8.
Parker, William N. 1975. "From Northwest to Mid-West: Social Bases of a Regional History." Pages 3–34 in Klingaman and Vedder 1975, *Essays in Nineteenth Century Economic History (q.v.)*.
Paullin, Charles O. 1932. *Atlas of the Historical Geography of the United States*. Washington: Carnegie Institution.
Potter, David. 1954. *People of Plenty: Economic Abundance and the American Character*. Chicago: University of Chicago Press.
Potter, J. 1965. "The Growth of Population in America, 1700–1860." Pages 631–88 in Glass and Eversley 1965, *Population in History (q.v.)*.
————. 1976. Review of Robert V. Wells, 1975, *Population of the British Colonies in America before 1776 (q.v.)*. In (London) *Times Literary Supplement*, 15 October 1976, 1314.

Rabb, Theodore, and Robert I. Rotberg. 1971. *The Family in History: Interdisciplinary Essays*. New York: Harper & Row.
Reinhardt, Marcel R., André Armengaud, and Jacques Dupâquier. 1968. *Histoire générale de la population mondiale*. Third edition. Paris: Montchrestien.
Reps, John W. 1979. *Cities of the American West: A History of Frontier Urban Planning*. Princeton: Princeton University Press.
Ricardo, David. 1815. *An essay on the influence of a low price of corn on the profits of stock; shewing the inexpediency of restrictions on importation: with remarks on Mr. Malthus' last two publications. . . .* London: Printed for John Murray, Albemarle Street.
————. 1887. *Letters of David Ricardo to Thomas Robert Malthus, 1810–1823*. James Bonar, editor. Oxford: At the Clarendon Press.
————. 1966. *Works and Correspondence*. Piero Sraffa, editor. Vol. II: *Notes on Malthus' Principles of Political Economy*. Cambridge: At the University Press, for the Royal Economic Society.
Rindfuss, Ronald R., and James A. Sweet. 1977. *Postwar Fertility Trends and Differentials in the United States*. New York: Academic Press.
Rodgers, Daniel T. 1978. *The Work Ethic in Industrial America, 1850–1920*. Chicago: University of Chicago Press.
Rorabaugh, W. J. 1979. *The Alcoholic Republic: An American Tradition*. New York: Oxford University Press.
Runblom, Harald, and Hans Norman, editors. 1976. *From Sweden to America: A History of the Migration*. "A collective work of the Upp-

sala Migration Research Project." Minneapolis: University of Minnesota Press, and Acta Universitatis Upsaliensis, University of Uppsala.

Rutman, Darrett B., and Anita H. Rutman. 1976. "Of agues and fevers: Malaria in the early Chesapeake." *William and Mary Quarterly*, 33 (January), 31–60.

Ryan, Mary P. 1975. *Womanhood in America: From Colonial Times to the Present*. New York: New Viewpoints.

———. 1979. "Reproduction in American history." Review article of Judy Barrett Litoff 1978, *American Midwives*; James C. Mohr 1979, *Abortion in America*; James Reed 1978, *From Private Vice to Public Virtue*. In *Journal of Interdisciplinary History*, 10 (autumn), 319–32.

Sallume, Xarifa, and Frank W. Notestein. 1932. "Trends in the size of families completed prior to 1910 in various social classes." *American Journal of Sociology*, 38 (November), 398–408.

Senior, Nassau W. 1928. "The Pressure of Population on the Means of Subsistence." Pages I:283–375 in S. Leon Levy, editor, 1928, *Industrial Efficiency and Social Economy*. New York: Henry Holt and Company.

Sennett, Richard. 1970. *Families Against the City: Middle-Class Homes of Industrial Chicago, 1872–1890*. Cambridge: Harvard University Press.

Seward, Rudy Ray. 1978. *The American Family: A Demographic History*. Beverly Hills: Sage Publications.

Sharlin, Allan N. 1977. "Historical demography as history and demography." *American Behavioral Scientist*, 21 (November-December), 245–61.

Shortridge, Ray Myles. 1976. "An assessment of the frontier's influence on voter turnout." *Agricultural History*, 50 (July), 445–59.

Shover, John L. 1976. *First Majority–Last Minority: The Transforming of Rural Life in America*. DeKalb: Northern Illinois University Press.

Smith, Daniel Scott. 1970. "Cyclical, secular, and structural change in American elite composition." *Perspectives in American History*, 4:351–74.

———. 1972. "The demographic history of colonial New England." *Journal of Economic History*, 32 (March), 165–83.

———. 1978. "A community-based sample of the older population from the 1880 and 1900 United States manuscript census." *Historical Methods*, 11 (spring), 67–74.

———. 1979. "The estimates of early American historical demographers: Two steps forward, one step back, what steps in the future?" *Historical Methods*, 12 (winter), 24–38.

Smith, Daniel Scott, and Michael S. Hindus. 1975. "Premarital pregnancy in America, 1640–1971: An overview and interpretation."

Journal of Interdisciplinary History, 5 (spring), 537–70.

Smith, Timothy L. 1978. "Religion and ethnicity in America." *American Historical Review*, 83 (December), 1155–85.

Socolofsky, Homer. 1967. "Land disposal in Nebraska, 1854–1906: The homestead story." *Nebraska History*, 48 (autumn), 225–48.

———. 1968. "Success and failure in Nebraska homesteading." *Agricultural History*, 42 (April), 103–09.

Spahr, Charles B. 1896. *An Essay on the Present Distribution of Wealth in the United States*. New York: Thomas Y. Crowell and Company.

Spengler, J. J. 1935. "Malthusianism in eighteenth century America." *American Economic Review*, 25 (December), 691–707.

Stearns, Peter N. 1978. *Paths to Authority: The Middle Class and the Industrial Labor Force in France, 1820–48*. Urbana: University of Illinois Press.

Stephen, Leslie. 1893. "Malthus," in *Dictionary of National Biography*, XXXVI:3. Sidney Lee, editor. London: Smith, Elder & Co.

Stiles, Ezra. 1799. A Discourse on the Christian Union: The Substance of which was delivered before the Reverend Convention of the Congregational Clergy in the Colony of Rhode Island, assembled at Bristol, April 23, 1760. Brookfield, Mass.: [n.p.] September 1799.

Stilwell, Lewis D. 1937. "Migration from Vermont (1776–1860)." *Proceedings of the Vermont Historical Society*, 5 (June), 63–245.

Stolnitz, George. 1979. "Population trends in eastern and western Europe." Address delivered at Indiana University. Bloomington, 5 November 1979.

Stommel, Henry, and Elizabeth Stommel. 1979. "The year without a summer." *Scientific American*, 240 (June), 176–86.

Taylor, Philip. 1971. *The Distant Magnet: European Emigration to the U.S.A.* New York and London: Harper & Row.

Thernstrom, Stephan. 1973. *The Other Bostonians: Poverty and Progress in the American Metropolis, 1880–1970*. Cambridge: Harvard University Press.

Thernstrom, Stephan, and Peter Knights. 1970. "Men in motion." *Journal of Interdisciplinary History*, 1:1–35.

Thomas, Brinley. 1973. *Migration and Economic Growth: A Study of Great Britain and the Atlantic Economy*. Second edition. Cambridge: At the University Press.

Thompson, Warren S., and P. K. Whelpton. 1933. *Population Trends in the United States*. New York: McGraw-Hill Book Company.

Tocqueville, Alexis de. 1840. *Democracy in America*. "Part the Second, The Social Influence of Democracy . . . translated by Henry Reeve, Esq." New York: J. & H. G. Langley.

Tomaske, John A. 1971. "The determinants of intercountry differences in European emigration: 1881–1900." *Journal of Economic History*, 31 (December), 840–53.

Tuchman, Barbara W. 1978. *A Distant Mirror: The Calamitous Fourteenth Century*. New York: Ballantine Books.

Turner, Frederick Jackson. Manuscripts, Henry E. Huntington Library, San Marino, California.

———. 1920 [1893]. "The Significance of the Frontier in American History." In F. J. Turner, editor, *The Frontier in American History*. New York: Henry Holt and Company.

Ubelaker, Douglas H. 1976. "Prehistoric New World population size: Historical review and current appraisal of North American estimates." *American Journal of Physical Anthropology*, 45 (November), 661–66.

———. 1976. "The Sources and Methodology for Mooney's Estimates of North American Indian Population." Pages 243–88 in Denevan 1976, *The Native Population of the Americas in 1492 (q.v.)*.

United Nations. 1979. "World Population Trends and Prospects by Country 1950–2000: Summary Report of the 1978 Assessment." New York: United Nations.

United States. Manuscript censuses 1840–1900, selected tracts. Microfilm.

———. 1872. Ninth Census. Vol. I, Population. Washington: Government Printing Office.

———. Census Bureau. 1975. Historical Statistics of the United States, Colonial Times to 1970. Washington: Government Printing Office.

———. Census Bureau. 1976. "The geographic mobility of Americans: An international comparison." Current Population Reports, Special Studies.

———. Census Bureau. 1978a. "Geographical mobility: March 1975 to March 1977." Current Population Reports, Population Characteristics, series P-20, no. 320, February.

———. Census Bureau. 1978b. "Geographical mobility: March 1975 to March 1978." Current Population Reports, P-20, no. 331, November.

———. Census Bureau. 1979. "Estimates of the population of the United States and components of change: 1940 to 1978." Current Population Reports, P-25, no. 802, May.

———. Census Bureau. 1980. "Estimates of the population of the United States to March 1, 1980." Current Population Reports, P-25, no. 881, May.

Unruh, John. 1979. *The Plains Across: The Overland Emigrants and the Trans-Mississippi West, 1840–60*. Urbana: University of Illinois Press.

Vedder, Richard K., and Lowell E. Gallaway. 1975. "Migration and the Old Northwest." Pages 159–76 in Klingaman and Vedder 1975, *Essays in Nineteenth Century Economic History. (q.v.)*.

Veysey. Lawrence. 1979. "The autonomy of American history reconsidered." *American Quarterly*, 31 (fall), 455–77.

Vinovskis, Maris A. 1971. "The 1789 Life Table of Edward Wigglesworth." *Journal of Economic History*, 31 (September), 570–90.

———. 1972. "Mortality rates and trends in Massachusetts before 1860." *Journal of Economic History*, 32 (March), 184–213.

———. 1976. "Socioeconomic determinants of interstate fertility differentials in the United States in 1850 and 1860." *Journal of Interdisciplinary History*, 6 (winter), 357–96.

———. 1978. "Marriage patterns in mid-nineteenth-century New York State: A multivariate analysis." *Journal of Family History*, 3 (spring), 51–61.

Wade, Richard D. 1959. *The Urban Frontier: The Rise of Western Cities, 1790–1830*. Cambridge: Harvard University Press.

———. 1972. "Violence in the Cities: A Historical View." Pages 475–91 in Kenneth T. Jackson and Stanley K. Schultz, editors, 1972, *Cities in American History*. New York: Alfred A. Knopf.

Walker, Mack. 1964. *Germany and the Emigration, 1816–1885* Cambridge: Harvard University Press.

Walsh, Lorena S., and Russell R. Menard. 1974. "Death in the Chesapeake: Two life tables for men in early colonial Maryland." *Maryland Historical Magazine*, 69 (summer), 211–27.

Ward, David. 1971. *Cities and Immigrants: A Geography of Change in Nineteenth-Century America*. New York: Oxford University Press.

Warden, G. B. 1970. "L'urbanisation américaine avant 1800." *Annales E.S.C.*, 25 (July-August), 862–79.

Weber, Adna Ferrin. 1899. *The Growth of Cities in the Nineteenth Century. A Study in Statistics*. New York: Published for Columbia University by the Macmillan Company.

Weber, Eugen. 1976. *Peasants into Frenchmen: The Modernization of Rural France, 1870–1914*. Stanford: Stanford University Press.

Wells, Robert V. 1971. "Demographic Change and the Life Cycle of American Families." Pages 85–94 in Rabb and Rotberg 1971, *The Family in History (q.v.)*.

———. 1974. "Household size and composition in the British colonies in America, 1675–1775." *Journal of Interdisciplinary History*, 4 (spring), 543–70.

———. 1975. *The Population of the British Colonies in North America before 1776*. Princeton: Princeton University Press.

Welter, Barbara. 1966. "The cult of true womanhood, 1820–1860." *American Quarterly*, 18 (summer), 151–74.

Westoff, Charles F. 1978. "Marriage and fertility in the developed countries." *Scientific American*, 239 (December), 35–41.

White, Philip L. 1979. *Beekmantown, New York: Forest Frontier to Farm Community*. Austin: University of Texas Press.

White, Richard. 1978. "The winning of the West: The expansion of the western Sioux in the eighteenth and nineteenth centuries." *Journal of American History*, 65 (September), 319–43.

White, Theodore. 1978. *In Search of History*. New York: Harper and Row.

Wiener, Jonathan M. 1976. "Note: Marxism and the lower middle class: A response to Arno Mayer." *Journal of Modern History*, 48 (December), 666–71.

Williams, William Appleman. 1966 [1961]. *The Contours of American History*. Chicago: Quadrangle Paperbacks.

Winters, Donald L. 1976. Review of Seddie Cogswell, Jr., 1975, *Tenure, Nativity and Age . . . in Iowa Agriculture (q.v.)* In *Agricultural History*, 50 (October), 656–57.

Wirth, Louis. 1938. "Urbanism as a way of life." *American Journal of Sociology*, 44 (July), 1–24.

Wishart, David J. 1973. "Age and sex composition of the population on the Nebraska frontier, 1860–1880." *Nebraska History*, 54 (spring), 107–19.

Yasuba, Yasukichi. 1962. *Birth Rates of the White Population in the United States, 1800–1860: An Economic Study*. Baltimore: Johns Hopkins Press.

INDEX

Abortion, 130, 140, 142, 174n26
Abundance, 111, 114–15
Adolescence, 44, 68, 109, 116, 142
Africans, 37–38, 48, 59
Age: median, 56, 108, 116, 130, 140, 142; -related behavior, 86, 133; structure, 135–44, 161n16
Aggregate data, problems with, 159n1
Agriculture: changes in, 50–51, 75–76, 79–85, 104, 122, 132; semisubsistence, 81, 83, 85, 112; stabilizes in 20th c., 29, 85, 121, 175n36
Alabama, 73, 76, 103
Amerindians, 36–39, 155n6, 155n9
Annales history, 21–24
Apprenticeship, 63, 66, 102, 162n27
Arieli, Yehoshua, 16
Arkansas, 38, 77, 84
Atlantic economy, 2, 10, 176n53

Baby boom, 29, 32, 115, 122, 126–34, 142, 143; defined, 127–28; echoes of, 137–38; and middle class, 144; and opportunity, 145; and population pyramid, 137
Beethoven, Ludwig van, 4–5
Belknap, Jeremy, 52, 75
Bender, Thomas, 9
Berger, Peter, 6
Birth rates: foreign, 138, 160n3; in frontier-rural period, 28, 44, 46, 49, 54–55, 92; since 1870s, 101, 126, 130–31, 134, 140; also 68–69, 78, 84, 95, 108
Births, 50, 57, 120, 122.
Blacks: demography of, 48, 78, 107, 122; and frontier, 78–79, 169n98; and middle class, 124–25, 130–31, 146; migration of, from South, 31, 103, 112, 114, 117, 123, 131; also

76–78, 102–03, 119–20, 126, 179n15. *See also* Slavery
Bledstein, Burton, 120
Bloch, Marc, 22
Boston, Mass., 40, 45, 48, 51, 87, 96–97, 107
Bowen, Ian, 21
Braudel, Fernand, xii, 23, 40, 108, 146, 155n6
Britain, 7, 115, 127, 128
British, 107, 138
Bushnell, Horace, 93

Canada, 14, 20, 37, 51, 55, 71, 79, 84, 101, 138; fertility in, 128; French, 20, 55, 148n19. *See also* Ontario
Capitalism, agricultural, 79
Cassedy, James, 50
Chesapeake region, 10, 40–45, 55, 68, 80
Chevalier, Michel, 11, 62, 96
Chicago, 1, 60, 92, 95–99, 104, 107
Childhood, 42, 44, 116, 122, 135
Children, 57–58, 99, 118
Cholera, 28, 39, 56
Cities: before 1870, 63, 87; in late 19th c., 87, 105; become metropolises, 97; foreignness of, 60; manufacturing and commercial, 95; natural increase in, 92
Civil War, American, 63, 77, 93, 96, 152n74
Class, social, 14–16, 109, 164n50. *See also* Middle class
Class conflict. *See* Engels; Gramsci; Marx
Colonies, English, 4, 17, 20, 40–41
Columbus, Christopher, 14, 16, 36, 61
Community, idea of, 9–10
Conjoncture, 23
Connecticut, 45–46, 64–65, 68

Scandinavians, 60, 105
Scotch-Irish, 47, 59, 160n4
Senior, Nassau, 19, 21, 151n49
Settled-rural areas, 5, 84, 87, 92, 98–102, 111
Sex ratio: colonial, 42–43, 57, 68; in 19th c., 72–75, 91; also 94, 99, 101
Slavery, 44, 63
Slaves, 42–43, 48, 56, 76–78
Slave society, 5, 98, 102–03
Smallpox, 28, 37–38, 47, 49, 51, 56, 61, 155n5
Social order, 85–86
Sombart, Werner, 16
South, the, 51, 63, 66, 73, 76–77, 98, 110, 112–13, 131
Stamford, Conn., 45
States (of the U.S.): central, 62, 72–73, 76, 80, 81, 84, 104, 132; eastern, 45, 48, 51, 76, 103; southern, 38, 48, 66, 76, 106; western, 28, 41, 60, 68, 104, 105, 111, 113. *See also* specific states
Steamboats/ships, 96, 108
Stiles, Ezra, 20, 38, 46, 50, 52
Stilwell, Lewis, 69, 71–72
Structures, 23, 53
Suburbs, 29, 31, 122
Suicide, 123, 134
Sweden/Swedes, 12, 47, 81, 107, 113, 138, 166n66

Texas, 28, 60, 77, 84–85, 99, 104, 112, 168n85
Tocqueville, Alexis de, 11, 79, 116, 145
Tönnies, Ferdinand, 5–6, 9–10
Town-congregation settlement, 41, 44, 46, 64
Towns, boom and frontier, 31, 98–100
Traditional society, 6–12, 34, 102
Transportation, 79–80, 92, 95, 110
Travel time, 96
Turner, Frederick Jackson, xii, 4, 12–17, 21–22, 25, 32–33, 100, 104, 113, 163n34, 175n36, 177n69

Urban: proportion of population, 29, 30, 32, 95, 122; takeoff in 1840s and 1850s, 63, 91–92
Urbanization, 29, 95

Vermont, 64–73, 76, 100, 167n73
Violence, 86, 95, 109–10, 119, 133
Virginia, 19, 38, 40, 42, 48, 52, 76
Vorzeit: in Chesapeake, 42–44, 57; in general, 25, 42, 54, 61, 80, 143; in Middle Colonies, 63, 158n41; in New England, 42, 44–46, 64, 87

War of 1812, 71, 90
Wars and population, 153n77
Wealth, per capita, 63, 138–40
Weber, Eugen, 7
Weber, Max, 6, 10
Webster, Daniel, 100
Wheat exports, 80
Wisconsin, 62, 74, 104
Womanhood, ideas of, 74, 171n7
Women: in Chesapeake colonies, 43; enfranchisement of, 120; as farm workers, 113, 162n27; frontier-rural, 58–59, 73; Great Plains, 75, 168n86; and households, 162n28; independence of, 59; in labor force, 59, 90, 92–93, 118, 124, 127, 134, 140, 145; in metropolitan period, 143; productivity of, 142; proportion marrying, 134–35; also 119, 146
Workers: blue collar, 112, 114; wage, 90; white collar, 33, 112, 114–15, 118, 121, 124, 144; also 117, 149n33. *See also* Apprenticeship; Indentured servitude
Work ethic, 11
World War I, 16
World War II, 22, 59, 126–28, 132–33

Yellow fever, 28, 37, 39
Youthful disorder, 85–86
Youthfulness of settlers, 56, 69